Backpacking through the Anglican Communion

A Search for Unity

Jesse Zink

Morehouse Publishing
NEW YORK · HARRISBURG · DENVER

Morehouse Publishing, 4785 Linglestown Road, Suite 101, Harrisburg, PA 17112

Morehouse Publishing, 19 East 34th Street, New York, NY 10016

Morehouse Publishing is an imprint of Church Publishing Incorporated.
www.churchpublishing.org

Cover design by Laurie Klein Westhafer
Typeset by Rose Design

Library of Congress Cataloging-in-Publication Data

Zink, Jesse A.
  Backpacking through the Anglican community : a search for unity / Jesse Zink.
    pages cm
  Includes bibliographical references.
  ISBN 978-0-8192-2901-4 (pbk.)—ISBN 978-0-8192-2902-1 (ebook) 1. Anglican Communion—History—20th century. 2. Anglican Communion—History—21st century. I. Title.
  BX5005.Z56 2014
  283—dc23
                          2013037208

Printed in the United States of America

for Debbie
who endured many absences so this could be written
and whose support remained unwavering

"How can we show forth the one body of Christ in the incredulous eyes of a world which now takes the separation of nations and races and classes for granted? How can we . . . express the underlying oneness of Christ's Church which is subservient to no national boundaries and obeys no national will?"

— STEPHEN BAYNE

Contents

Preface

This is a book born of the deep joy found in honest and mutual relationships with sister and brother Anglicans around the world. In travels that have introduced me to some of the diversity of people who are linked in worldwide Anglican fellowship, I have time and again seen the face of Christ. But it is also a book born of a deep frustration with the narrative of disunity that dominates the highest levels of the Anglican Communion. I know I am not alone in my experience of the joy of relationship. Yet none of these experiences appears to penetrate the echo chamber that encompasses those people who debate the future course of the Anglican Communion.

Looking for an outlet for both this joy and frustration, I found a model in a book I stumbled across in a library. Between 1959 and 1961, a priest named Howard Johnson, then canon theologian of the Cathedral of St. John the Divine in New York City, went on one long trip to visit every province of the Anglican Communion—200,000 miles, 730 days, 294 beds, and, he wrote, "more mosquito bites than I could count." The result was a book titled *Global Odyssey: An Episcopalian's Encounter with the Anglican Communion in Eighty Countries* that sought to describe the life of Anglicans in every corner of the world. To my knowledge, there is no other book like it. But the Communion has changed since Johnson wrote. There were sixteen provinces when he traveled. There are thirty-eight today, along with six extraprovincial jurisdictions. Moreover, Johnson's travels, though extensive, were incomplete. He was unable to visit Sudan and spent hardly any time in Nigeria, two places that figure significantly in the Anglican Communion of the twenty-first century. But the impulse behind Johnson's travel remains right. Anglicans really do not know all that much about each other. Like Johnson, I believe that sharing the experience of Anglicans in unique contexts around the world will enrich conversations about our future direction as a worldwide body.

One question I have deliberately not engaged in this book is the question of Anglican identity: What makes an Anglican an Anglican? Much has been written about this question. But I defer answering it here. This is not to say Anglican identity is unimportant. But it is a question, I have found, that quickly leads one into argumentative cul-de-sacs. Much more interesting to me is the question of how those of us who claim membership in the Anglican tradition are to relate to one another. Put another way, I am more interested in the nature and quality of our belonging than I am in articulating just what it is we belong to.

My understanding of the Communion has been shaped by my background and upbringing. As a result, the book begins with two chapters that share some of my formative experiences in the North American church. I hope these chapters give readers outside the Euro-Atlantic world a look into grassroots life in a church about which they may have only heard its leaders speak. After that, the chapters describe, in a more or less chronological fashion, my travels and life in various parts of the Anglican Communion. Except for the portions about South Africa and Uganda, all the travel for this book took place in the period between January 2010 and July 2011 while I was studying for ordination. The chapters describe experiences of church that lasted from a few days to a few years, so the comparisons with Howard Johnson, who was constantly on the move, are inexact. But as near as I can determine, this book is the result of 88,682 miles of air travel on 55 different flights that took me to 33 different beds (not counting airplane seats), cost me more than my fair share of mosquito bites—though none, thankfully, resulting in malaria—and left me with one beat-up backpack. It is offered to those of us in the Anglican portion of the body of Christ as we seek to understand how God is calling us to relate not only to one another but also to the rest of that wider, global body of Christ.

Jesse Zink
Advent I, 2013
Emmanuel College
Cambridge, England

Why Anglicanism? Why Unity?

If there is a center to the Anglican Communion, a simple stone chair in Canterbury Cathedral might be it. Up six steps from the quire to the cathedral's high altar and then another ten steps beyond that, this is the Chair of St. Augustine. It takes its name from the Benedictine monk whom Pope Gregory the Great sent to bring the gospel to the Anglo-Saxons in the late sixth century. The chair—a cathedra, to give it its proper name—is the chair of Augustine's successor, the archbishop of Canterbury. When seated in the cathedra, its occupant looks down the cathedral's quire, through an ornate screen, and into the nave. But if he—and the chair's occupant has always been male— stares straight ahead, he can see the lowest level of the stained-glass windows in the far west wall of the cathedral. The window most clearly in view depicts Adam. The first man is not relaxing in the garden, but is hard at work hoeing the land after his expulsion from Eden. It is a continual reminder of the challenges of human existence that confront the cathedra's occupant.

Directly behind the chair is the site of the former shrine to Thomas Becket, a twelfth-century archbishop. Becket's tenure was marked by conflict with King Henry II, which culminated in Becket's murder while he was saying Vespers in the cathedral on December 29, 1170. Almost immediately, Thomas's memory was venerated, and he was canonized in 1173. Canterbury became a pilgrimage site for people from across Europe. The stone floor behind the cathedra has been worn away by centuries of knees, as pilgrims supplicated their saint. The stained-glass windows around the shrine tell of how pilgrims were healed after praying to Thomas. A later king, Henry VIII, ordered the

1

shrine destroyed in the early years of the English Reformation. While there is a new shrine down the steps from the quire, the single flickering candle at the site of the original shrine remains an emotional heart of the cathedral.

More so than any other ancient and imposing English cathedral, Canterbury Cathedral is central to Anglicans around the world. To be Anglican, bishops once declared, means to be in communion with the see of Canterbury. Bishops gather here once a decade for the Lambeth Conference. When troubles arise among Anglicans around the world—whether in a dispute about integrating traditional cultures into the South African church that, in the mid-nineteenth century, led to the first Lambeth Conference, or the episcopal consecration of Gene Robinson, a partnered gay man, in New Hampshire in 2003—Anglicans look first to the bishop who sits in the Chair of St. Augustine. The cathedral is a place of authority, of grandeur, of history.

Half a world and a lifetime of experiences away is the village of Panyakwara Abarra in the governmental district and ecclesiastical diocese of Torit, South Sudan. I found myself there one September morning only after bumping down a major unpaved highway for several hours and then turning on to an even bumpier and narrower dirt road that led to Panyakwara. My guide was Robin Denney, an American missionary working on agricultural programs for the Episcopal Church of the Sudan. As we made our way down the road to Panyakwara, I saw a collection of log benches under a large tree. A dog sniffed around a table at the foot of the tree. "What's that?" I asked.

"The church," Robin said, as she steered around a particularly big hole. "That's where the community worships on Sunday."

In the middle of Sudan's two-decade-long civil war, Panyakwara emptied. Its residents fled to northern Uganda, seeking refuge both from the warplanes of the government army and a rebel army that made their life unbearable. The years in exile meant that much of the agricultural knowledge that had for generations provided the basis of their livelihood began to evaporate. Refugees dependent on food aid and living in crowded camps have neither the incentive nor the space to grow their own food. Gradually, during the war, people with agricultural knowledge died without being able to pass it on to another generation. When the war ended, people began to return to

Panyakwara. They found their village destroyed and overgrown. Food assistance from international agencies was insufficient and people began to starve. A survey showed the average household in Panyakwara lived on less than fifty dollars a year.

Enter the church. On a few acres of land just outside the village, there are rows of sorghum and sesame, growing neatly under the equatorial sun. In the rich and loamy soil, residents of Panyakwara are growing their own staple crops. Under the direction of the church's agricultural education officers, people in Panyakwara cleared the tall grasses and trees from the land, learned about the importance of sustainable agricultural techniques, and applied them to their own fields. The crops on these few acres of land are testament to the success of the work. With the church's help, and the considerable motivation and drive of the people in Panyakwara, no one is starving any longer, new shops are opening along the main road, and there is an energy and excitement about the future there was not before.

St. Paul and the Redeemer Episcopal Church on the South Side of Chicago sits right in the middle of the many contradictions of American urbanism. On one side, it draws its members from the prestigious University of Chicago. Barack Obama's home is only a few blocks away. Less than a block from SPR (as the church likes to be called) in the other direction is Shoesmith Elementary School, a school that ranks near the bottom of the academic achievement tables in the city. Its students are predominantly African-American and live in difficult homes surrounded by crime and drugs on a daily basis.

SPR is the rare American parish that manages to cater to both constituencies at once. When I was a member there, the music in its services blended old standards from the *Hymnal 1982*, English choral pieces, and the African-American hymnal, *Lift Every Voice and Sing*. Its young adult group was made up of graduate students at the U of C who joined with retired professors to tutor students from Shoesmith after school. Members of the congregation gathered on evenings and weekends for earnest discussions on social justice and what the church was being called to do in response to the world around it. A few years before I arrived, several members had noticed the absence of public pools in the African-American-dominated sections of the city and during the hot summer months led a campaign for more pools on the South Side. Two years after Gene Robinson's consecration, the congregation gathered in the parish hall to consider whether the rector should bless a union between two women. There was almost no debate. "These are the values we stand for," was the refrain from those who spoke. The rector received the near-unanimous backing of the congregation to proceed with the service.

Canterbury, Panyakwara, and St. Paul and the Redeemer are each authentic expressions of Anglicanism in the twenty-first century. Yet they appear to have little in common. The imposing history of Canterbury differs from the instability and turnover of Panyakwara. The urbane congregation at SPR contrasts with the poverty of Panyakwara. The liberalism of SPR is at odds with ostensibly conservative values in South Sudan and even—perhaps—Canterbury. Yet each belongs equally to the Anglican Communion, a global body that claims to hold together such diversity in one entity. Such a claim seems a recipe for ambiguousness at best, incoherence at worst. It is a claim that has been tested almost to its limits by debates over the last decade and more. Why not let each go its own way? What is to be gained by claiming each belongs to the other?

Answering these questions is the task of this book.

⟨⟩

The Anglican Communion is said to be coming apart at the seams. The collection of churches with some common connection to the archbishop of Canterbury has been split in the past over debates about biblical interpretation, the ordination of women, how to relate to cultures encountered in the process of missionary expansion, and much, much more. But the 2003 ordination of Gene Robinson as bishop of New Hampshire—the first openly partnered gay man to be bishop in the Anglican Communion—along with moves to bless same-sex relationships in a Canadian diocese and interventions by some bishops outside their ecclesiastical jurisdictions, took these tensions to a new height and brought about the widely bruited threat of schism. Commissions were appointed, studies conducted, meetings held, and denunciations spread as various sides angled for position and supremacy. Human sexuality is the presenting issue this time around—what should be the church's response to homosexuality?—but this conceals deeper issues: How do Anglicans around the world relate to one another when more and more Anglicans live in the Global South but the money and power remain—apparently—in the Euro-Atlantic world?*

Sex sells in the news business and the more church leaders talk about sex—especially other people's sex lives—the more it appears in newspapers and on television screens, even if this obsessive focus on sex pushes others away. As an Anglican from birth—baptized at Christ Church Cathedral in Vancouver, British Columbia, at the age of fourteen weeks—I cannot help but have followed these events over the years. As I have, I have developed a deep interest in the forms that Christianity takes around the world and how people can honestly and fruitfully communicate across cultural differences. In the decade since Gene Robinson was ordained bishop, I have pursued these interests and traveled to places that at one time I barely knew existed: Gulu, Uganda; Guamote, Ecuador; Waciri, Nigeria; Mangshi, China; and many others. These travels have introduced me to the wide diversity of Anglicanism. Whether marching for peace with Ugandan bishops or standing in the middle of an overflowing church in South Sudan, it has been difficult to reconcile the dominant images I had learned about the so-called "African church"—homophobic, unreflective, somehow not truly Anglican—with the reality I was experiencing. Anglicanism is vibrant around the world. But it is also different. I began to ask how we all ended up together.

ᏬᎥᏯᎶ

To subtitle this book "A Search for Unity" is, I have been told, problematic. The word unity has acquired negative connotations. Some gay and lesbian Christians have told me when they hear a call to unity, they hear a call to delay or hold off on what they feel are justifiable and holy desires to be fully included in the life of the church. Unity is interpreted as a call to preserve the unjust status quo. A

---

* "Homosexuality" is an imperfect word to describe the issue Anglicans are debating. It does not appear in the Bible and was first used only in the late nineteenth century. But I use it in this book for lack of a better alternative that is as widely understood. Similarly, there are almost no good words to refer to geographical divisions in the world. In this book, I use "Global South" to mean those parts of the world in Latin America, Africa, and Asia that are traditionally outside of the "developed" areas of Europe and North America. I use "Euro-Atlantic world" and occasionally "Western" to refer to this latter grouping of countries. And as much as I have tried to avoid unhelpful labels, I occasionally use "liberal" and "conservative" to refer to the ethical stances of two broad parts of the church.

similar dynamic was at work during the American civil rights movement. African-Americans demanding equal rights were told to wait. Martin Luther King Jr.'s prophetic "Letter from a Birmingham Jail" explained why black people heard the word "wait" to mean "never." It is instructive that King was responding to a letter from Alabama religious leaders—including two Episcopal bishops—titled "A Call for Unity."

Beyond those who find the word unity unappealing or offensive, many Anglicans appear to care little about their worldwide Communion. It is, I believe, axiomatic to Anglican existence that most Anglicans identify first with their local parish. A small percentage of those are invested in the local diocese. A smaller percentage of those are interested in the workings of the province or national church. A yet smaller percentage still are interested in the workings of the worldwide Communion. It is understandable. The Anglican Communion is sprawling and amorphous, difficult to wrap one's mind around. Far preferable is the life of faithful Christian witness in a particular location.

For those who do pay attention to events in the wider Anglican Communion, a not uncommon response to the divisions in the church is to shrug and assert that different groups can go their separate ways without much harm coming to anyone. The differences dividing Anglicans can seem extreme. Liberal Americans look to African bishops they see as bigoted and behind on the times and say "good riddance." Conservatives around the world look forward to the opportunity to "cleanse" the church of what they see as an unbiblical quasi-faith. In this context, even basic agreement on the importance of unity is elusive. It is easier to point to superseding values—inclusion and justice on the one hand, orthodoxy and faithfulness on another—and assert fidelity to those. Yet it is the basic contention of this book that the life and faith of Anglicans and those we encounter would be enriched were we to live in the unity that is God's gift to God's people.

This argument is based on theological claims, but it has its roots in my own experience of being a Christian. Although I was raised an Anglican, when I went to university I joined the local chapter of Inter-Varsity, a conservative evangelical campus group. With my mostly liberal, university-town upbringing, I stuck out like a sore thumb. Many of my peers had grown up in rural farming communities. More than once, people told me they were "praying for me." No doubt something I said convinced them that prayer was something I—especially—needed. But I was convinced I had something to learn from InterVarsity. And I did. I learned about new forms of worship, the importance of seriously reading the Bible, and why extemporaneous prayer matters. At the same time, one of my closest friends was an active member of the Church of Jesus Christ of Latter Day Saints. I attended church with him on a handful of occasions, visits that often ended in prolonged conversation about the particulars of our faith. Even as I was put off by some of his beliefs, I remained committed to him as a friend and fellow member of the body of Christ. My Christian faith is one that has been constantly enriched by people who think differently than me but in whom I nonetheless recognize a similar effort to live a life shaped by the good news of Jesus Christ.

It was at this time that I first became drawn to Jesus' prayer for his followers: "That they may all be one." This prayer, I came to realize, is a prayer about mission. Jesus prays that his followers may be one "so that the world may believe" (John 17:21). Our relationships with our fellow followers of Christ are connected to our witness to the world. Looking around the church, however, one could be forgiven for thinking otherwise. Even as mission and evangelism have again become prominent buzzwords in Anglican circles, the connection between unity and gospel witness is rarely discussed. Instead, a firm belief about the importance of proclaiming one's convictions and finding allies for one's views takes precedence. When Jesus prayed these words, his followers were confined to a small part of the world. Now his followers cover the globe, in countless languages, cultures, and contexts. There are more Christians in the Global South than in the church's historic heartlands in the Euro-Atlantic world. The center of gravity of the church continues to move south and east. These changing circumstances only heighten the difficulty of living in unity. But in a globalizing—and fracturing—world, I began to wonder what unity in a worldwide Communion might mean as part of that Communion's witness to the world.

I also began to ask myself when else Anglicans have confronted similar issues. Surely, I thought, this is not the first generation to be asking itself what it means to be a worldwide Communion? Indeed, it

most certainly is not. As I have continued to think about the Anglican Communion in the early twenty-first century, my mind has gone
often to the mid-twentieth century. The dissolution of the British
Empire, the new independence of many countries, and a growing
ecumenical movement challenged Anglicans then to think about
what it was that united them. They no longer had a common tie to
the British monarch—sundered, in any case, by the Americans a
century and a half earlier—and increasingly recognized that they did
not even share a common language. English was no longer the first
language of most Anglicans.

Anglicans responded to these changing times with two large international gatherings. Anglican lay people, priests, and bishops gathered first in 1954 in Minneapolis, Minnesota, and again in 1963 in
Toronto, Ontario. The first Anglican Congress, as it was called, led to
the recommendation for more ways to bind Anglicans together, particularly a secretariat that could oversee the work of the Communion.
In 1960, Stephen Bayne, then bishop of the Diocese of Olympia in
the United States became the first executive officer of the Anglican
Communion. In this role, he travelled widely, meeting with church
members, listening to their needs, and facilitating communication
among the different provinces of the Communion. Bayne's central recognition was that Anglicans are part of a body of Christ that spans the
globe. "There are not many bodies in many cities," he told the 1962
General Synod of the Anglican Church of Canada. "There is one
Body, one Lord, who walks with His immense strides over every middle wall of partition between us, who brings us all together by baptism
into His Body so that when we celebrate His Supper it is not just those
we see who share it with us."

Bayne's work led to "Mutual Responsibility and Interdependence
in the Body of Christ," a manifesto unveiled at the 1963 Toronto
Congress. MRI, as it came to be known, was hailed as a watershed in
Anglican thinking. It called on Anglicans to do away with old patterns
of relationship and form new ones based on "mutuality, equality, and
interdependence." In keeping with what Bayne had been teaching,
MRI urged all Anglicans to acknowledge their common membership
in a single body. MRI languished in the years following the Toronto
Congress but the vision it set forth remains challenging for—and
unrealized by—Anglicans of our own day.

Anglicans again confront shifting times and a changing world that challenge our traditional understandings of how we relate to one another. The Internet, the airplane, and a growing global consciousness have brought together people around the world in ways that would never have been possible in the past. In another era, it is doubtful the ordination of Gene Robinson would have generated a response so well organized and well calibrated to cause quite so big a crisis. The pre-Internet debate over the ordination of women proceeded at a pace that is glacial by comparison. Women were ordained in the United States in the mid-1970s, the topic generated resolutions at Lambeth in 1988, and the Virginia Report that responded to these resolutions did not come out until 1997. By contrast, Anglicans moved from the consecration of Bishop Robinson to a final draft of a proposed covenant in fewer than seven years.

Yet even as the world moves faster, it is not clear we actually know more about people in other parts of the world than at previous times in history. When visiting with South Sudanese seminarians, I was asked, "Is Gene Robinson the bishop for only the gay people in New Hampshire or all the people in New Hampshire?" The answer is obvious to me, but it was a serious question, asked earnestly. Westerners, similarly, can have little knowledge of life in other countries. A Nigerian priest once told me of a conversation he had with a European on a visit to Britain. The priest, who lives in a medium-sized city with five universities, mentioned his two postgraduate degrees. His conversation partner cut him off: "You have universities in Nigeria?" he asked incredulously. If Anglicans are actually serious about being a worldwide Communion of Christian believers, a good first step might be more knowledge of the Anglican experience in different contexts.

I have not been to all of the Communion's thirty-eight provinces or even most of them. But I have had sustained exposure to some of the great diversity that is the foundation of the Communion: England, the mother church of Anglicans, struggling to adjust to a new, secular age; Sudan (and now South Sudan), at one point the fastest-growing church in the world, now rebuilding after devastating civil wars; Nigeria, the largest province in the Communion ministering in an unstable political environment; South Africa, a church dealing with the legacy of entrenched racial discrimination and rapid social change. What I have learned as I have travelled challenges the narrative of disunity and fracture that dominates the debate about global Anglican futures. When the focus shifts away from our purple-clad leaders, I have found space for conversation and relationship that is at once holy, fruitful, and undeniably hopeful. Although bishops do appear in this book, the focus here is not on who takes communion with whom, who boycotts which meetings, or who issues the speediest denunciation of the other. Instead, the focus is on the much more interesting—but far less headline-grabbing—daily life of local Anglicans around the world.

As I have travelled, I have been repeatedly aware that who I am matters a great deal in shaping the experiences I have. I am a man, well educated and wealthy by the standards of most of the world, heterosexual, and white. I have an able body, which means I can visit churches that are well off the beaten path. I have friends, supporters, and access to organizations that can fund my travel and bring me home safely. These factors combine to give me a great deal of power and flexibility. I can talk about homosexuality with seminarians in South Sudan and not feel personally threatened by the conversation because I am heterosexual. I can witness unequal treatment for women in patriarchal societies and avoid speaking out because the treatment does not directly affect me. Qualities and aspects of my being, many of which I have little or no control over—sex, sexual orientation, wealth, education—mean I can have experiences that few others are able to. I can fit in and make myself feel at home in situations where others can not.

At the same time, who I am hinders me. In societies where gender roles are sharply delineated and barriers between the sexes still tall, I have found it difficult to engage in lengthy or serious conversation with women. As a man, there are places that I am told, directly or otherwise, to avoid. As a result, what follows is primarily a male—and thus minority—perspective on global Anglicanism. It is an acknowledged failing of this book.

⁂

Half a mile from the Chair of St. Augustine are the ruins of an ancient abbey. Now a national heritage site, this is the place where the monks who founded the cathedral first lived, worked, and prayed. Tourists can walk among the stone remains and crumbling walls. The soaring arches and looming towers of Canterbury Cathedral, the legacy of the monks' efforts, are visible from the ruins. Along one side of the ruins is a series of small rock piles, each no more than eighteen inches off the ground. These simple markers are the graves of some of the first monks who brought the influence of Rome to the British Isles. A modern engraving next to one such pile reads: "St. Augustine, site of the grave, 1st Archbishop of Canterbury, 597–605, d. 605." Looking at the jumble of stones, it is hard not to contrast it with the graves of other church founders—St. Peter's Basilica in Rome, for instance—or even the tombs of some other archbishops in the cathedral itself. The founder of Anglicanism, the first occupant of the Communion's defining see, gets a modest pile of rocks, no different than that of any of his other fellow laborers.

Perhaps the great mistake Anglicans have made in recent years has been listening to our loudest voices and thinking they are the most representative in the Communion. They are not. Instead, there is a deep and holy humility at the heart of what it means to be Anglican. I have found this humility in the lives of faith lived by so many around the world who are linked to the legacy of St. Augustine. This book is a journey shaped by those stones, both the ones that make up Augustine's grave and the ones that are the building blocks of the Anglican Communion.

My travels have not been comprehensive. Who I am has shaped the research for this book. This book cannot pretend to be the final and definitive answer to the divisions that threaten the Anglican Communion. It is necessarily subjective and impressionistic. But I do hope to offer windows into the life of Anglicans around the world, glances into a truly global Communion, in the hopes that this knowledge will enrich conversations about the future of our portion of the worldwide body of Christ, and so lead us into that missional unity for which Christ himself prayed.

CHAPTER 1

Growing Up with Difference

Diocese of Western Massachusetts, The Episcopal Church

One of my first memories of church revolves around a handshake: one very long, hard, and energetic handshake.

I was five or six and my family belonged to St. John's Episcopal Church in Northampton, Massachusetts. St. John's is an imposing, century-old building with a tall granite bell tower. It sits on the edge of Smith College, an elite women's school, and just on the edge of the downtown core of Northampton, the heart of what is known regionally as the Five College Area, after the many institutions of higher education nearby. Parishioners at St. John's include more than the average number of university professors, and the city is more liberal and left-wing than the rest of rural, agricultural western Massachusetts.

On Sundays, I waited in line at the end of the service to shake the rector's hand, as the adults did. The rector was a young man named Jim Munroe, a Marine veteran of Vietnam who had been wounded in combat and attended seminary after his long convalescence. He had arrived at St. John's a few years earlier with a reputation for his preaching, praying, and wonderful sense of humor. Already he had endeared himself to our family with his uproarious laugh and the need to tell the exact same four jokes again and again and think they were just as funny as the first time he told them.

Other people in line, I knew, usually exchanged polite, restrained handshakes with Jim. This was not for me. When it came my turn, I pumped his hand enthusiastically. Up and down, up and down, I shook his hand for all I was worth, week in and week out. Jim was always more than willing to play along, laughing uproariously every time. But this Sunday morning in late August was different. Jim was saying farewell to the congregation before a sabbatical. It was the late 1980s and he was headed to New York City to volunteer at a hospice for people with AIDS. Standing on the top step of our granite church, I asked Jim how many Sundays he would miss. "Twelve," he said. "I'll be back just before Christmas."

"Well," I said. "I'll have to shake your hand twelve times as hard."

And I did.

And Jim laughed. Uproariously.

◦⟋ɱɯ◦

My entry point to the body of Christ and the Anglican Communion came a few years prior to that handshake on the other side of the continent. I was three months old and my parents took me to Christ Church Cathedral in Vancouver, Canada, where they were living and where I had been born. Graham Witcher, a priest at the cathedral, asked my parents and the aunt and uncle who were serving as my godparents if they would raise me in the life of faith. He asked the congregation if they, too, would support my walk in faith. Evidently, everyone agreed because water was sprinkled on my head. I died the death of Christ and was raised to new life through the waters of baptism. It sounds dramatic. I wish I remembered it.

Within a year, my mother, father, and I resettled in Northampton so my father could go back to school. Soon enough, our family had a deepening relationship with St. John's.

When I became old enough, I gathered with the children of the Sunday school in the parlors of the church house. We listened to Mrs. Jones, the Sunday school director, welcome us and lead us through the Lord's Prayer. During the week, she taught at a school for deaf children so her enunciation was perfect, tending toward the overexaggerated. "Ow-er Fah-ther," I learned to say, drawing out each syllable carefully. When we reached "Ah-men," we were off, a confused mass of children and teachers headed up the stairs to our classrooms.

Church involved my whole family. My father and mother served on the vestry and taught Sunday school. When my brother was born, he was baptized with a splash of water from the Jordan River that Jim had collected on a recent visit. At Christmas, we geared up for the annual pageant. There were the costumes to be dusted off and lines to be learned. By age twelve, having worked my way from innkeeper to shepherd to wise man, I graduated to the role of narrator. Standing in the pulpit, I did my best to intone in my unbroken, twelve-year-old voice such weighty lines as "A decree went out from Emperor Augustus . . ." and "Far away in the East . . ." It was a heady moment, standing where I had only ever seen Jim and other priests stand.

One spring, when I was nine or ten, my parents took me to the home of the deacon three Wednesday afternoons in a row. Mel, a retired banker, had been ordained when he retired. One of his responsibilities now was to teach us how to receive communion. Sitting on his living room floor, he carefully set out a silver chalice and paten and began to explain what Holy Communion was and why it was important. The first time he taught us to sip from the chalice he used water. The next time, though, he poured a dark liquid in. "He's using real wine!" my friend whispered to me, excitedly.

"I know!" I whispered back, equally excited, but also nervous at the thought of drinking real alcohol. I tried to play it cool, but I still sputtered when the cup first touched my lips.

I do not remember any of the teaching we learned on that living room floor. But I do remember that on my first taste of the burn of the alcohol, I thought to myself, "Ugh. Why would anyone want to drink that?" But from that first Sunday and ever afterward, I did, dutifully tipping the chalice closer to my mouth, sipping, tilting it back, pausing, and waiting until the chalice-bearer had completed serving the person next to me before returning to my seat. It was just as I learned on the living room floor.

With First Communion behind me, on one Sunday a month I missed Sunday school, pawed through the closet of white robes, found one that more or less covered my growing limbs, lit my candle, and prepared to serve as an acolyte. At first, it seemed a fairly important affair—exactly how to bow and when, on which verse of the final hymn to begin marching out of the church, how to tell the water from the wine so you did not wash Jim's hands with wine before Communion—but the seriousness did not last long. There were just too many things that went wrong during a church service for it to be anything other than funny—and fun. The priest chugged the chalice wine at the end of the service! My friend got caught by his mother picking his nose during the sermon! The oldest lady in the choir snapped at us for whispering to one another during the prayers! At a late-night Christmas Eve service I lifted the fully loaded offering plates high over my head as the congregation sang the doxology. My mind was focused more on the presents I was to receive than on keeping the plate parallel to the floor. Right around "above you heavenly hosts," a magnificent stream of bills, envelopes, and coins came pouring out, raining down over my head and shoulders.

As the years passed, I became aware that my Sunday school class was getting smaller. The number of available acolytes was shrinking too. There were just fewer and fewer people my age in church. But when I turned fifteen, the number of people my age in church surged. It was another rite of passage: confirmation. In a year-long course, I prepared for confirmation with twenty-five other young people, many of whom had returned to church only at their parents' instigation. Once a month, we got together to learn about Henry VIII and Thomas Cranmer, the Wesley brothers, and Samuel Seabury. We looked at the Nicene Creed and thought about what it means to say "Light from Light" or "Begotten not made." Once a month, I met with three other confirmands and our two sponsors for dinner. We talked about what it meant to be confirmed and what it meant to be Christians—and Episcopalians—in our daily lives at school. We did not, as I recall, reach any satisfying conclusions.

Then, on an April evening, I knelt in front of the bishop of Western Massachusetts, holding a small card with my first and middle names on it. I felt his heavy hands on my head and the light touch of my two sponsors' hands on my shoulder. In his sonorous voice, the bishop intoned, "Strengthen, O Lord, your servant Jesse Andrew with your Holy Spirit; empower him for your service; and sustain him all the days of his life." The congregation responded with a loud "Amen."

The duress under which my peers completed the course quickly became apparent. Most of those who were confirmed that evening seemed to see the service as akin to a graduation. They were finished with church and never needed to return again. Of the four people in my small group, I was the only one who showed up at church the next Sunday. I had to. By that point, I was helping to teach Sunday school to the three-, four-, and five-year-old class. I did so partly because I enjoyed it but partly because there was nothing else for high school students to do on a Sunday morning at church except sit through the service, and I was not quite ready for that. Less than a year after my confirmation, I was the only person my age left on the acolyte roster and the only one still in church on a regular basis. There were sporadic efforts to have a youth group with lots of fun activities planned—climb the rickety wooden steps in the bell tower and look over the lights of downtown Northampton; play Sardines and hide under the pews in the church; have sleepovers in the parlors. But my peers were busy. They could find fun in other places.

There was one trip that managed to draw back some of my confirmation colleagues. With a handful of other parishes, Jim organized a week-long trip to Washington, DC. We slept on the floor of the basement of a suburban parish and cooked meals in its kitchen. On the night before our visit to the Vietnam Veterans Memorial, Jim sat with us and told us how it felt when the grenade went off in his foxhole, killing the friend who was with him. It was a riveting story for a group of teenagers and we listened intently.

But it was the coda to the story that I remembered most. Some years after his discharge, Jim was in Nairobi with a group of Episcopalians visiting a companion diocese. While walking through a park, the group was mugged. No one was hurt, but the experience made Jim flash back to Vietnam. For the next few days, he was paralyzed by fear, unable to do anything without help from his travel companions. The group continued its trip and arrived in one particular village to a warm greeting from local church members. Jim described how he was wrapped in a giant hug by a woman who spoke only one word of English, "Welcome."

"In that moment," Jim said, "the fear and anxiety I had been feeling since the mugging in Nairobi melted away and I knew that I was loved and welcomed. The only thing she and I have in common is that we are both Christian. But on that day, that was all that mattered. I'll never see her again in this life, but she is a dear sister in Christ and I can't wait to see her in heaven." The story left me transfixed. I had never before thought that I had something in common with people in other parts of the world.

This was not the only time I learned that I might have something in common with people who seemed different than me. The congregation itself contained a good deal of difference. Sometimes I served as acolyte with a pair of identical twin brothers, each of whom was profoundly deaf. At first, I was put off by the difficulty of understanding them and working with them. Slowly, however, I realized they were not much different than me. On the youth group trip to Washington, DC, they taught me to swear in sign language. We became fast friends.

Other forms of difference were more challenging. The state mental hospital in Northampton closed in the mid-1980s and a whole host of people who needed psychiatric care ended up on city streets with little support. Several made their way to St. John's with some regularity. Len sat in the very front row every Sunday. I knew it was impolite, but my young eyes could not help but stare. He was overweight, his hair askew, and his face never seemed quite right. He had a vacant expression, but his eyes always seemed a little bit crazed. He was not like me and he was not really like anyone else I knew. But somehow, maybe, he was. He did go to St. John's, after all.

St. John's hosted a soup kitchen in its undercroft every Sunday morning. We passed the guests on our way out of church. They were also not like me. They smoked, swore, laughed too loud, smelled bad, and carried all their possessions with them in a single bag or two. But even if they were not like me, I was learning, they could still be part of St. John's. Not only could they be, I realized, they already were.

When people for the soup kitchen were not coming to St. John's, we were going to them. My first experience sorting cans of food at a food pantry and working for Habitat for Humanity came with the youth group. In addition to carefully enunciating the "Ow-er Fah-ther," the Sunday school collected school supplies for children affected by hurricanes in Florida or in new schools in Tanzania. When we marched into the service at the offertory to join our parents, we often rolled wagons full of canned food for the food pantry down the center aisle while the ushers carried the plates of money.

Carved in stone over the main entrance to St. John's were the words "Given to hospitality." Hospitality, I was learning, meant that everyone was welcome at St. John's—even people I did not usually meet in my life outside of church. They may have seemed different than me, but they were still, somehow, part of my life.

There was one aspect of life in Northampton whose difference some people found to be challenging. I learned this when my cousins came to visit when I was about ten. Sandy rushed in the door and breathlessly told me what he had seen on the drive in. "Jesse! There were two women walking down the street." He paused to make sure the significance of what he was about to say would sink in. "And they were holding hands!" To a young boy raised in a rural farming community, this was a piece of exceptional news. But Northampton is known for its tolerance of same-sex relationships. When Sandy told me the news, I shrugged.

Growing up in Northampton—which I heard described more than once as the "San Francisco of the east coast"—meant that a major part of the difference I encountered while growing up involved sexual orientation. Classmates of mine in school had two mothers. There were same-sex couples living in our neighborhood. They were friends we invited over for parties and saw walking their dogs. They were our fellow worshippers at St. John's. One woman in a lifelong relationship with another woman sponsored me for confirmation. By the time I graduated from high school, both the mayor and city council president were openly gay people. Homosexuality was not something foreign or unusual to me. Rather, it was the opposite—so commonplace as to attract hardly any notice, except from a visiting cousin.

But the issue took a surprising turn the autumn after I turned thirteen. The city council proposed an ordinance that would legalize what were called "domestic partnerships." The law would allow same-sex couples to have hospital visitation rights and share custody of children. The ordinance did not call the relationships marriages, and same-sex marriage was not then seriously on the political horizon. But the ordinance was an opening salvo in a debate that would take shape around the country a decade later. The ordinance ended up on the November ballot and the city was consumed with debate.

The opposition was led by Northampton's Catholic parishes and the one evangelical church in town. They called their coalition Northampton for Traditional Values and ensured the ordinance received major attention in the media. At the time, I had a school assignment to research an issue where people had "taken a stand." I chose the ordinance, though it is no longer clear to me if I thought those opposed to or in support of the ordinance were the ones taking a stand. I followed the news closely and clipped articles from the newspaper relating to the proposal. A week before the vote, I interviewed Jim to ask him why he supported the ordinance. "This is something we can do," he said, "to honor and include people who have often been excluded and rejected by society." On election day, I accompanied my father to the polling station and interviewed a man holding a sign opposed to the ordinance. "This is not just about same-sex partnerships and allowing gay people to register," he said. "This is about the values we have as a community. We need to remember Christian values."

To the surprise of those who took its passage to be a foreordained conclusion, the ordinance was defeated by a single percentage point. The church-led opposition was the decisive factor in defeating the measure. I finished my assignment and moved on to other projects. What I did not do, in retrospect, is consider the sharp divide the vote revealed. Jim was a church leader and he—and many other clergy in town—supported the ordinance. Yet other priests and other churches did not. I had heard both support and opposition to the ordinance defined in explicitly Christian terms. What explained this division? Why was there no consensus on the issue? At the time, I asked none of these questions. Whether they could register their relationships or not, gay people were going to continue to be a part of my daily life. In some ways, they seemed different than me and my family, but so did a whole host of other people I was encountering at St. John's. Having people from different backgrounds and walks of life all together in one place was just what it meant to be the church.

◦✠◦

One Sunday morning when I was nine, we had a guest at our morning gathering of the Sunday school. He was tall, played the guitar, and told us about a place named Bement—"like a B on cement"—the diocesan summer camp. Over dinner that evening my parents asked if I was interested in spending time away from home that summer. I was. That summer, I swam, shot archery, paddled a canoe around the lake, and fell in love with Bement. Bement became a regular part of my summers and before too many more had passed that same tall man, whose name was Mark, was back in the parlors at St. John's with his guitar. This time he pulled me aside and said, "You know, Jesse, you're old enough to be on staff. How would you like to work at Bement for the summer?" My mind boggled. The whole summer? At Bement?

I spent the next eight summers on staff at camp. My fellow staff members became some of my closest friends. We accompanied one another through high school, college, and into graduate school, and the romantic entanglements, challenging home situations, and life transitions that ensued. The staff was a mixed lot. On the one hand were the evangelical Episcopalians. They were part of nondenominational campus ministries at their colleges and intent on "saving" the children in our charge. One young camper, whose father had died not long before she came to Bement, asked a staff member if her father was in heaven. The counselor asked if her father believed in Jesus. "No," said the young camper, her lip quivering. "Then he's not in heaven," replied the staff member perfunctorily.

On the other hand, and by far the larger portion of the staff, were those who had been raised in their local Episcopal congregation but, like many of my fellow confirmands, had drifted away. Their parents were eager to feel as if they were raising them in the church but lacked, it seemed, either the ability or the resources to do the work themselves. Having their children spend a whole summer at a Christian camp no doubt gratified the parents and reassured them that their children were being raised right. These staff members believed—if they believed at all—in what one friend of mine called "stealth Christianity." "We don't have to talk about it openly," he said. "We show them God in the wonder of nature around them and in how we run our programs."

Standing in the middle of this divide was that tall man with the guitar, Mark Rourke. Mark laughed at dirty jokes and threw his elbows around on the basketball court—hard. The stories of the practical jokes he played when he was a younger staff member were legendary. But none of that meant he was not a deeply religious man. "Stealth Christianity" was not for him. When he was diagnosed with the brain tumor that would eventually kill him, he wrote the Bement community lengthy e-mails while he underwent radiation:

> As I walk through the door to radiology, I want two powers with me—God and therapeutic radiation. I make eye contact with other patients in the clinic on the way. We share smiles, winks, or other signs of support and understanding. I get a clear sense and some

signals from many of the people there that "feels" like prayer. At
other times it feels very important to pray silently for a patient
nearby. I wonder to myself what people who have not had a chance
to know Jesus might be saying or thinking at these moments. I am
left only to pray that there is something that supports and accom-
panies them on this journey. I pray that Jesus is riding shotgun
with them!

This last line was an allusion to a game that children play when
they argue over who should sit in the front seat of the car:

Think how blessed we all are as Christians to have Jesus riding
shotgun for us, every day, no matter where we are. Feel deep in
your heart for a second, feel very deeply, at how we might take that
precious gift for granted in our lives and how we might bring more
people to know that incredible blessing of Jesus riding shotgun.

I promise you this—it doesn't take lots of money or high
priced guest lecturers to come into relationship with other Christians. It requires only this: your time and willingness to be open to
saying YES when God says: "I got shotgun."

As I leave for my appointment the front seat of my car is always
gloriously filled with the echoes of: "I Got Gun."

His letters were a testament to the enduring power of God to
transform even the darkest situations into moments of hope. In his living and his dying, Mark showed that there was nothing to be ashamed
of in being a Christian or an Episcopalian. We could take deep comfort and courage from our faith—and still have fun while doing so.

The staff community tried to put some of this into practice
in the way we ran our summer programs. We met weekly in small
groups to study the Bible, address conflicts, and reflect on how the
week was going. The faith we live, I was learning, we do not live
alone. We live it within a community and our faith is strengthened—
and can be weakened—by how others in the community live. We
tried to explain this to our campers as well. I grappled with themes for
our evening devotions, haltingly encouraging campers to think about
where they had seen God during the day or why it was important to
try to share a cabin with other campers who might seem different than
them. Sometimes, I got so tangled up in my words, I barely made it

through a closing prayer. Sometimes, though, it worked. Giving good-night high-fives to a group of campers one evening, a young camper rolled over in bed and said contentedly, "When I get home, I'm going to have to ask my mother to take me to church more often. I've got a lot of catching up to do!"

This was the flavor of Anglicanism in which I was raised. At its best, it was open to all comers, regardless of mental ability, age, gender, sexual orientation; focused on those who did not have what we did; and community-centric, knowing that a healthy community leads to a deeper faith. On its less good days, however, it was a faith that struggled to understand how believing in Jesus affected one's Monday-to-Saturday life and grappled—but never very seriously—with the challenge of keeping young people in church. Still, we were Christian and we knew our bishop made us Episcopalians. But we did not have to go around telling everybody about it.

CHAPTER 2

An Unexpected Visitor

Diocese of Nova Scotia and Prince Edward Island, Anglican Church of Canada

After I graduated from high school, I moved to rural Nova Scotia in Canada to attend university in the small town of Wolfville. This meant I was again an Anglican, a change I first became aware of when I drove into Wolfville with my parents and we passed a wooden church surrounded by a large cemetery: "St. John's Anglican Church," the sign read. I resolved to come back to learn more.

My resolve was tested the first Sunday morning of the term. There was no one around to wake me up, no activity that indicated it was time to go to church. Instead, my residence hall was dead quiet. I got out of bed only because I had made a new friend in the first week of school. Fisher was from the Solomon Islands and in conversation we learned that we were both Anglican. I told him about the church I saw on the way into town. We decided to visit it together.

Wolfville has one main street that stretches for a few blocks of banks, shops, and city offices. That Sunday morning, our walk down Main Street was quiet. The only substantial activity was in front of the two other churches we passed on our way out of town: the large Baptist church on the corner of campus and the United Church next to the fire station. We kept going out of town, up a slight hill, and into the parking lot of the wooden church I had seen a few days earlier. We were there for the middle of three services, the one that was called the Family Service. Looking around the parking lot that morning, there was not much activity, certainly not of the kind I associated with families at St. John's in Northampton. Most of the parking spaces were empty and the only person I saw heading for the door was using a cane.

Inside, the wood was dark and lent a kind of suffocating gloom to the interior. But what really surprised me was the size: it was tiny. I was familiar with the airy buttresses and high ceilings of St. John's in Northampton, which had an aisle down the middle and one on each side, leading to a raised chancel that could easily accommodate a large choir. Looking around, all I saw was a single aisle down the middle, with about eight plain wooden pews on each side. The aisle ended in a small chancel, with barely enough room for a pew or two on each side for the choir and a single aisle to reach the communion rail. At the foot of the chancel was a small wooden pulpit, set to one side. There was another difference with Northampton, I realized, in the chancel. Not only was it small, it was more ornate and more decorated than anything in Northampton. The altar, backed against the wall, was the chancel's centerpiece. It was decorated with fine green cloth.

Given the number of cars in the parking lot, it was no surprise that there were about twenty people in the pews and a handful of children. Fisher and I walked across the creaky wooden floor and found seats toward the back just in time for the first hymn. The woman at the organ played with skill, but I could barely hear anyone singing. People had hymnals in front of them, but I could not hear much above a soft mumble rising from each pew. As the mumbling continued, the priest came down the aisle. There was no procession, no acolytes or lay people. Neither was there a choir, which explained the mumbling. Just a single man, older and graying, but still trim and limber. His vestments hung on him like they had been worn many times before.

Once he launched into the liturgy, some of the feelings of foreignness began to fade away. The words he was saying were largely familiar and the actions he led us in felt comforting. Yes, the church was smaller than I expected. Yes, I did find it a bit odd that the priest celebrated communion with his back to the congregation and a bit more bowing and genuflecting than I knew in Northampton. But as we mumbled the last stanza of the concluding hymn, I had a feeling— vague and hard to pinpoint—that, somehow, this was the right place to be. Afterward, Fisher and I were greeted by several people on our way out the door. They invited us to stay for coffee and as I mingled with them, I knew I would be back.

The priest who processed in that first Sunday was named Doug Hergett. He was in his thirtieth year as rector of the congregation. His ministry, I later learned, had been marked by a deep commitment to the needs of the least and the poorest in the community. He had, for instance, played a pivotal role in ensuring affordable housing was built in the area. But on my fourth Sunday at St. John's, he had an announcement. "Many of you know that my wife and I have been building a home for many years. It is nearing completion and with it my time in St. John's. I'll be retiring at the end of the year." The congregation took the news with equanimity. Apparently, the end had been in sight for some time.

Doug's retirement was the end of an era, and the congregation knew it. It is not clear to me what they expected to happen after he left. But whatever it was, it almost certainly is not what they got. After an interim period that stretched over the summer, I returned to Wolfville and found a new rector. Cathy Lee was young. She was a woman. She had short, fashionably cut blond hair. At the middle service, which I still attended, she put a small table between the two front pews at the foot of the chancel and celebrated communion facing the congregation. This was her first rector position so she was new to the whole business of being in charge of a congregation and she knew it. She made mistakes during the service and laughed at them. The change from Doug—who had been doing the same thing for so long it was impossible for him to make a mistake—was dramatic. The church remained as creaky as ever, but there was a new kind of energy in it. Attendance crept upward as husbands returned to church. A young female rector was certainly more interesting than a grey-haired priest.

Some of Cathy Lee's energy produced wonderful results. On her first Easter, a respectable portion of the congregation turned out for a 5 a.m. sunrise service. Standing in the cemetery in the predawn chill, we kindled the first fire of Easter. We processed toward the church doors, reading the lessons of Israel's deliverance. Once inside, we turned on the lights and proclaimed that the Lord was risen indeed. The organist had not been persuaded to get out of bed so Cathy Lee led the congregation in *a capella* rounds. Startlingly, people sang and sang well. In that little church in the early hours of Easter morning, these were Anglicans rejoicing in the first and best service of the new Christian hope.

But not every innovation worked out so well. Perhaps buoyed by the success of the music that Easter morning or simply tired of the mumbling, Cathy Lee persuaded the organist to add some new hymns to the congregation's repertoire. And so, one morning before the service began, the organist came out from behind the console and taught us to sing, "Will You Come and Follow Me?" a hymn text written by John Bell of the Iona Community and set to a Scottish folk tune. The congregation picked it up quickly and soon it was a regular part of our repertoire. In fact, it was too regular. Every other Sunday, it seemed, we were singing the same five verses in which Jesus asks us to follow him. The tune, once pleasantly catchy, quickly caused my heart to sink when I heard its first notes. The more frequently we sang it, the more the energy we once had began to dissipate.

Cathy Lee brought her new energy to the little wooden pulpit as well. Doug's sermons had been fine: they reflected on the Bible passages and, importantly, they were short. But Cathy Lee was different. Her energy in the pulpit was infectious. As I listened I realized something new was happening. She was not just talking about the Bible and the passages appointed for that day. She preached about the world, and one part in particular: Israel, or, as she said, Palestine. It was the beginning of the second *intifada* in the Holy Land. Bombs were exploding in Jerusalem and Tel Aviv and the Israeli army was pushing deeper into Gaza and the West Bank. Cathy Lee was on an e-mail list and received updates from the Anglican bishop in Jerusalem. Sometimes her sermons consisted simply of reading his e-mails. She prayed pointedly for peace, and often.

This kind of sermon was novel for me. In Northampton, Jim usually preached about daily life and the way in which God's grace can transform our experience of life together. Mostly, I remembered the illustrations he used from movies he had recently seen. I listened to Cathy Lee's sermons and was surprised at the ways she made it seem self-evident that our Christian faith compelled us to be interested in, pay attention to, and pray for people in the Holy Land, and work actively for peace here and there. But the emotion of the sermons was unusual—and discomfiting—for me. Cathy Lee bore each development in the Holy Land, it seemed, as a personal burden. Her voice had more than the usual modulation I was used to from a preacher. She closed her eyes at times, as if overcome with emotion.

Cathy Lee's focus on peace extended beyond the pulpit. In her continuing effort to expand the musical selection, she invited a congregant to play the offertory anthem on guitar. It was Steve Earle's "Jerusalem," a folk-rock ballad about the need for peace in the holy city. The woman on the guitar sang well. Cathy Lee sat back in her chair, her eyes closed, soaking in the music. Such overt sentiments in church were unknown to me. As I looked around the congregation at other people shifting uncomfortably in their pews, I thought that I was not alone.

⁂

The more Sundays I spent at St. John's the more I became part of the congregation. I was no longer a newcomer to be greeted and welcomed back but a familiar face to chat with over coffee after the service. I came to know my fellow congregants. There were a few teachers and one or two nurses. The chair of the economics department at my university was one of the husbands who came wandering back into church when Cathy Lee arrived. The president of the local chapter of the Progressive Conservative political party belonged. It was a reasonable cross section of the population of Wolfville, a modest-sized hub community in the midst of miles and miles of agricultural land.

What there were not a lot of, I quickly realized, was people like me. There were enough young children to sustain a Sunday school. But I fell in the vast chasm between those children and their parents. If I had felt lonely during my last years at St. John's in Northampton, I felt positively abandoned once I arrived in Wolfville. When I woke up on Sunday morning, my residence hall was silent, a stark contrast to the loud partying of the night before. Occasionally, a few students from the university wandered out to St. John's, but they did not often come back. The walk was too far, the congregation too old, the worship too old-fashioned, the liturgy too confusing, the music not good enough—whatever they wanted, St. John's did not have it. Even Fisher, my once stalwart companion, gradually began to attend the Baptist church on the corner of campus.

There were Christians my own age at university. I found many of them at InterVarsity, the evangelical student fellowship. The praise choruses, guitar music, and extemporaneous prayer were quite different from what I found on Sunday mornings. But I liked the people, made good friends, and appreciated the diversity the group brought to my life. From time to time, I even broached the idea with friends of coming to St. John's with me on Sunday. My invitation was usually met with derision—polite and kind, but derision nonetheless. Anglican, my friends knew, meant boring liturgy and stultifying sermons that lacked energy or enthusiasm. I tried to explain that Cathy Lee was different, but it was not to be. On Sunday mornings, my InterVarsity friends either joined Fisher at the church on the corner of campus or, more likely, climbed in the van that drove around campus on Sunday mornings and picked up students to take to the Baptist church in a neighboring town. That church, I knew, did not have an organ or a confusing liturgy. They had a praise band with drums, guitars, and a keyboard, and almost no liturgy to speak of. They sang songs, listened to the Bible, heard a long sermon, prayed, sang some more songs, and then went to the hall for lunch. Against that, how could St. John's compete? But I was not overly disappointed with the situation. St. John's was the steady anchor of my worship week. InterVarsity let me become close to the other Christians on campus. I studied the Bible and prayed with them. If none of them wanted to come to St. John's on Sunday morning, that did not mean they could not still be my friends and my sisters and brothers in Christ. In my bifurcated religious life, I thought I had found more or less the same thing: Christians, different, but united by a common bond.

The more time I spent alternating between these religious worlds, however, the more I realized that for a lot of people being a member of the two divergent groups was too much to hold together. The more I heard people talking about theology in InterVarsity, the more I wondered just where I fit in. In one group conversation, a friend noted how many wonderful people there were in her residence hall. They were friendly and nice, but "they don't believe in Jesus so they're going to burn in hell." My theology was still forming, but this struck me as too far out of bounds. I had not heard much talk about hell at either St. John's. It was not necessarily that what she said was wrong so much as making such a categorical and definitive statement about something so difficult to comprehend seemed unwise. As I looked around, however, people were nodding as if the truth of the comment was obvious. The conversation was indicative of what my InterVarsity friends focused on in their theology: salvation, heaven, hell, Jesus, atonement.

There was a personal focus as well in the way they concentrated on the individual's relationship with God and were less concerned—if at all aware—of the rest of the world that did not share the relatively comfortable style of life to which we were all accustomed. What I almost never heard mentioned were the issues Cathy Lee emphasized in the pulpit: peace, reconciliation, and the world around us.

One issue was mentioned at InterVarsity only in tones that indicated the matter was settled and not up for debate. The Bible, it was plainly asserted, condemned homosexuality. Therefore, it was impossible to be both gay and Christian. In rural Nova Scotia at the time, I knew only a few out gay people in the student body and I never remember hearing the issue discussed at St. John's in any form or fashion. Nonetheless, it attracted major attention at InterVarsity. What I heard was out of keeping with what I had intuitively learned growing up in Northampton. There were gay people in the congregation there; how could homosexuality be incompatible with the Bible? But when I broached this with my InterVarsity friends, the conversation rarely went far. Bible passages were quoted and the matter deemed settled, although I doubt many of my InterVarsity friends had ever encountered a same-sex couple in their life. Occasionally, with people I was closer to in InterVarsity, I pressed the question, genuinely interested in trying to reconcile what I learned growing up in Northampton with what they learned growing up in their churches. No one's mind was ever changed, but I like to think the act of conversation deepened the relationship. The conversations, at least, were both respectful and honest.

The divide between my Sunday mornings at St. John's and my Friday evenings with InterVarsity were teaching me there were at least two different kinds of Christianity. There was the kind I knew from both St. John's: older, liturgical, shrinking, and broadly liberal. There were other churches like this in Wolfville, I knew. My roommate Tom went to the United Church and had a similar experience of sticking out in the congregation on account of his age. Then there was the kind of Christianity I was encountering in InterVarsity: younger, growing, and broadly conservative.

The divide between the two was laid starkly bare for me on a Sunday evening in January. Tom and I—both serving as assistants at the university chapel and preaching occasionally at our churches in town—were asked to preach at the community's Week of Prayer for Christian Unity service held at Tom's United Church. I remember looking out at the pews as we preached—the parish was quite full—and being struck by just how many grey-haired and no-haired congregants there were. Except for our third roommate, Andrew, no one else of our generation was present. (That it was Super Bowl Sunday likely did not help.) As I accepted the good wishes of people on the way out the door, I had the sense that Tom and I were people on whom these older parishioners were pinning their hopes for the future. We were welcome in the church insofar as our presence absolved the older people of any sense of failure at not ensuring their own children and grandchildren still went to church. Our words about Christian unity and togetherness were fine, but they manifestly failed to address this gap between the two separate and distinct Christian worlds I moved in.

So I kept moving between Sunday mornings and Friday nights. Sunday mornings at St. John's were like a familiar blanket I could wrap myself in for warmth and comfort. Friday nights were the bracingly cold shower that kept me fresh and on my toes. In truth, it was invigorating—if not always easy—to encounter people who so consistently held different views than me and to seek to understand one another in prayer and Bible study. There were two Christianities, I knew. But I was no closer to figuring out how they fit together.

But then one Sunday in my fourth year in Wolfville, not long before I graduated, I had an experience that showed some kind of integration might be possible. Cathy Lee had asked me to preach, which meant being part of all three services at St. John's, an unusual occurrence. After the early service, I noticed a familiar face in the line at the door. It was Pastor Morrison, the minister at the Baptist church on the corner near the university. He shook my hand and thanked me for my sermon. I mentioned I had not expected to see him at an Anglican church on a Sunday morning. "I often come to this service," he said. "We don't have communion every Sunday at our church and it's important to me that I do." With that, he was out the door to hurry to church and prepare for his services.

The thought of why he did not institute a more regular communion service in his congregation passed through my head. Mostly, however, I was struck that something I took completely for granted—that each service on Sunday would include the celebration of the Eucharist—was valued so highly by him that he made time for it on a busy Sunday morning. The more I thought about it, the more it seemed right and appropriate that he should have been there. Communion, I knew, is a marker of relationship and community between people. That is one reason we confess our sins and make peace with our neighbor before we partake of the meal together. If Pastor Morrison wanted to be part of that, there was no reason he should not join in with us. Whatever the distinctions and differences that may have separated us, if we could share this common meal, surely we truly were united and part of the same body. It did not seem like much and it seemed to go no distance at all toward lessening the divisions I was experiencing elsewhere in my life. But Pastor Morrison's example of showing up in an unexpected place remained with me long after I left church that morning.

CHAPTER 3

"Bind Us Together, Lord"

*Diocese of Mthatha, Anglican Church
of Southern Africa*

"Uxolo lweNkosi malusoloko lunani" says the priest, spreading his arms wide. "The peace of the Lord be always with you."

"Lube nawe kanjalo," we respond in Xhosa, the language of the congregation, linking hands with our neighbors. "And also with you."

"Bind us together, Lord," sings the choir leader in a high, clear voice.

"Bind us together," we sing as we join in, "with chords that cannot be broken. Bind us together, Lord, bind us together, bind us together with love." As we sing, we raise and lower our hands, an unbroken chain stretching through the church. Mine are the only white hands in the chain.

For the two years that I lived and worked in Mthatha, South Africa, this was the guaranteed highlight of each week: the passing of the peace at St. Andrew's Anglican Church in Ngangelizwe township. It usually came around the two-hour mark of what was routinely a three-hour service. As a result, it functioned as something like the seventh-inning stretch of a baseball game, a chance for us to stand up, stretch our legs, and greet our neighbor. More importantly, the peace tangibly represented the feeling I had at St. Andrew's. Yes, my skin was a different color than that of my fellow congregants and my first language was not theirs. They lived in a township in a city that had once been the capital of the Transkei, the neglected and forgotten "homeland" of the Xhosa people during apartheid.

But none of this mattered when we exchanged the peace. In singing about being bound together, we anticipated the unity that would come at the altar rail. After the last note of "Bind us together" faded, we launched into Xhosa-language choruses and greeted each other while the altar was prepared. The warmth and enthusiasm with which people greeted me, and which I tried to equal in my greetings to them, showed me that I was welcome here.

Different, yes. But still part of the same body of Christ.

∽§∾

The path that led me to St. Andrew's was a winding one. I arrived in Mthatha as a fresh-faced, young adult missionary of the Episcopal Church to work at a community center in a shantytown known as Itipini, a community built on a garbage dump. The scale of the cultural, racial, and linguistic barriers I faced immediately overwhelmed me. Everyone spoke Xhosa, a language I had no background in. I struggled to adjust to the new work, and the reality of HIV/AIDS, poverty, and illness that were part of life in Itipini. I had some friends, but I longed for a church to belong to, to help me process what I was encountering.

Just up the hill behind Itipini was Ngangelizwe. During apartheid, Ngangelizwe was the township where black people lived. The quality of housing was much worse than in town, and life was just generally harder than elsewhere. Much has changed since the end of apartheid, however. For one thing, I was allowed to roam freely in Ngangelizwe, though I still attracted stares. More importantly, the area has undergone what might be called a partial gentrification. People who have done well in democratic South Africa have built homes in the areas where they grew up. These new houses had running water and were surrounded by tall fences. The government was also paying more attention. There was a new health center in Ngangelizwe and some new schools had opened in recent years. From time to time, I drove past St. Andrew's, the Anglican church. But I knew its services were in Xhosa and I always dismissed it as a possible church home. However, as I gained functionality in Xhosa at work and found myself not satisfied with the limited English-language church services on offer in Mthatha, I thought it might be worth a try.

Still, I hesitated. Although my work took me through Ngangelizwe often and I was used to being the only white face around, I was uncomfortable at the thought of how I might stick out as the only white face in a large African congregation. I did a little research. One day when I was driving past, I saw that the doors were open. I parked the car and poked my head inside. The sanctuary was large and completely undistinguished architecturally. The building was made of cinder block and the painters had chosen a variety of citrus colors for the wall—a lemon yellow along the two sides, a sort of pink grapefruit tone behind the altar. The floor was linoleum tile and the pews were of plain wood. One long communion rail divided the chancel from the rest of the sanctuary. Seeing the inside was helpful but not enough to give me the courage to actually attend a service at St. Andrew's. Being in Ngangelizwe for work was fine, but I thought it would feel odd to be there on a Sunday.

Two weeks later, though, I was driving with Mkuseli, one of my coworkers, through Ngangelizwe. "Church Street," he said, as we drove past the turn-off to St. Andrew's. "That's where my church is. A church on Church Street!" he said with a smile.

Problem solved! I thought. If Mkuseli was a member, I could just go with him. At least that way I might seem marginally less out of place. "Mkuseli," I said casually. "Perhaps I might be able to come to church with you some Sunday?"

"Of course!" he replied.

It took another week or two but on a February morning, just before Ash Wednesday, I drove over to Mkuseli's house to pick up him, his wife, and daughter. Church Street was busy with foot and car traffic. The men were in dark suits and ties, and the women wore flowing dresses. I immediately felt underdressed. I had not even mustered a tie that morning, let alone a blazer. As I looked for a parking spot, I started thinking of ways to get out of the situation. Perhaps I could tell Mkuseli I was not feeling well, drop him off, and come back another time. Not only would I stick out because of my skin color, I would stick out because of my dress as well. But I at least had to try St. Andrew's before rejecting it. As I carefully nosed my car in among the dark, imported cars, I noticed a tin shack not far from St. Andrew's. It was a church, its name painted on the side: "Apostolic Faith Mission Zion." Well, I thought, I would definitely feel out of place there; best go for the Anglicans.

Mkuseli is quite short. I am not. We must have made quite the pairing as we walked into church together. "Where do you usually sit?" I asked him casually, trying to lighten the mood. He did not seem to understand me. Although he was competent in English, we still often had communication problems, so I thought nothing of it. Instead, he found a pew about two-thirds of the way back and sat down. I slipped in as well, nodding casually to the woman in the pew. Since I knew most churches in South Africa had a "bring your own" policy with prayer books and hymnals, I had bought my own Xhosa prayer book, hoping it would make me look like I belonged. Its cover was uncreased and its pages were gleaming white. The woman next to us held one that was dog-eared and well-used. I hoped she did not realize just how new I was to all this.

I just had time to notice that Mkuseli had neither a prayer book nor a hymnal, when I felt a tap on my shoulder. It was an usher. "Please, come with me," he said in English. "I'll show you where to sit." Had we sat in the wrong section? He pointed to the front of the church where the men in the nicest and darkest suits were sitting. "You can sit up there."

I started to protest. There must have been some mistake. I was not special or important in any way. But Mkuseli cut me off and stood up with an eager look on his face. "Come on," he said. I made some comment about leaving his wife behind, but he brushed it off. I reluctantly stood up and followed him toward the front, slouching as I went, as if that would somehow help conceal the awkwardness of my presence in the church. Fortunately, we were early and the sanctuary was still only half-full. The men in dark suits made way for us and we squeezed in with them. Some were wearing purple vests and ties, markers of their membership in the Bernard Mizeki Society, a group for men. Elsewhere in the congregation, there were women in the white and navy uniforms of the Mothers' Union. Looking around, I realized I was probably on the younger side of the congregation. For the most part, the congregation seemed to be made up of people of my parents' generation.

A crowd began to gather at the back of the church. This, I realized, was the beginning of the service. A young man in a red cassock and white surplice stood at the front, carrying a smoking thurible. He had his arm over a small boy, similarly vested, who was carrying a small silver boat in his hand. Behind them was a young man holding a tall silver cross, followed by six more young people carrying candles. If that was not enough, there was a small brigade of at least a dozen more acolytes behind them, all vested and looking serious. Behind the acolytes came a platoon of lay people, wearing white cassocks and carrying prayer books and Bibles. Behind them was a single deacon and behind him three priests, each wearing a cope. A male voice called out from the front of the church, "Hymn two zero three. Two. Zero. Three." There was no organ so the same voice sounded the first note and soon the congregation joined in. Neither Mkuseli nor I had a hymnal so we stood mutely as the procession marched past us. As they reached the front of the church, the brigade of acolytes turned to face one another, creating a corridor for the lay people and priests to process through. When the last priest in procession reached the front, he bowed deeply and everyone did the same, simultaneously. It was an impressive performance.

The opening of the service was familiar to me. There were the opening sentences, a short prayer, a hymn whose words I recognized as containing the word "glory," another prayer, and then we sat down. There were readings from the Bible, two sung canticles, and a sung psalm. I was following along in my prayer book and even managing to pronounce all the Xhosa words correctly, though usually a syllable or more behind the rest of the congregation. By the time we rose to our feet again and the gospel book was processed into the center of the church, I was beginning to feel comfortable. For all the uncertainty I felt walking into the church, once the service was underway, it felt like I was putting on a favorite old shirt that knew how to hang on me just so.

That feeling dissipated when the preacher ascended the two short steps to the pulpit directly above us. He began talking. And talking. And talking. Forty-five minutes later, he sat down. To that point in my life, it was the longest sermon I had ever heard. What his topic was I never knew. I had caught one word in ten and one sentence in fifty. But the sermon gave me time to think. During the epistle lesson, an usher had sidled up to us and asked Mkuseli and me to write down our names so they could announce us as visitors. This puzzled me. I thought Mkuseli was a member. But he had not exactly acted like a member to this point. He owned neither a prayer book nor a hymnal. At times, he did not seem to know when to stand or sit during the liturgy, though those actions came naturally to me. He was not dressed as nicely as many of the men in the church. Neither usher recognized him. To be sure, there were three or four hundred people in the sanctuary, but I still thought that if Mkuseli was a regular member of this church the usher would have at least known his face. Still,

I did not think much about it. By the time the passing of the peace rolled around and I linked hands with Mkuseli and my neighbor and sang "Bind us together" for the first time, I was feeling like I belonged. When we went forward to the communion rail, it felt almost natural to be in this place.

The announcements came at the end of the service. Mkuseli and I were introduced and made to stand up. I did so reluctantly, but Mkuseli gave a big smile and waved. He was announced as being from the village outside Mthatha where he grew up. When we greeted each other on Monday morning at work, I told him how thankful I was for taking me to church. He acknowledged my thanks, but we never spoke about the subject again. Neither did we ever go to St. Andrew's together again.

I never did figure out what the story was with Mkuseli and St. Andrew's. Though we became close colleagues, there was still a cultural and language barrier between us and I never felt like I could ask why he said he was a member. Maybe I had misunderstood him. More likely, I realized, Mkuseli thought of himself as Anglican but never went to an Anglican church. He was not rich. He and his family survived on the salary he was paid at the community center. It was enough for him to afford to rent a ten foot by ten foot cinder-block room that he, his wife, and daughter shared. One weekend a month, he took the family back to his rural village to see his mother. That, I knew, was what he thought of as "home."

St. Andrew's—to judge from the cars outside and the clothes the men wore—was a church by and for people who were at least in the middle class. To be a member, one essentially had to purchase a prayer book and hymnal, each of which cost about seven dollars. For people who lived on a dollar or two a day, like the ones I worked with at the community center, this was simply out of reach. They were not irreligious, I knew—many had a deep and abiding faith—but if they owned a book, it was a Bible; that was sufficient for their religious needs. At St. Andrew's, there was an implicit expectation that one would, in time, join the various guilds and groups of the church—the Mothers' Union or Bernard Mizeki Society, for instance. But there was a uniform for each group and those clothes cost money, not money that people like Mkuseli and his wife had to spare. Perhaps Mkuseli's grandfather had been Anglican or he was baptized in an Anglican church. He remained firmly Christian—he led our morning prayer circle at the community center and in other circumstances I often thought he would have been a fine priest—but as an adult he simply had not risen to the class necessary to be a member of a place like St. Andrew's. When he went home, he probably attended a local church not much different than the tin shack behind St. Andrew's. In South Africa, being Anglican was likely out of Mkuseli's budget.

⌀⟶⟵⌀

The thoughts about Mkuseli aside, the first Sunday at St. Andrew's left me buoyant. The comfort I felt at being wrapped in a familiar liturgy made me resolve to return the following weekend. But when my alarm went off that Sunday morning, I hesitated. All I could think of was how awkward I felt when I walked in the door the first time. No matter how comfortable the liturgy felt, I was not sure I could stomach another lengthy sermon in a language I barely spoke.

I fought back the thoughts and climbed out of bed. When I entered St. Andrew's, I again made for the pew two-thirds of the way back. Again, before I could get comfortable, I was being shown to the second row. This Sunday, I had pulled out my only sport coat so I would not stick out quite as much. Still, it was more than a little awkward. These men, presumably, had earned their spot in the front of the church. The senior warden who made the announcements the previous Sunday sat up here. I imagined the other men were members of the vestry. Who was I to join them? Once the service began, however, these thoughts began to fade and I felt more comfortable once again. We exchanged the peace and received communion together and soon were jostling out the door together. For all that I had wanted to stay in bed, it had been the right decision to come. I went back to St. Andrew's every Sunday for the next several weeks. Each time I made for a back pew, I was directed to the front. Eventually, I stopped even trying to sit anywhere else. It was an example of the unearned privilege I encountered in many places I traveled, and it made me feel like the opposite of Rosa Parks: I wanted to sit in the back, but they made me sit up front.

The Sundays passed and the seasons changed. We celebrated Palm Sunday by marching around the block with our palms. It was early April, the beginning of autumn, and the weather was quite chilly that morning. On Easter morning I was aware of the way the grass was turning brown in the fields around my house. The winter dry season was coming. There was no new growth of spring to provide the preacher an easy metaphor for his Easter sermon. Otherwise, the rhythm of life in St. Andrew's was much as I imagined it would be. There was little change in the liturgy from week to week, and I began to develop a facility with singing certain hymns and belting them out with my fellow men up front. As my Xhosa improved, I even managed to catch up to the congregation on the prayers.

After several Sundays, the senior warden took time during announcements to point me out to the congregation and introduce me again. "This is Jesse," he said in English. "He has been coming here for many weeks, he speaks Xhosa, and we are glad to have him." It was a bit of an exaggeration. I was able to greet my pew mates and have short conversations with them in Xhosa, but they all spoke English and that was usually the language we chatted in. Still, I appreciated the recognition.

The senior warden had an ulterior motive. At the end of the service, he pulled me aside and handed me a blue card. The writing was in Xhosa, but he gave me a quick explanation. "You write your name here," he said, "and the amount you want to pledge here." There was a series of check boxes below those two lines. "When you bring in that amount of money each month, we check the box." If I was going to be a member, I was going to be a pledging member!

᳁᳁᳁

Although South Africa's apartheid past is formally behind it, the country is still riven by deep poverty and social division. I saw the effects of this at work in Itipini, the shantytown where our community center was located. St. Andrew's was not far away and for a time I naively hoped I might see some people from Itipini at church on Sunday. But if Mkuseli could not manage it, the others definitely could not. I also hoped that people at St. Andrew's might show an interest in a place like Itipini. But in this, too, I was disappointed. It is not that newly successful South Africans are unfamiliar with the challenges facing their country. People with jobs, I knew, supported large, extended networks of family members who were not so fortunate. The work of simply getting by and keeping an extended family going was exhausting for many of my fellow parishioners. Still, I longed for people at St. Andrew's—and Anglicans more generally—to know more about the lives of the people I worked with in Itipini.

Each morning at the community center, I saw two young children, Asange, a little girl, and Esinakho, who I initially thought was her brother. They showed up together in the morning for preschool and went home together in the afternoon. I saw them play together and fight with one another the way siblings do. In time, however, I learned that, in fact, it was their mothers who were siblings. Kholeka and Xoliswa were sisters in their early twenties. The fathers of their children were no longer involved in their lives. Not long after I arrived, Kholeka and Xoliswa's mother died in a cooking accident. Their father—Asange and Esinakho's grandfather—left his daughters for another woman soon after. The two sisters lived together and raised their children together, making no distinction in their parenting. Each was equally the mother of both children. Though Asange and Esinakho acted like siblings, they were—nominally, at least—cousins.

Beginning with Northampton's debate over the Domestic Partnership Ordinance, I had heard about the "two mommies" situation, that is, two lesbian women raising children together. I had heard arguments made and denunciations issued that children need both a male and female presence in their lives as they are growing up. Church leaders—Anglican leaders—have made precisely this argument. Yet I have never heard any Anglican leader mention the problem of two mothers when the women are sisters who have been dealt a difficult hand by the combination of fate and the dismal performance of the men in their lives. As I encountered it at work, however, Asange and Esinakho's situation seemed far more tragic and serious—and far more worthy of attention from the church—than the more frequently mentioned "two mommies" scenario.

Even when my Xhosa was strongest, I never could make much sense of the sermons I heard at St. Andrew's so I never really knew how or if homosexuality figured into the content of the church's teaching. I knew from my work in Itipini which way the general cultural bias leaned. Once when I was in town with a group of students from Itipini, they suddenly broke into a fit of whispering and giggling. They pointed at two women walking down the street together. "Gay!" they whispered, as if it was the most hilarious thing they had seen that day.

I imagined some of my fellow parishioners shared a similar belief, if expressed in a less juvenile fashion.

Neither, however, did I ever see the church make much response to situations like that faced by Asange and Esinakho. And that is disappointing. If sex and sexuality are truly to be focal points for the Communion, the conversation is too narrowly focused. Teenage pregnancy, absent fathers, and struggling mothers may not be mentioned in the Bible in the same, direct way as same-sex relationships ostensibly are, but they are surely a part of the reality of family life in many parts of the world. As I watched Kholeka and Xoliswa raise their children, I thought that surely this was a place for a thoughtful, compassionate response from the church's leaders. I have yet to hear it.

Despite some of these frustrations, there was much I learned to love about St. Andrew's, and it became my church home in Mthatha. Some mornings I struggled to get out of bed and get up the energy to attend a three-hour service in a language I was, at best, barely functional in. But I became more comfortable and even began to bring other friends. This proved to be a brilliant move. When I showed up with a female friend, I realized we would not be able to sit in my usual spot up front because it was clearly only for men. She was my excuse to sit further back. After a few Sundays of this, even when my friend did not come, I still sat halfway back and no usher ever tried to move me again. Never have I felt so relieved to be seen as no one special.

On my final Sunday, the senior warden made a big deal of my departure. "He has been a full pledging member of this church," he said, never one to miss an opportunity to remind his congregation of the importance of their tithes. The priest prayed over me and said I had to come back. I was asked to write down my contact information for the church so they could have it on file after I left. For some reason, I wrote down my full name. When I handed it to the senior warden, he pointed to my middle name. "Andrew!" he said. "You clearly belong at this church."

Whether it was my name or simply divine providence, he was right. I had belonged to this church.

CHAPTER 4

Blessed Are the Peacemakers

Diocese of Northern Uganda, Church of Uganda

The harried-looking police officer, I am sure, was wishing he had not gotten out of bed that morning. Standing in the central traffic roundabout in Gulu, Uganda, he found his usual traffic-directing job slightly more complicated than usual. Marching down one avenue leading to the roundabout was a parade I was part of. We were a hundred or so people led by a handful of interfaith religious leaders, marching—as our signs and banners made clear—for peace in a region emerging from a ruinous civil war. But coming down another avenue leading to the same roundabout was another parade. This one was larger and had several drummers and dancers at its head. Its purpose was less clear. Based on its signs, it looked like it might be a march against poverty or in support of a microcredit program. No matter the worthiness of our causes, the two parades were on a collision course.

The police officer blew his whistle and motioned for our parade to stop. The bishops in their purple cassocks and the imams in their flowing robes obediently came to a halt at the head of the line, as did the small truck that was carrying our sound system. We watched the drummers and dancers pass. Even as we cheered for their cause—and they boisterously returned our greetings—I felt a brief stab of envy at their louder sound system and the energy of their drummers and dancers. Still, we had the bishops and imams and, anyway, marching for peace was a lot punchier and more to the point than marching against poverty or for microcredit or whatever it was they were doing.

Our leaders may have obeyed the police officer's directions, but others did not. Boda-boda motorcycle taxis weaved in and out among us, not letting the parade traffic disrupt their fares and daily routines. A truck full of construction materials tried to slip through a corner of the rotary, though the driver only succeeded in further snarling traffic while the marchers passed around him. Finally, the last of the marchers against poverty had passed by and the police officer motioned for us to carry on. On we marched, proclaiming the need for peace in northern Uganda, a land that has known war for far too long.

It was Christmastime and my work in Mthatha was on hiatus for two weeks. I had come to Gulu to visit my friend John, a fellow young adult Episcopal missionary. With our friend Matt, also a missionary in South Africa, I wanted to catch up with John and see what he had been up to in his work. Gulu has a difficult history. Beginning in the late-1980s, Gulu served as the center of the Ugandan military's campaign against the Lord's Resistance Army, a rebel group that ostensibly sought to establish an independent state based on the Ten Commandments, though it became infamous more for its breaking of those commandments than its observance of them. Both sides were brutal in their conduct of the war, but the LRA was particularly noteworthy for the way it pressed thousands of children into service. Whole communities sought refuge in cities like Gulu. In 2006, aid agencies estimated 1.7 million displaced people lived in more than two hundred camps across northern Uganda. The military action did not conclusively defeat the LRA, but it did succeed in pushing it out of Uganda and into the neighboring Democratic Republic of the Congo and southern Sudan. (Some years later, I would find myself in southwest South Sudan and learn about the havoc the LRA continued to wreak there.) By the time I visited Gulu, the city was emerging from the war years to a new phase of rapid growth. New buildings were going up and scaffolding made of tree trunks rose high around construction zones. Roads were being paved, banks and restaurants opened, and a lively hum was returning to the city.

To this point, my experience of Africa was confined to Mthatha. Although the people in Itipini were proof that Mthatha was not rich, South Africa still counted as a modestly prosperous country on the continent. Gulu was a different story. White SUVs emblazoned with the logo of the United Nations or other well-known nongovernmental organizations sped around town. Not far from the traffic roundabout where the two parades had crossed, the World Food Program stored its wares in a sprawling camp of canvas tents. It was the dry season and dust was everywhere, giving the tents an ochre shading. There were still several camps for internally displaced people around Gulu and the needs of the people there were great. Things I had come to take for granted in parts of Mthatha—hot water, ovens, potable water, wide-spread indoor plumbing, pasteurized milk—were not to be found in Gulu. More importantly, there continued to be unresolved political tensions. Northern Uganda's largest group of people is the Acholi. The LRA's success had grown, in part, out of a general feeling among some Acholi of discontent and exclusion. That feeling had not entirely—or even mostly—disappeared.

A few days before the peace parade, John met Matt and me in Entebbe, the international airport outside Kampala, Uganda's capital. We spent the night with an Anglican priest friend of John's who was building a new home and had moved into the partially finished building just a few weeks prior to our visit. Electricity had only been connected to a single bulb in the room downstairs. John, Matt, and I rolled our sleeping bags out on the concrete floor of what was to be the main bedroom and talked by the light of our headlamps under our mosquito nets. It was a slumber party, Episcopal missionary style.

Gulu is three hundred kilometers north of Kampala. In the United States, this trip might take three hours. When John had first been driven to Gulu, the journey stretched over one very long day and into the night, slowed by breakdowns and the poor roads. We traveled on the early morning post office bus. The only seats left—and later I learned to be grateful there were any seats at all—were in the far back. We squeezed into the second-to-last row, my knees bumping uncomfortably against the seat back in front of me. People in Gulu later told me the journey between Kampala and Gulu at one point had taken as little as four hours. Now, however, thanks to a combination of war, neglect, and corruption, the road had deteriorated so much that only patches of pavement remained. Long stretches were unimproved dirt. In search of the best—meaning fastest, not necessarily smoothest—path north, the bus driver freely crossed from the left to the right side

and back again, apparently uncaring about other traffic and swerv-
ing at times perilously close to the gullies on either side of the road.
More passengers joined us as we headed north and soon there were
several standing in the aisles. Before long, the bus was so full, John and
I offered to take two small children on our laps. Sitting in the back of
the bus made the swerves swervier and the bumps bumpier. With two
small children on our lap, the experience alternated between painful
and hilarious. When we pulled into Gulu more than seven hours after
we first left, we were cramped, dusty, and exhausted. "Welcome to
Gulu," John said, mustering the last remaining reserves of his energy.

John's boss and host was Bishop Nelson Onono-Onweng, then-
bishop of the Diocese of Northern Uganda and one of the bishops at
the head of our parade a few days later. The Church of Uganda is one
of a handful of provinces in the Anglican Communion that acted to
end high-level links with the American church in the wake of the ordination of Gene Robinson as bishop of New Hampshire. But Bishop
Nelson was interested in having a mission volunteer from the United
States to work with diocesan youth, and John accepted the position.

Although Ugandans have been in charge of their church for fifty
years, the legacy of the mission era remains strong. The church's close
historical ties to the colonial power means it functions at times as a
quasi-established church for the country. Indeed, its official name—
the Church of Uganda—is an indication of this. In Kampala, we had
seen evidence of its outsized role in society. There was the tall cathedral in the center of the city and the major university in which the
church took a leading role. This prominence has not compromised its
independence in the past, however. The second Ugandan archbishop
of the church, Janani Luwum—himself a former bishop of Northern
Uganda—was ordered killed by Idi Amin in 1977 for his outspoken
opposition to the regime. Luwum's statue now stands with that of
other martyrs of the twentieth century at Westminster Abbey.

Gulu is a long way from those corridors of power. But the legacy
of mission is still present, particularly in the enduring nature of the
mission compound. When missionaries arrived, they concentrated on
establishing centers of activity that could house a school, a hospital,
and other church-related activities in one place. They induced the
people they encountered to listen to their preaching by providing a
host of services not directly related to the church. When Ugandans

moved into positions of ecclesiastical leadership, they occupied these same compounds.

The headquarters of the Diocese of Northern Uganda are in a former mission compound, a few kilometers outside of the center of town. A handful of years before my visit, it was not safe to travel this far out of town for fear of the LRA. But with the advent of peace, people felt comfortable moving farther out of town. Riding out to the compound from the bus depot on a motorcycle taxi, we passed the new homes and huts that were being rebuilt, the mud brick and thatch surrounded by leafy palm and banana trees. There was cassava and sugar cane growing in the yards. A few huts now had small businesses, some selling soft drinks and candy, others homebrew.

The idea of a diocesan compound is, in a sense, no different than the idea of a cathedral close in a place like Canterbury or St. John the Divine in New York City. But differences began to be apparent as we pulled into the compound in Gulu. Over John's house stood a tall, leafy mango tree. The cathedral was a brick structure, painted orange, with a tin roof. Surrounding Bishop Nelson's modest house was a forest of black water tanks on stilts. Putting the tanks at a height meant gravity could bring the water into the house's taps. The color of the tank meant the water heated up in the afternoon sun so that evening showers were warm.

The exhaustion of the travel left me with little energy to appreciate these details. What mattered was we had arrived. After our long day, that warm shower was particularly pleasant.

The peace march was on New Year's Eve, a few days after our arrival. When one of John's coworkers came to pick us up, he gave us each an official T-shirt for the march. On the front was the logo of the Acholi Religious Leaders Peace Initiative, the organization the local bishops and imams formed at the height of the civil war to press for peace. On the back was the theme of the march: "Women are peace-builders by nature." Marchers were gathering on the edge of town. Bishop Nelson looked appropriately episcopal in his purple cassock except for one detail. Instead of the shiny black shoes I was accustomed to seeing professional men wear, he had on a pair of New Balance sneakers. The bishop was a practical man. There would be a lot of walking today.

Bishop Nelson moved to the front of the procession, joining an Anglican bishop from a neighboring diocese, two Roman Catholic bishops, and the local Muslim imam. For all that women were being called peace-builders by nature, all the religious leaders were men. We began moving slowly down the road, the bishops leading the way. In our midst was a small truck with outsized speakers. A man walked alongside with a microphone, calling out to the people we passed, explaining who we were and exhorting them to join in. A woman in the market waved her hand ecstatically and began shouting her support. Others were less interested. A few boda-boda drivers waiting for their next fare looked on disinterestedly.

We paused in front of Gulu's public hospital, the place that had for so many years borne the brunt of caring for war victims. The religious leaders took turns praying. They prayed for an end to the war, for the peace to endure, for safety, for healing, and for return for the still-displaced. For Bishop Nelson, I knew, these were prayers with human faces attached to them. Although I was unable to see it on my visit, the church had an active ministry in the camps for displaced people. Not long after my visit, the church began a healing program for people who had suffered from the trauma of the war.

The patients came to the windows to see what was going on. A gaunt woman leaned on her too-thin arms and stared out the window at us. An older man rested wearily on his crutches and looked on. What were their stories? How many things would I never know about the toll the war had taken in this part of the world? Apart from the statistics that were used to summarize the war, the people in the hospital were the very personal faces of the devastation. Some years later when an Internet video about the LRA went viral, I thought back to these patients and wondered where they were. I prayed for the Diocese of Northern Uganda and its work, which I knew continued regardless of the Twitter and Facebook interest that quickly moved on.

The tie-up at the roundabout happened not long after we left the hospital. Once clear, we wound up at the field in the center of Gulu where cattle were grazed. An array of tents and musicians awaited our arrival. The religious leaders began to speak, taking turns to summarize—and expand upon—parts of the press release they had ready to distribute to the local media who were covering the event: "For nearly twenty-one years, the need and cry for 'lasting peace' in

North and North-Eastern Uganda has been on the top of our agenda," the release said. "The urgent need for 'lasting peace' is the reason why we should, collectively, say 'NO TO VIOLENCE.' . . . The long years of suffering in our region is a challenge to all of us peace loving Ugandans to become 'PEACE BUILDERS' through dialogue, forgiveness and reconciliation."

The leaders played on the theme of the march and highlighted the role of women in society, and particularly in Acholi culture. In that culture, they said, "grandmothers are the ones who give blessings of success to all who go for hunting expeditions. On the same note, a man who quarreled with his wife at night before the day of hunting was not allowed to go for blessings from the grandmother until after reconciliation with his wife. Also during the planting season, the grandmother gives blessings upon the seed before it is planted. At birth, women are the ones who play a great role in assisting fellow women to deliver peacefully." This peaceful role was no surprise, the religious leaders said. They highlighted examples from the Qur'an and the Bible that spoke of the important role of women. Mary Magdalene, they noted, was the first to see Jesus at the empty tomb and "was commissioned to be the messenger of peace to the Apostles and the whole world."

From the holy texts, they turned to a larger theme: the particular devastation and suffering that war has on women and children. "Women and children are the most affected groups who suffered greatly from the twenty-one-year-old conflict in our region. Yet their aspiration and desire for peace through dialogue, forgiveness, and reconciliation occupy their hearts. To you, dear women of peace, ARLPI asks for forgiveness from you on behalf of those who committed crimes and atrocities against you and the innocent children in this conflict and at home through domestic violence."

The final section of the day's program was an exhortation to men to change their relationships with women. It was repeated and direct. "Reconcile with them," the men were told, for, in an echo of Desmond Tutu's theology, "'there is no future without reconciliation.'" Moreover, they had to "respect the dignity and recognize the rights and God-given talents of women in peace building." Speaking directly to the young men, the religious leaders told them they must "become fully committed to peace building like women who are peace builders by nature. . . . Above all, do everything in your power to become peace builders like women."

Before moving to Mthatha, I had heard the phrase the "African church" used in conversations about the Anglican Communion, as in, for instance, "The African church doesn't understand the American church." Some of these comments were unthinkingly derogatory, like ones that highlighted the alleged misogyny of the leaders of the "African church." I thought about those charges as I listened to the speeches. In truth, there was something a bit jarring in hearing a message about the important role of women from a panoply of male religious leaders. (A few women did take to the microphone earlier in the rally but that was mostly to read Scripture passages.) Still, the gender of the messengers did not detract from the truth of their message, one that was not all that different than what any major nongovernmental organization or development expert says about the role of women in society. As the religious leaders spoke, I looked around the large crowd that was listening. Most were women. Perhaps, I thought, these women would hear this message and feel empowered to press these male leaders for further change. For societies to make progress and work toward peace, women cannot be in a subjugated position. To hear that basic truth preached so honestly and repeatedly from a group of male church leaders was nothing short of refreshing.

When John took us to church on Sunday, I saw again what a mistake it was to lump the "African church" into a single, undifferentiated mass. St. Andrew's and the other Anglican congregations I knew in South Africa practiced a particular style of worship: liturgically formal, heavy on incense, and featuring an array of clergy and lay leaders in matching vestments. It was high churchmen of the Society for the Propagation of the Gospel who first brought Anglicanism to South Africa and their legacy was apparent in the worship. It is how South Africans know how to "do" church.

When John took us the few steps over to the tin-roofed cathedral for worship on Sunday morning, it was for an Anglican service alright—but one that was nothing at all like what I knew in Mthatha. Instead, the worship was authentic to the heritage of the evangelical Church Missionary Society. The small handful of clergy came in with hardly any procession. There were almost no lay people on the altar party, not even a thurifer, *de riguer* in any Anglican church I had visited in South Africa. The clergy wore simple vestments and passed by the altar with a modest reverence. There was no cope or even a chasuble. Moreover, the color of stole they were wearing varied. This was not, I surmised, because they did not know the seasonal color or failed to check what their colleagues were wearing, but because the priests did not have a complete set of vestments. If on this Sunday there was one priest in a purple stole and another in a white one, that was just the way it was.

In South Africa, I barely spoke the language of the services I attended. But there, the services followed the liturgical formulae I knew closely enough that I always had an idea where we were in the service. At the cathedral in Gulu, however, I found this much harder. Perhaps it was because it was the Sunday after Christmas and the energy in the congregation was subdued. Still, it was clear the liturgy was being taken with something less than the earnestness with which people in South Africa approached it. What mattered was the closeness of connection with God and the devotion of the prayers. It also meant that I had trouble figuring out exactly what was going on. Were these prayers we were saying or was this the creed? Was the priest making announcements or was this the sermon? The service was in Luo, the language of the Acholi people, and I realized we were at the sermon only when the preacher was kind enough to translate a few passages of his sermon for us. The Eucharist felt rushed and slightly haphazard, but only compared to the ceremony that accompanied it in South Africa. For the cathedral parishioners, it was what they knew and it was how they marked the death and resurrection of Christ.

When the service was over, we spilled into the big grassy field that served as a soccer pitch for the diocesan school on weekdays and an impromptu coffee hour location on Sundays. We were overwhelmed by attention from members of the congregation, who came to greet us warmly—shy and timid children, older women missing teeth and limping, and men who courteously welcomed us to Gulu and the diocese. For all the talk of impaired relationships in the Anglican Communion, there were none here, though it was obvious we were American and had been introduced as such. What these people knew about me was that I was John's friend, that I was an American, and that

I was a Christian, a fellow member of the body of Christ. That was enough for them. We stayed long on that field after the service, chatting and meeting John's friends and fellow parishioners.

We were not the only visitors in the diocese that weekend. Three siblings, son and daughters of a missionary bishop in Gulu in the 1950s, were making their first return visit to the region since their family moved away fifty years earlier when they were children. This called for great celebration. The lunch laid out in Bishop Nelson's house was a feast. We lingered over the meal while the visitors shared their memories of growing up in this same compound. The bishop told them about what the diocese was like today and explained the work he still hoped to do. It was an involved vision, including the work in camps for displaced people, as well as assistance for people to return to their home communities and reestablish life there.

Sadly, the lunch that afternoon came toward the end of my time in Gulu, a visit that was ending almost before it began. John's work with diocesan youth was paused for the holiday and I had not been able to see much of what he did. Indeed, the visit was barely enough time to begin to truly understand what ministry was like in this part of the world. But my appetite was whetted for more. The experience of church I had had in the peace march and on the field after the Sunday service was starkly different than what I had been led to believe would be true. I knew I needed to see more, read more, learn more about this thing called the Anglican Communion.

As I sat, comfortably full, and listened to the conversation between Bishop Nelson and his guests, I knew that here was something significant. In the two generations since these missionary children had left Gulu, the church had undergone a transition, from foreign leadership to indigenous, from mission control to self-governance. In this meal, that transition was complete. The former mission children were guests of the confident, capable, and welcoming Ugandan bishop who was a successor to their father. They were all Christians, all members of the same body of Christ, united in a way that had never been true before.

CHAPTER 5

Going Forward with the Gospel

Bishop Gwynne College, Episcopal Church of the Sudan

The twenty students look at me expectantly from their motley collection of worn wooden seats and aging desks. They are seminarians at Bishop Gwynne College, the leading theological school of the Episcopal Church of the Sudan (ECS). For a week and a half, over meals and on walks between classes, they have peppered me with questions about life in the American Episcopal Church. There has been no hostility in their questioning, just eagerness. They are as eager to learn about my background and my church as I am about theirs. At last, on this Thursday afternoon, we have found time in the schedule to address these questions in a sustained fashion.

I put some figures on the chalkboard. The U.S.-based Episcopal Church, I tell them, has about two million members, a number that is declining. Statistics are harder to come by for ECS, but educated guesses place the membership at two to three million and growing. There are over one hundred dioceses in the American church; there are thirty-one in Sudan, a number that is likely to grow in coming years. I ask them to brainstorm what it is our two churches have in common with each other and with other Anglicans. "The Bible," says one student. "Holy Communion," says another. "A connection to the archbishop of Canterbury," says a third. Before long, they have named the elements of the Chicago-Lambeth Quadrilateral that nineteenth-century bishops agreed constituted the basis of the church and the grounds from which Anglicans would pursue ecumenical relationship: a belief in Scripture, the creeds, the sacraments, and the episcopate. That last point prompts a conversation on how our two churches choose bishops. Each follows a similar, though not identical, process of nominating candidates, praying, voting, and consecrating the winner as bishop.

With these points on the blackboard, I look again at the students. "What else do you know about the Episcopal Church?"

There is silence for a moment. Eventually Gabriel tentatively raises his hand.

"You have homosexual bishops," he says.

"Right," I say and write that on the board. "In fact, there are two." There is giggling and guffaws as I write this, as if one partnered gay bishop isn't scandalous enough. "Does anyone know their names?" There is silence. No one does. It occurs to me that "gay bishops" has become more of an epithet than a descriptive term. It is an issue Anglicans can fight over, one onto which they can project their understandings and misunderstandings of the Communion with little regard for the individuals who embody the issue on a daily basis.

"Their names are Gene Robinson and Mary Glasspool," I say as I write those names on the board. "In 2003, the people in the diocese of New Hampshire nominated several candidates for bishop, prayed, and then decided Gene Robinson was the one God was calling to be their bishop. He is a gay man and has a husband." Something similar happened in 2009, I explain, when Episcopalians in Los Angeles elected Mary Glasspool bishop. Episcopalians in each diocese, I explain, discerned that God was calling someone to be bishop who happened to be in a committed relationship with someone of the same sex. This time the guffaws in the room are of disbelief.

My explanation has opened the floodgates. In between deep skepticism at the thought that the Holy Spirit could act in such a way, hands shoot up around the room. The questions—and statements—come quickly.

"We hear that if you keep doing this, before too long a man will be able to marry a cow. In a church!"

"Is that man, Gene Robinson, just the bishop for the gay people in New Hampshire or for all the people in New Hampshire?"

"When God created people, he made a man and a woman, not a man and a man!"

"What parts of the Bible say it is alright to be gay?"

They bring up Sodom and Gomorrah, the first chapter of Romans, and passages from Leviticus and assert with varying degrees of vehemence that the Bible condemns homosexuality. Nothing here is new to me; these same passages had been quoted to me by friends in InterVarsity in Wolfville.

When I was planning this session, I never imagined it would change anyone's mind. The questions indicate that would, in any event, be an impossible task. Instead, after the initial questions have run their course, I try to explain some of the ways in which Episcopalians have concluded that what they have done is, indeed, what God is calling them to do. I tell them about the Council of Jerusalem recorded in the fifteenth chapter of Acts in which the early Christians had to decide whether God could be working among people who were outside the Jewish covenant. Peter and Paul testified that they had seen the Holy Spirit at work among such people and that these people should be allowed to follow Christ as well, without conforming to Jewish practices. It was a challenge for the early Christians, but they eventually saw the truth of Peter and Paul's testimony and their understanding of the faith changed. In the same way, I said, some Anglicans in Canada, the United States, and elsewhere were convinced they were seeing the Spirit at work among people who have traditionally been excluded from the church. The decisions these churches have made in recent years are akin to what that council in Jerusalem decided. My explanation is listened to attentively and when I am finished, there are more questions and references to other verses in the Bible. But the mood in the room is still good. Our basic task is an attempt to understand the Bible together. Christians have been doing this for centuries without yet reaching agreement on core matters, I remind them. What is significant about our conversation is that no relationships have yet been sundered.

Moses stands up next. He is one of the oldest students and his years show in his body. His right hand—the hand he extends to greet me each morning—is twisted in on itself, the result of an old accident. "When the missionaries came to the Dinka, to my people, they told us we had to give up polygamy to be Christians. This was very hard for us because when a man had many wives it meant he was rich and important. But we did give it up and now we only have one wife. We changed our culture to be Christian." This history has all been a lead-up to his question: "Why don't you have to give up homosexuality in the United States to be Christian?"

There is no quick and easy answer for this. I think back to my time as a missionary in Mthatha and how uncomfortable I felt at times to stand in the mixed history of Christian mission. At times, then, I thought past missionary behavior needed an apology. Except in the instance Moses described I thought the missionaries had been right, though their methods may have been problematic. I consider mentioning to Moses that gay friends of mine had told me part of the realization of their sexual orientation was the acknowledgement that it was not something they could choose. Polygamy, on the other hand, did seem to be something that could be chosen. But as I stand there with Moses facing me, I realize I am not sure I wholly believe this. Biologically speaking, Moses's people may have been able to choose monogamy. Culturally speaking, however, they likely could not. The transition from polygamy to monogamy in Dinka culture had been— and continues to be—wrenching, I knew. Culture can be almost as confining as biology.

Instead, I answer Moses by talking about culture and its relationship to what we read in Scripture. In some cases, I say, the Bible trumps local culture. Moses had pointed to one such example. In other cases, however, culture is heeded. There is not one universal name for God, I point out. In English, we say "God." But in Dinka, the word for God is Nhialic. But Nhialic was the word for god in the Dinka traditional religion before Christianity ever came to Sudan. The Dinka had taken an integral part of their culture—their name for and understanding of a supreme deity—and transferred it to their Christian beliefs. Dinka culture and Christianity came together as new traditions were created. This brings us back to the Council of Jerusalem and the ongoing debate in the early church about whether the new Christian religion would be confined only to Jewish people or spread among people of other cultures. There is no easy way to settle these questions, I tell Moses, and point him to some of the many instances when Paul has to address these concerns. Instead, people like us have to decide where homosexuality—and a whole host of other questions—fits into this relationship between Bible and culture.

Moses seems satisfied—at least for the moment—so we turn to another question. "Many other churches in Sudan say we are apostate," says Samuel. "They say we have broken away from the church and have gone very far away from the Bible and that soon we are going to practice here what you are practicing in America. I have heard other people say, 'Don't join ECS—that is the gay church.'" Samuel's question comes from experience. When he was on the bus ride from his home village to come to school for the beginning of the term, a fellow passenger learned he was a member of ECS and accused him of being part of the "gay church." Samuel argued back and said he would not allow homosexuality in his church. The argument became so heated the driver of the bus threatened to kick them both out unless they changed the topic. Other students are nodding their heads as Samuel speaks and I can tell this is not an isolated incident. It is hard to know what to say in response. The actions Americans take—in church or otherwise—have consequences on people around the world. Rarely, however, have I heard these consequences considered.

Samuel's question is far from the final one. We cover a huge range of issues, moving between Bible, culture, sexuality, church polity, Anglican identity, and much, much more. I do not—cannot—answer every one. Mostly, I try to share my experience. I tell them about classmates of mine at seminary who are gay. "In my time here," I tell them, "I've heard you speak about your experiences during your civil war. Some of what you have said is so difficult to hear it is almost unbelievable. But I trust what you say because I recognize you as fellow followers of Jesus Christ." The same is true for my friends who are gay in seminary, I say. Because I see in them the pattern of a life following Christ, I believe them when they tell me that God created them to love people of the same sex.

Our conversation in the classroom that afternoon is long and involved, not unusual for a topic on which so many people so clearly disagree. But as the afternoon wears on, what I am most struck by is the way in which our conversation is free of any kind of sustained posturing or polemic. The students' questions are pointed and direct, but they are not mean-spirited. They are uncomprehending but not deliberately so. There is laughter to leaven the conversation. Never once do I feel as if my position in this community depends on my position about gay bishops.

The conversation could go on for hours, but Evening Prayer is approaching. As we move out into the courtyard for the service, I ask gamely, "So, did I change anyone's mind?"

There is a chorus of replies: "No!"

"Good," I smile, "that wasn't my job. Did anyone learn anything new?"

The chorus of replies is equally emphatic: "Yes!" The students call out some of what they learned—that Gene Robinson is bishop for all of New Hampshire, that the presiding bishop did not have veto power over his election, and that Americans are not seeking to impose gay bishops on the rest of the world. We leave the classroom, picking up the pamphlets of prayers we use for the service and the green paperback hymnal in Arabic and English. As the students' strong voices begin the first hymn, I realize I am no less welcome in this community than I was before I opened my mouth about Gene Robinson and Mary Glasspool. Indeed, I am probably more welcome. Our relationships had not fractured in talking about these difficult issues. They had deepened.

〜〜〜〜

I arrived at Bishop Gwynne College in Juba, Sudan, ten days prior to that afternoon conversation. I had left St. Andrew's, Ngangelizwe, a year earlier and was now a student at Yale Divinity School. But given my experience of the diversity of the "African church" in South Africa and Uganda, Yale was hardly sufficient. I arranged to come to Sudan for several weeks to experience the life of an Anglican seminarian in another part of the Communion. BGC, as everyone called it, was named after the first missionary bishop to Sudan. It was founded in the late 1940s and its history was intertwined with the history of the country. An earlier site in southwestern Sudan was destroyed during the country's first of two civil wars. The second war forced the college to move to Juba, where it endured the deprivations and oppression of life in what was then a tightly controlled government garrison town. As part of its rebuilding effort after the war ended in 2005, ECS had temporarily closed the college, allowing it to take stock, refocus its efforts, and eventually reopen shortly before my arrival with great energy and enthusiasm about the future. During my visit, that future was right around the corner. Juba was then a regional capital in southern Sudan. Within a year, it would be the capital of the world's newest nation, South Sudan, after southerners voted overwhelmingly in favor of independence in a referendum.

In some ways, life at BGC did not seem terribly different than what I knew from Yale. The students studied the Old and New Testaments, church history, theology, and many other familiar topics. The first lecture I walked into was about Perpetua, Polycarp, and other early martyrs. I heard a lecture on the exact same topic a year earlier in my first week of class at Yale. But there was no concealing the obvious differences at Bishop Gwynne. There was no electricity while I studied there. When the equatorial sun rapidly set each evening, we switched on flashlights so we could continue to study. The only running water came from a tap in the courtyard from which we filled buckets to bathe and wash our clothes. The library had about three hundred books. This made it one of the best libraries in Juba but left it a long way from the resources available to me at Yale.

The most significant difference was in my new classmates. Although the fifty or so students were all in seminary, most were already ordained, including the two female students. During the civil war, bishops ordained people to preserve the ministry of the church. Now, some of these clergy had the opportunity to fill in the training they had not previously been able to receive. Though the students represented a wide range of cultures, experiences, and backgrounds, each had been shaped in some way by the devastating civil war. Many had spent part of the war as refugees, either internally in cities like Khartoum, or externally in refugee camps in Ethiopia, Uganda, and Kenya.

One evening I sat with John, a student from Aweil, a town near the border with northern Sudan. He traced the route he had followed as a child into exile, first across the Nile River, then through an active war zone and past unwelcoming villages, all with little food. It was in a refugee camp that John went to school for the first time. He also learned about something else for the first time: Christianity. Growing up, there had not been a church in his village. First in refugee camps in Ethiopia and then in Kenya, John learned about the gospel, was baptized, and became a leader in the church. Some of John's friends in the refugee camps were resettled in the United States, but John returned to his village as the war was ending and began to share the message he had learned about Jesus Christ. Eventually, this led to the construction of a church, close to the border with northern Sudan. One Sunday, militias allied with the northern government showed up at his church. "They came with horses and made a circle around the church. They started shooting. Then they went to where we kept our cattle and they took our cattle, and then they left most of the people in the bush." The church was in time rebuilt in cinder blocks, rather than mud brick and thatch, by the evangelical relief organization Samaritan's Purse. Like every other student at BGC, John is a nonstipendiary priest but only because his diocese does not have any money to pay him. Because there are not many other jobs available, he is a subsistence farmer, like his congregants. When the opportunity to study at Bishop Gwynne arose, John jumped at the chance, though it meant leaving his new wife behind. "I think education is the key to life," he told me. "When you are in school, you will be changed."

Samuel, who had told me about the debate he had about homosexuality on the bus ride to school, was from Nzara in southwestern Sudan. Although the Sudanese civil war was ostensibly over, the northern government was supporting the Lord's Resistance Army, the brutal rebel army whose impact I had first encountered in Gulu, Uganda, and using them to terrorize southerners. Two years earlier, Samuel was kidnapped when the LRA came through his village. He escaped, but not before they shot at him, wounding him in the abdomen and wrist. He was hospitalized for a month and showed me the scars from the wounds. Needless to say, these were not the sorts of stories I often heard from my classmates at Yale.

But the students were also different from one another. South Sudan is not a monolithic block. Indeed, its diverse mix of peoples and languages is an important cause of the violence that has plagued the region. John was Dinka, a pastoral people, who live in the low-lying region around the Nile River. Samuel was Zande, who along with many other ethnicities live farther south and are dependent on their crops, rather than cattle, for sustenance. In many ways, Samuel has more in common with the peoples of central Africa than with his compatriots to the north. Each evening at BGC, a different group of students would share a hymn in their own language with the entire student body. I could not understand the lyrics, but I did note the ways in which the musical styles differed. The large contingent of Dinka students sang a rhythmic and pulsing hymn on a five-note scale. When the Zandes sang, their hymn was more melodic and familiar-sounding to my ear. During the civil war, the northern government was able to exploit the divisions between peoples to pit them against each other. The civil war had left lingering and deep-seated grievances in southern Sudan that will take generations to heal.

This diversity was well represented in the student body at BGC. Not only was it well-represented, it was a reality of even the quietest moments. Students whose people had previously warred with one another now had side-by-side beds in the long and narrow dormitory. Conversation in the evening was a conflicting mix of a number of different languages, breaking occasionally into English or Arabic, the languages the students shared. I mentioned this diversity to Simon one day, in a quiet moment between classes. Simon was a Dinka and came from a part of the country that bore the brunt of interethnic violence. "It's so interesting to me," I said, "that all of you live so closely together and come from such different backgrounds. Is it difficult for you?"

"That is the past," he said. "I have no problem now with people from a different tribe. Our tribe now is Christ." It was a good answer but a little too neat and pat. Millions of people had been caught up in the violence and hundreds of thousands had been killed. Was it really so easy to look past it? Simon pressed his point. He told me about the long-standing conflict between his own Dinka and the Nuer people, a division that provoked some of the most catastrophic violence of the civil war. "Now," Simon said, "there is a diocese in a Nuer area of the country. But the bishop is Dinka. No one ever thought it could happen, but it is." Simon told me how the church was growing rapidly and the bishop had sent several students to BGC to study. He concluded by quoting Galatians. "'In Christ, there is no longer Jew or Greek, slave or free, male and female.' We are one people now."

If the students were divided, it was in the same way my fellow students at Yale and I were divided: they disagreed in class and argued over matters of theological interpretation. No class sparked more of this than the one titled "Theology from the Perspective of African Women." The instructor was Daniella, an Italian woman married to a Norwegian diplomat stationed in Juba. Happily for BGC, Daniella had a graduate degree in theology and offered to teach. The topic the day I attended was what the Creation narratives in Genesis have to say about the relationship between women and men.

Daniella began by asking the students to offer their opinions. Since everyone came from a patriarchal society and there was only one female student in the class, the initial comments were fairly predictable. Since God created men first, men take priority. The woman is a helper for men. The class knew that there were two different Creation narratives—one in which God creates all that is in six days by word alone, and a second in which God creates man and woman from dust and the man's rib. The usual explanation for this is that the two accounts come from different sources, which the students knew. But it did not pose a problem to their interpretation. The most common opinion, it seemed, was that the second account expanded upon a moment in the first.

But then Daniella started writing some Hebrew on the board. She showed the class all the different words for "humankind," "male," "female," "man," and "woman." She explained that the Hebrew word "adam" is used differently in the two accounts. In the first account, it means "human being" in general and the account says God created humankind "male and female." In the second account, the word "adam" is used as if it is the name of a person. A separate word is used for "man." Much of this was familiar to me from my Old Testament class at Yale when we read the article by Phyllis Trible that first laid out this interpretation.

I looked around and saw a classroom full of engaged students. From their questions, it was clear they were following the Hebrew and understood the implications of how the words were used in the two different accounts. Daniella moved from Genesis to some passages from St. Paul's letters in the New Testament about gender relations. There were places—well known to the students—where writings attributed to Paul took a hard line against the role of women in the church. In many other places, however, Paul praised individual women for their leadership roles in the community. Seeing the contrasting passages side-by-side was a new experience for several students. "It is the same Paul who is writing this!" exclaimed one student in disbelief as he flipped back and forth in his Bible. The class began to wrestle with the implications of the passages.

To this point, the lesson had all been material I had covered in my education at Yale. But as the conversation continued, I realized it was taking a turn I had not anticipated. The students began to think out loud about how their cultural backgrounds influenced how they read the Bible. Since there were so many different cultures represented in the room, each brought a different shade to the conversation. If their different cultural backgrounds influenced their understanding of the passage, they asked, how did the cultural background of the authors of the Bible influence the original text? They wondered what is lost and what is gained by looking at gender relations in a new light, and they shared how their cultures treat the different genders. They questioned whether this new interpretation was just another imposition of white people, something to be rejected out of hand or considered seriously and integrated into their understanding. I stayed quiet and listened, slightly jealous at how far the conversation ranged. In my experience of similar conversations at Yale and in the American church more generally, the trenches on these questions are deeply dug and few people are interested in changing their minds. Even fewer ever bother asking how their cultural background influences their interpretation of the text.

The class produced far more questions than it did answers, and there was little consensus by the end of class. Moses, the older Dinka student, quietly reflected that his culture was already changing. Women used to be seen as a man's property. Now, in some places, there were schools and girls were being educated. "We are going to lose our culture if we keep going this way and say men and women are equal," he concluded. It was not said with sadness, however. He was acknowledging what was already taking place around him. Another student was eager to point out that the world had changed since the time of the Bible and that in his church men and women shared roles and responsibilities. "We need to treat women as if they are one of us, not as if they are less important or second class," he said. The one conclusion everyone agreed on was that if they approached the Bible with preconceived notions, they would likely find them confirmed in the text. One student, realizing this, asked, "What in our culture is going along with the Bible? What is not? How can we challenge our people to follow along with the Bible and do away with what is not following the Bible?"

They were good questions, I thought, and I was asking them of myself on the way to Evening Prayer.

The days were passing and I was being drawn closer and closer into the community. Students began vying to take me to church services in their native languages on Sunday. Some invited me over to the homes of relatives for meals so I could learn more about their cultures. They told me more stories about what it had been like to grow up in the war. They talked about their dreams for the future of their new country.

Shortly after our afternoon question-and-answer session about the American church, Gabriel, who had first tentatively broached the subject of gay bishops, said he was going to the store for a soda and offered to get me one. When he came back, we sat in his room together and he peppered me with more questions about the Episcopal Church. What were our seminaries like? How were gay students allowed in? What did we learn in our training? How were we going to address the decline in membership? It reminded me of being in college again, staying up late and discussing issues that seem profoundly important long into the night. Gabriel finally ran out of questions when I could barely keep my eyes open. As I sleepily headed off to bed, I gave thanks for what I considered to be an example of what happens when Anglicans honestly exchange opinions even when they disagree. Gabriel knew we disagreed on sexuality-related questions but that did not obstruct our developing friendship. He had been eager to buy me the soda, no insignificant thing given how little money the students had. As I reflected on it, I knew none of this would have been possible if I had shown up and started talking about gay bishops on the first day. Over the course of a few weeks, however, I had become a known quantity by eating, living, and praying with the students. The students trusted me and listened honestly to what I had to say, even though they continued to disagree. As if in confirmation of my thoughts, one student offered up a prayer at Compline the next evening. "We give thanks for our brother Jesse who has come all the way from the U.S. We know we don't agree on everything, but we see him sharing our burdens and hardships and we know he is one of us. We pray that when he goes back, he will remember this time in a different place as a blessing."

Two nights later, I was reading in the library. Changkuth, a student I had not yet come to know well but who had been particularly pointed in his opposition to my comments in our question-and-answer session, walked in. Although he acted like he was looking for a book, it was clear he wanted to talk. I set aside my reading. That was all it took for him to launch into conversation. We rehashed a little of the question-and-answer session, and he restated his opposition to homosexuality in the church. With that out of the way, he started broadening the conversation.

"If there is some point that the two of us reach that makes us disagree, we have to come to agreement," Changkuth said. "Let us not reach that point where we go apart."

It was refreshing to hear him put so much emphasis on unity. But there was a problem. "We already do disagree," I said.

"OK, OK!" he said with exasperation, as if I was reminding him of something unpleasant. "You say you are fine with gay bishops and I say no. So let us agree—don't practice it. Just don't practice it."

This was a familiar line in these sorts of conversations and I had heard it before, the idea that it is acceptable to be homosexual so long as one is not a "practicing" homosexual, as if there is some sort of difference. I tried to shift the conversation. "I think we can say that there are important things that we agree on: that Jesus Christ is the Son of God, that Jesus Christ wants people to be reconciled to one another, that Jesus Christ preached about a new and different kingdom that we try to realize in our lives and in the church's life. We can agree on all of that and also say, 'Well, we disagree about some things, but we stay together on big things.'"

Changkuth listened carefully and then nodded his head. "So we agree that we can live as the people of God faithfully," he said.

"Yes!" I said eagerly. "Amen!"

"This is correct," he said.

"We agree."

"And we agree that if it is a matter of the gospel, you are carrying the gospel and I'm carrying the gospel. Let us go forward with the gospel together."

"Yes!" I said, emphatically.

"There is not any difference between us. We agree," he said, still sounding a little surprised.

"We agree," I said. "We have not reached the point where we go separate paths."

"Let us not reach that point," he said.

"Let us pray that that day never comes."

There was a brief pause while we soaked in our surprise at reaching a point of agreement. Then I decided to provoke the conversation just a little bit further. "What does it mean to go forward with the gospel?" I asked.

This sparked another argument. He started quoting Bible passages and emphasizing the parts of Jesus' message that concern salvation and the promise of life after death. In a society where death has been so overwhelming in recent decades, this is not surprising. Students who converted during the war told me that after seeing close family members and friends die, hearing "whosoever believes in me shall not perish but have eternal life" was especially appealing. I quoted more passages back at Changkuth and challenged him to think about other parts of Jesus' message, especially Jesus' concern with the way people live here and now and the new kingdom he preached. In the grand scheme of things, however, the differences between us were in degrees of emphasis. We each understood and recognized the truth of what the other was saying. Our differences in understanding the gospel are not even close to schism-causing matters of interpretation. And, for once, we are not talking about sex, sexuality, and gay bishops. We are talking about the real-life impacts of scriptural teachings that have been passed down across centuries. We are talking about core elements of our faith. We are talking about the gospel of Jesus Christ.

There is daylight between us, sure. But there is also unity.

CHAPTER 6

A Growing Church

Diocese of Yei, Episcopal Church of the Sudan

Partway through my time at Bishop Gwynne College, I accompanied two staff members from the ECS office in Juba on a weekend trip to check on a project in Yei, a town one hundred miles south of Juba, not far from the border with Uganda. We stayed in the Diocese of Yei's guesthouse near the cathedral. I asked what time services were on Sunday morning. "In what language?" was the reply. There were five services in four languages, it turned out. Two were in English, the first at 7:30 in the morning and the second at 9:15. I mentioned I would be inclined to go to the latter: 7:30 is awfully early. The response of my hosts was firm. "You definitely want to be at the 7:30 service. Make sure you get there early too, at least by 7:15 but probably earlier." This I could not believe. At St. Andrew's in Mthatha the service may have been three hours long, but many people did not show up until at least an hour into the service. I presumed it would be the same in Yei.

In any event, 7:15 was a little too much for me. By the time I was ready to go on Sunday morning, it was 7:25. My travel companions and I walked the short distance to the cathedral and were there at 7:28. I was completely unconcerned. "No one shows up to church on time," I thought. "I'm sure there will still be a good seat."

We walked through the church doors and into a sea of humanity. Beginning at the crossing and moving back, there was row after row of people, over a thousand sitting on the hard benches that served as pews. They were young, the vast majority of my generation, and about evenly divided between genders. For once, I did not feel conspicuous by my gender in a church service. We looked around for seats. In the entire cathedral, the only seats remaining were in the second-to-last row. We took them just in time for the opening hymn. As we did, I noticed ushers walking up and down the aisles. It was not immediately clear what they were doing until I saw one motion to a man in a pew, who shifted closer to the person next to him. They were packing the pews as tight as possible so not a single seat was wasted. How could I explain in a place like this that where I went to church I could reasonably expect to have an entire pew to myself?

Our seats were not terrific, but as the service got underway, I realized we were comparatively fortunate. Latecomers crowded into the door and peered in through the open windows. On this early Sunday morning in Yei, church was the hottest ticket in town. Though the service was in English, I had trouble following along from so far back. It seemed like the Bible was being read, a sermon was preached, and hymns were sung, though I could not figure out the content of any of it. It was clear when the offering happened, however. Baskets were placed at the front of the church and the congregation surged forward almost as one to deposit their contribution. As I fought my way back to my pew against a tide of others moving in at least three different directions, I thought that this was what a mosh pit must feel like.

Within an hour and a half, the service was over—there were four more to go that day, after all. The clergy recessed down the aisle and out of the church where they took seats under a tree. They chatted with us briefly, but their main purpose seemed to be to catch their breath for the next service. When I glanced back at the cathedral, it looked like it had never really emptied: as the first congregation left, the second was streaming in. When the second congregation was more or less arranged, the clergy thanked us for coming, stood up, and processed back into the building to begin again. We went to have breakfast.

The liturgy had been mostly unclear to me, but what I had seen reminded me of the service at the cathedral in Gulu. There was no incense, and the priests wore a simple robe and stole. There had not been communion, though I suspected that was mostly because of the logistical difficulty of communicating such a large congregation and still being done in time for the next service. As in Gulu, it was the Church Missionary Society that had been active in Sudan and this worship was true to that heritage.

The character of Sudanese worship became more clear to me the following weekend when I was back in Juba. Samuel, the student who told me about his experience fleeing the Lord's Resistance Army, took me with him to the church in Juba that people from his Western Equatoria State attended. The church was a small building made of mud bricks with a simple tin roof and dirt floor. There had been wooden pews in Yei. Here, little mounds of dried mud served the same purpose. There was no need to cram them full: the congregation fit snugly but not overwhelmingly in the building.

As a guest, I was shown to a seat of honor. In this instance, that meant I was relieved of the need to sit on the mud pews and instead could sit in a plastic chair near the front. Samuel often assisted on Sundays, but on this day he took a seat next to me so he could translate. The service, Samuel whispered as we began, was Morning Prayer, and I recognized many of its familiar elements—a psalm, canticle, collects. Few people had prayer books; many just seemed to know it by heart. If they did not, they learned from listening to their neighbors. When Samuel whispered in my ear that we had reached the pronouncement of the Grace, just an hour after the service began, I imagined we were getting close to the end.

The formal liturgy, it turned out, was merely the warm-up for the main event. Thirty-odd children from the Sunday school came singing and swaying down the aisle. They performed a few songs with dances to accompany them and then retired. Next came the introduction of newcomers, in which a handful of others and I were given a few minutes each to greet the congregation. Then there were announcements, followed by the offering. Finally, there was more singing and dancing, this time from the "youth," a group generously defined to include anyone under the age of forty-five or thereabouts who, it seemed, was not married and did not have children. Not to be outdone by the Sunday school, these young people sang several numbers, each with complicated dancing and choreography, backed up by music tracks played over the church's scratchy sound system. The service I thought was ending after an hour had turned into a knock-down, drag-'em-out three-hour affair.

The length of the service was not really a problem. After all, services at St. Andrew's in Mthatha routinely ran as long as this one had. But at St. Andrew's, the prayer book liturgy pervaded the entire service. The service was long because there was Eucharist every Sunday and the majority of it was sung. In this service at Samuel's church, on the other hand, the liturgy seemed to be regarded as something to be gotten through so they could move on to other things. The differences between the looseness of Samuel's church and the structure of St. Andrew's are due to many things. Training in liturgical practice is not one of the things that easily survives when bishops ordain clergy in the middle of a war. South Africa has a liturgical commission that produced a prayer book and translated it into many languages. Such liturgical uniformity is another casualty of Sudan's civil wars. But the differences were also another indication of the legacy of the mixed Anglican mission effort around the world. As I had seen in Gulu, the legacies of the Church Missionary Society and the Society for the Propagation of the Gospel, both equally Anglican, differed widely. At St. Andrew's, the amount of incense used during a service was enormous. Bells rang repeatedly during the Eucharist. In Juba, I never smelled the faintest whiff of incense nor heard a single bell in a church service. I doubt many students at BGC would have recognized a thurible. At St. Andrew's, the small army of acolytes that served faultlessly in worship every Sunday led me to jokingly think that one way to promote Anglican unity might be synchronized acolyting competitions. The team at St. Andrew's would put to shame any motley group of confused adolescents in middle-American, suburban Episcopal churches. But that idea died in Sudan. Aside from an occasional server to help out around the altar, there were hardly any acolytes at all.

Anglicans are rightly proud of their legacy of common forms of prayer. Indeed, it is said to be one of the defining features of Anglicanism. How we pray shapes what we believe. The languages in which we pray may be different but, we have led ourselves to believe, the form of worship is broadly the same Sunday to Sunday around the world in the churches of the Anglican Communion. The influence of successive Books of Common Prayer was the reason I could feel at home in places as diverse as Mthatha, Gulu, and Juba.

In none of the services did I ever doubt the authenticity of these forms of prayer. No matter that they trace their roots to the Euro-Atlantic world, these liturgies are clearly an integral part of how African Anglicans worship God. Even when the hymns were translated versions of English-language standards, they had been so integrated into the worship life of the community that they might as well not have begun anywhere else but there. But the way in which these liturgies became part of differing cultures varied widely. In South Africa, the prayer book is a central and deep part of the worship. At Samuel's church in Juba, on the other hand, enculturation took a different approach: begin with the liturgy and then tack on additional items. Both are legitimate approaches to worship and both clearly help people connect to God in Christ. But I would be hard-pressed to articulate what else the two had in common that made each distinctively Anglican.

∽∾∽

One thing was clear, however: in South Sudan, people go to church. The cathedral in Yei was not an exception. A Dinka congregation I visited in Juba spilled out the doors. On a later visit to a diocese in the remote southwest of the country, I would preach to a congregation of nine hundred. People sat on windowsills and stood around the outside of the church to at least listen to what was going on. These services are indicative of the growth of the church in South Sudan. But it was not always so.

Anglican, Catholic, and Presbyterian missionaries had some success in planting an indigenous church in southern Sudan in the first half of the twentieth century. Some peoples, like Samuel's Zande, were eager to hear what the missionaries had to teach. But for the most part the missionaries were seen—and saw themselves—as failures. Children they educated in mission schools either returned home and forgot about the Christianity they had been taught or grew to positions of prominence in colonial society while losing their connections to their traditional culture. When the independent Sudanese government expelled the remaining missionaries in 1964, some thought the church's future was imperiled. Shortly afterward, the south was consumed by the first of the civil wars. Hundreds of thousands of Sudanese were displaced.

The wars transformed the church. The experience of exile—a biblical concept if there ever was one—not to mention the destruction and suffering caused by the wars led many southerners to look anew at Christianity. In refugee camps and in communities that moved deep into the bush to hide from the violence, evangelists spread the gospel, people sought baptism, and an indigenous church was truly born. Shortly after the first war ended, the Episcopal Church of the Sudan was born as an independent province of the Anglican Communion. The second war challenged the church's structures and placed great strain on its leaders, but the rapid growth continued. At one point, the church in Sudan was thought to be the fastest-growing church in the world. Now, as I was seeing in Yei, Juba, and elsewhere, as South Sudan takes its first steps as an independent nation, it does so with a vibrant and growing church that is central to the life of its people.

The growth of the church is a fortunate development. "Enormous" barely begins to describe the scale of the challenges facing South Sudan. The two civil wars devoured most of Sudan's years of independence, leaving little time for the country to make development plans. The situation since independence has not been much better. The social indicators in the country are abysmal. More than ninety percent of the population lives on less than a dollar a day. South Sudan is an area slightly smaller than Texas but lacks sufficient critical infrastructure, like hospitals, schools, and paved roads. The overwhelmed government struggles to administer the region. An Oxfam report concluded that a teenage girl has a greater chance of dying in childbirth than completing primary school.

But where there is need, there is also potential. South Sudan has incredible agricultural opportunities that are not immediately obvious to those for whom the word "Sudan" conjures up images of the desert north. But on the flight to Juba, one sees only vast expanses of green, acres and acres of land waiting to be cultivated. Development experts have long recognized the potential for the area to be a "breadbasket" for the region. Even if southerners never export food, they need it for themselves. The war prevented the transmission of agricultural knowledge from one generation to the next. As a result, as people return from refugee camps, many remain dependent on food aid, or, in places where such aid does not or cannot reach, many go hungry. The result is perverse: huge tracts of fertile land sit uncultivated while bags of sorghum, beans, and vegetables are trucked or barged in. The lack of infrastructure compounds the hardship. The punishing journey over bumpy dirt roads in old trucks means that by the time the food reaches the market its price has shot up. "It's silly," one church member told me. "We have good soil. We could be growing fruit and vegetables here."

In South Sudan, the church is uniquely placed to address this situation. It has a presence in even the most remote communities.

Indeed, some people refer to the church as the country's "largest non-governmental organization." In fact, it may be the largest organization, period. Congregations exist in places where even the government does not. So the church—almost by default, for lack of anyone else to fill the role—has become committed to teaching its people how to feed themselves. No matter the overflowing services, church is not just for Sunday morning; it pervades daily life in a way quite unlike anything I had ever seen.

The trip to Yei was an indication of this. I was traveling with Robin Denney, the American missionary working as an agricultural consultant for ECS at the central office in Juba. She had come to Yei to visit a government-run Crop Training Centre. Some of the many crops able to thrive in different parts of the country were growing on its large demonstration farm—coffee, pineapple, cassava, bananas. There were dorms for the students and a dining hall with a television. On the Saturday we visited, the students crowded around the television watching Manchester United play Chelsea. An approaching storm kept interfering with the satellite signal, eventually shutting off entirely just as ManU tied the match.

ECS's agricultural department had paid for a dozen students from eleven dioceses to enroll in a three-month course to learn about such topics as pest control, vegetable production, forestry, and marketing. The course had just begun and Robin's visit was to check in on them. "This is the next step forward for us in agriculture," she said when she met with them. These men and women were the first of a network of diocesan agricultural coordinators across the church. When they complete the course, they are to return to their dioceses to share their knowledge with others. Gabriel, a young priest from Rumbek in the center of the country, told me the course is exactly what he needed. "All over the country, there is land," he said. "But there are no trained people to work the land and no trainers. We will be trainers." Justin, another student trying to start his life again after the war, told me enough people in his community knew how to grow subsistence crops but did not know what to do with the surplus. "People in my village don't know how to sell them. I'm taking marketing here." The model for these students was Panyakwara Abarra, the village of returned refugees Robin had taken me to on a separate trip. The students at the Crop Training Centre will return to their dioceses with knowledge that will allow them to begin their own projects like the one in Panyakwara. But they are not the only ones.

The trip to Yei helped me see the situation of the students at Bishop Gwynne College in a new light. When they finished their studies, they would be returning to deeply impoverished situations. Their status as clergy afforded them little protection. Each student was intimately familiar with eking out a living on subsistence agriculture and trying to fit in work for their church amid the daily chores necessary to survive. The students who were married and had children told me stories about babies who had not lived longer than a few months or family members who had died young, victims of malaria or any number of other tropical diseases. One student, I knew, regularly purchased medicines in Juba that were not available in his village and arranged for them to be sent home to family members. In a context like this, conversations about gay bishops could seem somewhat out of place. At the very least, it was far from the most important of the possible topics of conversation. It was easy to see how these students, and their many colleagues throughout the church, could hear news about "gay bishops," reject it as incompatible with what they understood the Bible to say, and move on to thinking about more pressing issues: the next meal, for instance, or the health of a child.

The curriculum at Bishop Gwynne College responded to the context in which its students were to minister. In between their classes on Bible or theology, the first-year students met two mornings a week with Robin under the guava tree in the courtyard to learn about soil nutrients, photosynthesis, irrigation, pest control, and much more. On the day I attended, the lesson was about mulching. If farmers take discarded plant material and cover their fields with it, not only will it prevent the growth of weeds, it will return nutrients to the soil as the mulch decomposes. After a short lesson in the courtyard, Robin took the students to the demonstration garden she had been tending for several months and pointed to the rows of sorghum, a staple grain in South Sudan. The rows that had been mulched were clearly taller and healthier-looking than those that had not.

The rest of the class session was devoted to work in the garden. There was weeding to be done and new rows of tomatoes to be planted. A papaya tree planted a few weeks earlier had grown quickly but unfortunately turned out to be a male—that is, non-fruit-bearing—tree.

Robin gathered the class around and explained that one male can pollinate several females and pointed to another male growing nearby. "But," she said, "if you shock the male, it will sometimes regrow as a female." She pulled out her shears and quickly snipped the plant halfway up its stalk. "The truth is," she said, "when it comes to papaya, the males are fairly useless." There was some nervous laughter from the overwhelmingly male class, but Robin was already cutting the stalk into smaller pieces and letting it fall to the ground. "But you can always use it as mulch!" she added before turning to the next part of the lesson.

Later, there was a class for students who were about to graduate. In one lesson I attended, they talked through teaching techniques and how to write grant applications for more equipment and supplies. But rather than talking solely about the needs and shortages they confront, Denney encouraged them to think about the resources they already have. One student recalled how during the height of the civil war, the Mother's Union in his diocese planted two plantations of teak trees from wild seedlings. The trees grew through the war. In just a few years, those seedlings—now trees—will be harvested and generate substantial revenue for the diocese. The only need in that situation, Denney noted, was an investment of time. The women already knew how to recognize teak seedlings and how to plant them.

Like the good seminary students they were, the students had theological rationales for the church's investment in agriculture. For Richard, a priest from Yambio in the southwest, the interest in agriculture stemmed from God's creation of the world. "I want to teach that the land has been given to us by God," he said during class. "It is given to us to take care of and give back to God." The students, it was clear, were eager to return to their dioceses and homes and begin to put into practice some of what they had learned at Bishop Gwynne, not only the theology and history but the agriculture as well. "Nowadays, most of the pastors are asking for people to send money for them, to send things to them," Cimbir, one of the graduating students, told me. "But when they can grow their own things then they can feed other people. That's why it is important for the pastor to know about agriculture. He'll be able to tell them how to grow a lot of things. Then they can have a lot of things in their church to help other people."

The classes were interesting and the discussion, as always, fascinating. Still, it felt like whiplash to move from a jam-packed Sunday morning service to a lesson about mulching, two such seemingly different tasks joined into the same organization. Agriculture did not feature in my seminary curriculum. Liturgical practice certainly did. Was one more "churchy" than the other? As I looked through BGC's library one evening, I found an answer. In a book by former Archbishop of Canterbury Michael Ramsey, there was a quotation from Cyril of Jerusalem explaining what it means to say the church is "catholic." The church is catholic not just because it covers the earth but because it "teaches universally and without fail all the doctrines which ought to be brought to the knowledge of men concerning things visible and invisible in earth and heaven." In Sudan, agriculture, just as much as eternal life, is one of those "doctrines" that need to be brought to the knowledge of people.

Priests as theologians of creation and agricultural extension agents: I liked the sound of it. It is a contextual response to the realities of ministry in South Sudan. It is independent of liturgical variation and taste. Sisters and brothers in Christ from around the world could join in, sharing knowledge and learning from the situation. It is what it means to be the church catholic in a place like South Sudan.

CHAPTER 7

Holding Together Diversity

Diocese of Ely, Church of England

Cambridge is at the heart of both the Church of England and its history. King's College Chapel towers over the center of town. Its stonework is laced with the roses and portcullises that were the insignia of the Tudors, the family that, more than any other, established an independent church in England and set its contours for generations to follow. Not far from King's Chapel is St. Edward King and Martyr, an ancient church from whose pulpit Thomas Cranmer preached. On its wall is a memorial to Thomas Bilney, Robert Barnes, and Hugh Latimer, significant figures of the Reformation, who, along with Cranmer, were burned at the stake for their beliefs. Some of Cambridge's colleges were founded by leaders of different church factions to train candidates for ministry. Churches and church history surround and pervade Cambridge.

I was looking for a small piece of that history when I wandered into Holy Trinity Church on a Sunday morning in September. Holy Trinity was the parish of Charles Simeon, and the Anglican evangelical revival of the eighteenth century he helped spark began here. In the five decades he served as vicar, he made a habit of standing on the streets outside his church—the very streets I was now walking to church—and disputing with those who passed by. Henry Martyn, one of his protégés and one of the great early missionaries to the Middle East and beyond, served a time as curate in this parish. A century and a half later, Max Warren served a time as vicar before moving on to the Church Missionary Society, where as General Secretary he played a significant role in helping the Anglican Communion come to grips with itself in the mid-twentieth century.

I was warmly welcomed when I walked through the north door that Sunday morning. The greeters were young, in their early twenties, and undoubtedly were students at the university. Having learned nothing from my experience in Yei, I arrived two minutes before the service was to begin. As I stepped inside, I realized it was going to be difficult to find a seat. Most of the pews were already full. I found a single empty spot next to an elderly woman sitting alone. I smiled at her and sat down.

From the outside, Holy Trinity looks like many of the other churches in Cambridge; the stateliness and age of the building is evident in its ornate stonework and stained-glass windows. When thinking about "church" and "England," this is the sort of building that comes to mind. But if that exterior led me to certain expectations about what the interior would be like, they were misplaced. The normal ecclesiastical furniture I might have expected in the chancel—an altar, communion rail, side tables—was gone. The altar was pushed against the far wall. In its place, there were a handful of microphones, two or three guitars leaning on stands, a large drum set, and an electric keyboard. It was set up for a band, and, indeed, a group of musicians was just finishing their tune-up as I walked in. In front of the musical instruments stood a single glass podium. On each side of the chancel, there was a dark screen, hung high above the congregation.

My seat was in one of the pews arranged to face the chancel. Holy Trinity has a substantial crossing area and there were more chairs there, many, like the pews, already full. As much as the space permitted, the seating in the sanctuary had been arranged in a horseshoe around the glass podium. Seated in the pews toward the front were several elderly couples who would not have been out of place at any church I was familiar with in the United States. But much of the congregation was more like the two people who greeted me at the door: young, smartly dressed, and with a look of commendable eagerness on their face. There were several parents cradling infants, and there was the familiar hum in the air that told me children were around. I had come to England hearing about secularization, atheism, and, in the title of one well-known book, "The Death of Christian Britain." Looking around Holy Trinity that morning, I wondered if I was in the same country.

I knew something about praise and worship music from my time in InterVarsity. Unlike the music we sang at a place like St. John's in Northampton, this music was not played on organs but with guitars and drums. Singing it, it seemed, could lead to people closing their eyes and lifting their hands in the air. Although my liturgical horizons had been broadened in Juba, Gulu, and elsewhere, my ideas of what constituted Anglican worship in the Euro-Atlantic world centered on traditional hymns, the Eucharist, and very little else. So it was something of a surprise that shortly after I sat down, the band finished their tune-up, took their places at the microphones, and led the congregation in exactly this sort of music. "Come now is the time to worship," we sang, reading the lyrics off the screens at each side of the chancel. "Come, now is the time to give your heart." The band was good. The young man leading the worship knew what he was doing. The congregation sang loudly and well. Before long, I noticed a few hands being raised in the air, including from the older woman beside me in the pew. In between songs, the leader offered some extemporaneous prayers, while the person playing the keyboard kept a steady thrum of chords underneath his words. There was one song for which we were taught hand motions, led by a group of university students who came up on the stage—chancel—with the band. After that, the children departed for their Sunday school, the congregation sang one or two more songs, and then, nearly half an hour after the service began, we sat down.

The opening set had been a seamless performance but to my constricted sensibilities it had not seemed notably "Anglican." As we sat down, I thought that perhaps now was the time when we would turn to the "Anglican" portion of the worship. Even in Juba, despite the parade down the aisle from the Sunday school students or the songs from the youth, the liturgy still had a recognizably Anglican form. But at Holy Trinity, in place of any liturgical elements—or even any congregational response—there were two readings from the Bible in quick succession. Then the preacher came forward. He was wearing a purple shirt and a clerical collar—though no vestments—and the bulletin introduced him as the retired bishop of a neighboring diocese. He had a careful and deliberate style of preaching and I was reminded of being in a lecture hall. Several people around me started taking notes. The retired bishop made clear that he had five points to make that day about what we learned about our relationship with God from the passages we had just heard, particularly one from 1 Samuel about King David. At more than twenty minutes, the sermon was long by non-African Anglican standards, but it was clear from the attentiveness of the people around me that this was the high point of the service.

Following the sermon, there were some brief prayers. Then a man I had not noticed before came to the chancel from his seat on the north crossing. He was wearing a blazer over a sweater and an open collar, and carried a book in one hand. He draped a stole over his neck. Though he was not wearing a collar and had not taken any part in the service to this point I presumed he was Rupert, whom the bulletin identified as the vicar. Two young people carried forward a small wooden table on which there was a chalice and a paten.

Rupert stood over the table and introduced the meal as Communion, the Lord's Supper. "We're running a bit late," he said, "so I thought we'd just use the oldest recorded version of the Last Supper." The book he was holding in his hand was a Bible, and he opened it up and read from 1 Corinthians: "For I received from the Lord what I also handed on to you, that the Lord Jesus on the night when he was betrayed took a loaf of bread . . ." It was St. Paul's recollection of the Last Supper. Rupert read through the section and then stood back. Several more young people came forward, took the elements, and stood at the head of the aisles. I joined the congregation in coming forward. The young woman with the bread smiled at me. "The body of Christ," she said sweetly.

When we had all returned to our seats, there was a final prayer from one of the young women who had been most involved. As soon as she said, "Amen," she opened her eyes and said brightly, "Please join us in the back for tea and biscuits." Whatever reverence there may have been in the service immediately disappeared. Children dashed for the biscuits. Musicians started breaking down their equipment. I sat still, thinking that surely someone would dismiss me, tell me to "go forth in the name of Christ," but there was nothing. Instead, the woman next to me turned and introduced herself.

When I stepped outside a few minutes later, the tower of another church caught my eye. It was Great St. Mary's, the University Church, just a few hundred feet down the cobblestone streets from Holy Trinity. I wandered down the street for a closer look and realized they were in the middle of a service. I ducked inside, hoping to find a seat.

I need not have worried. In contrast to Holy Trinity, there were more empty pews than full ones. When I sat down, two thirds of the way back, I had the entire pew to myself. There were about forty people in the vast church. My presence significantly lowered the average age of the congregation.

The preacher, dressed in cassock, surplice, and tippet, was in the middle of his sermon. The bulletin I had been handed on the way in—by an older gentlemen, leaning on a cane—had a short text on its cover reflecting on the recent visit of Pope Benedict to Britain and the pontiff's call to "reflect on the place of faith in society." It was only because of this text that I could glean that the preacher was doing exactly what the pope had asked. The sermon wandered, making one point, moving on, coming back to a prior one, quoting Desmond Tutu, and then abruptly ending. True, I had missed the first part of the sermon, but I found myself missing the orderliness and deliberateness—not to mention the scriptural references—of what I had heard at Holy Trinity half an hour earlier. The choir was vested in cassocks and surplices, with ruffs at the neck. Following the sermon, they sang an anthem while the offering was collected. The congregation stood to sing a hymn that was played loudly on the organ. It was a Matins service, I realized, meaning there would not be communion. Shortly afterward, the altar party recessed from the church and the service ended.

My time in England followed closely my visit to Bishop Gwynne College. Thoughts about liturgical practice were fresh in my mind. In the contrast between churches in Mthatha and Juba, I had seen that liturgical similarity may not be as characteristic of Anglicanism as is often thought. But those were different churches in different provinces of the Communion with different historical backgrounds. On one Sunday morning in Cambridge, however, I had seen two services that could hardly have been more different. In the average age of the congregation, the type of liturgy, the musical choices, the vestments, the arrangement of the church, and the attendance, the two services were miles apart, even as they occurred in buildings that were separated by the length of a football field. Yet both, somehow, were claiming to be Anglican. If this kind of diversity existed within the Church of England—the mother church of the Anglican Communion—and existed in its very heart, what kind of diversity could exist in the world? And if liturgical uniformity did not hold in Cambridge, how were these churches to hold together?

⟨⟫⟩

I was in Cambridge for a term to study at Westcott House, a seminary of the Church of England. I had come because I wanted to experience the life of the Church of England in person. The contrasting experience of Holy Trinity and Great St. Mary's on my first Sunday was exactly what I was seeking. The diversity of those services was mirrored in the seminaries in Cambridge. There was Westcott, a moderate catholic, liberal place, whose ordinands worked at places like Great St. Mary's on Sundays. Then there was Ridley Hall, the evangelical training college on the other side of town. The young woman who led the concluding prayer at Holy Trinity that Sunday was a student at Ridley. To my American sensibilities, it seemed odd for there to be two Anglican seminaries in the same town. I presumed there would be at least some sort of fellow feeling between them, a sense that there was a common mission and a common church the two shared. It was this thought that prompted me, when I returned to Westcott that first Sunday afternoon, to share that I had been to Holy Trinity that morning.

It was as though I had dropped a filthy sock on the table. People looked at me with a pained and confused look on their face. "Why did you go there?" they asked, in a tone that mixed scorn, pity, and derision.

"It's an Anglican church," I said, somewhat defensively. "And it's historic. I wanted to see what it's like."

"Churches like that aren't really Anglican," I was told. "Those evangelicals are just taking over our empty churches and making them their own." My conversation partners proceeded to explain how Holy Trinity failed the Anglican test on multiple fronts. Liturgical practice was chief among the reasons. "You should have gone to Little St. Mary's instead," they told me. "That's the Church of England at its best." When I did later attend LSM, as it is known, I was enveloped in a cloud of incense as the priest and a small army of other ministers and servers celebrated the Eucharist at an ornate high altar.

With my Westcott colleagues, I stayed quiet and listened patiently. After all, these were precisely the sort of things I had come here to learn. But the more they spoke, the more I realized they were leaving out certain critical pieces of information. There had been a retired bishop at Holy Trinity that morning, and the former principal of Ridley Hall was now a diocesan bishop. If these people were not really Anglican, why were they rising to positions of leadership in the church hierarchy? Why were there so many young people at Holy Trinity and almost none—apart from some bored-looking choir members—at Great St. Mary's? Most importantly, why were these churches empty in the first place for the evangelicals to "take over"? Given the tenor of the conversation, it seemed advisable to keep to myself the thought that, of the two churches, I was more likely to return to Holy Trinity than Great St. Mary's. I liked its welcoming feel and the way it challenged my liturgical presuppositions.

The more time I spent in Cambridge that autumn, the more I realized that the divide I had seen between Holy Trinity and Great St. Mary's that first Sunday morning pervaded the entire church right up to the archbishop of Canterbury, a position that by tradition rotates between the evangelical and catholic wings of the church. It took me a while to figure this out, but when I told people I was studying at Westcott, they immediately made a number of assumptions about my liturgical and theological beliefs. The fellow feeling I thought might exist between Ridley and Westcott ebbed and flowed. There were many joint classes that produced friendships between the students. But in the term after I left, there was a great row when Ridley invited a preacher to a joint service who preached a condemnatory message about homosexuality. Some Westcott students walked out. The two schools also met on the football pitch. Ridley clobbered Westcott. "They believe in a more muscular form of Christianity anyway," sighed Westcott's captain afterward. "We never had a chance."

I thought back to my experience in Wolfville, where I had first come to be aware of two kinds of Christianity: the older, liberal type that I found at St. John's and in those who attended the Week of Prayer for Christian Unity service; and the younger, more conservative type I knew from my time with the InterVarsity chapter. In Wolfville, I associated the former with Anglicanism and the latter with non-Anglican denominations. In the Church of England, both types existed side-by-side, not always easily, happily, or with much direct communication. If both types could exist in one church—the one church to which all

Anglicans are ostensibly related—how could one possibly say what is truly Anglican and what is not?

☙❧

There were several popular conversation topics at the dinner table at Westcott that term. The pope's visit had sparked wistful longing among the few Anglo-papalists in the student body for reunion with Rome. The ins and outs of the interminable debate about ordaining women as bishops were also much deliberated. But the phrase that was on everyone's lips was "the new atheism." Names like Dawkins, Hitchens, and others were frequently mentioned, and Westcott sponsored a conference on apologetics that autumn. Far more than I had ever heard among my seminary colleagues in the United States, these Westcott students realized they were preparing to minister in an environment that did not look kindly on their faith and, at times, was actively hostile to it. I returned to Great St. Mary's later in the fall for a public conversation between then-Archbishop Rowan Williams and Terry Eagleton, a Marxist literary critic, about the new atheism. The church was packed to capacity, and the tone of the audience seemed to be far more suspicious of Christianity than supportive of it.

As I traveled around the church that autumn, there were signs of the shriveling of the established church. Only a handful of students came to the Sunday morning Eucharist services at the Cambridge college chapel where I worked. Some cathedrals I visited charged exorbitant admission fees to sustain their ancient buildings. Inside, the tour groups could make the experience feel more like a museum than a living place of spiritual nurture. Cycling around the countryside, I came across parish churches that were either closed permanently, or had posted notices from the wardens explaining just how much it cost to keep the church going and how the community needed to support the church if it was to remain open. I heard stories of large benefices, with four, five, six, or more parishes overseen by one or two clergy, who spent their Sunday mornings shuttling between churches, offering service after service to the small, grey-haired congregations that showed up. "How are you supposed to create disciples when you're just a roving Eucharistic minister?" asked one such priest in exasperation. "This is not what I signed up for." A friend at Westcott came from a particularly rural part of a nearby diocese. She lamented the difficulty of recruiting clergy to the rural areas of the country and said there were benefices that had been vacant for half a dozen years, limping along with lay leadership and supply clergy. "That means children are growing up without hearing about the gospel and without the church as an active part of their community lives," she said.

But there was hope to be found in the Church of England. With the growing secularization of the country and the split between wings of the church in mind, on a wet Sunday morning I cycled a dozen miles across the Cambridgeshire countryside, passing through three small villages along the way. Each had its own parish church, the youngest several centuries old. Like Holy Trinity or Great St. Mary's in Cambridge, they were buildings that testified to an imposing and august legacy of faith. In that context, the church in Cambourne, my destination, stood out. It was a large A-frame building. The concrete blocks that made up its walls were still visible from the outside. There was not a single grave or headstone in the churchyard. The turned earth and lack of significant growth around it told me that the church had been built only in the last few years. Indeed, all of Cambourne has this recent feel to it. A dozen years before my visit, the area was farmers' fields. Cambourne was created to respond to a growing population. Many of its residents work in Cambridge or one of the nearby hospitals. From the beginning of the planning process, churches expressed an interest in being part of the creation of the new community. Prophetically—or perhaps more prosaically as a practical response to the reality of diminished resources—several denominations realized the best way forward would be to work together. The resulting congregation combined Methodists, Baptists, Presbyterians, and Anglicans and began to meet first in the waiting room of the dentist's office. After a while, they moved to a slightly larger prefabricated building. At last, nearly ten years after the community first started meeting, they moved into the cinder-block building I saw in front of me.

Inside, the worship space was more like a multipurpose room of a recreation center than the sanctuary of a church. This was intentional. "Some of the funding for this came from the government," the minister's wife told me. "Everything that is specifically Christian has to be able to be removed when we are done." Not only was the space secular, it had to be interdenominational as well. There were posters on the bulletin board advertising a Catholic Mass on Saturday evenings in the space, as well as a monthly Indian Orthodox service on a Saturday morning. Another poster advertised a Quaker meeting.

When I walked in the door, I was immediately overwhelmed by activity. Children darted this way and that, chasing after one another while their parents chatted over tea or coffee. There was a band tuning up in one corner of the sanctuary. Several people were setting out chairs for the service and ensuring there was a Bible on each one. I was swept into the activity, offered tea, and shortly thereafter swept into the sanctuary—mug in hand—for the service.

Bringing together, as it does, such a variety of denominational backgrounds, I had little idea what to expect from the worship. The Diocese of Ely has designated Cambourne Church as the parish church—the minister read banns of marriage before the service began—but I wondered how Anglican the service would feel. When it began, I was reminded of the service I attended at Holy Trinity. The small band led praise and worship songs with the congregation singing along, using lyrics projected on the screen behind the portable altar. But there were important differences from what I remembered at Holy Trinity. When the music ended—and there was less of it than there had been at Holy Trinity, none of it involving hand motions— the minister led us in a call to worship that felt vaguely liturgical. There were congregational responses even, and these simple acts set the tone for the service: not somber, but devout and worshipful. I was not surprised to learn later that the set prayers used at several points in the service came from the Iona Community's resources.

The preacher was a Baptist minister associated with the congregation, who spoke about Jesus' famous teachings in John 3. He talked about how he had been asked once when he had been "born again." This, he said, was a question that could divide Christians. Many people could not remember a single moment when they had given their lives to Jesus. Others could pinpoint a specific minute, hour, day, month, and year. He expressed an interest to move beyond these debates. "None of us remembers our birthday," he said. "It doesn't matter when we were born again. What matters is that we are living the new life." It was a neat way between what can be a deceptively divisive question. And it was only the beginning of the sermon. He moved on to talk about what it means to share that new life together in community and how that worked itself out in this particular community. The sermon was good, instructive without being pedantic, thoughtful without being abstruse.

After the service, the swirl of activity that had preceded it returned with renewed vigor. A young father introduced himself to me. I had been looking at the posters on the wall, advertising the many midweek activities the congregation held—Bible studies, book groups, brainstorming sessions for how to encourage the businesses in town to stock more fair-trade products—and I mentioned what an impressive set of offerings it was. "This is fine for Sunday," he said, gesturing around at the sanctuary, "but this isn't all there is to church. It's not even the most important thing. What's important is people who gather around God's word and then seek to live Christian lives in the world."

Later, over lunch with the minister in charge of the congregation, I heard a similar view. Originally ordained in the Church of Scotland, Peter came to Cambourne with his wife and family because the questions he was asking about what the church is and how it relates to the world around it were best expressed and explored in this environment. He was a veritable fount of ideas, his words tumbling out in such rapid succession I was on the verge of asking him to slow down so I could understand them all. He was excited about having so many services from so many Christian denominations in the same building. He wanted to work more closely with them. He wanted to be part of Cambourne's growth as it continued to develop. "The church isn't just this thing that happens off to the side. The church needs to be part of the community, changing and shaping life as we can. If we're not, then we're not really being the church." He mentioned the church's push for fair trade in the community. "We need to be living kingdom values not only in church but in our lives as well. It's no good just staying off to ourselves." He wanted more Bible studies. A small group in the church had started a garden on the church's land. "It's been a great way to connect with new people," he told me. "They see the garden and they ask us about it and they want to learn more about why we're doing it." He wanted more men in the congregation. "Sometimes men don't like sitting around on Sunday in church because they feel like they're not doing anything. We need to give them something to do. It was great when we were building the church because so many of them could be involved." On and on and on he went, idea after idea, his passion and enthusiasm for his work so clearly evident. He ate, slept, and breathed this church, it was clear, and by "church" he did not just mean the usual routine of Sunday services, baptisms, weddings, and funerals. He meant life, all of it, in its many variations in this particular place.

Peter's energy, which was clear not only in conversation, but in the mood and tenor of the service and the congregation, was inspiring. Perhaps the most favorable thing one can say about the Establishment of the Church of England is that the parish system—in which every last bit of land in the country is under the care of some priest some-where—represents a profound incarnational commitment to each particular place. The ministry I saw in Cambourne was the logical out-come of such a commitment. The church exists in a particular place not to be one more social service provider—that is, in addition to the doctor's office for one's physical ailments, the grocery store for one's food needs, one also has a church for when one needs a child baptized or a relative buried—but to be a community that by its model of living changes the lives of those around it. The kingdom may be out of our reach, it is true, but by keeping a vision of it in front of the community, the church helps others continually move in its direction. It was this kind of vision, I thought, so much more interesting than interminable debates about others' sex lives, not to mention liturgical sensibilities, that could provide the ground for moving the church forward.

CHAPTER 8

An Andean Answer to the Ordinariate

Diocese of Central Ecuador, The Episcopal Church

Ecuador will never be mistaken for a hotbed of Anglicanism. Latin America has historically been Roman Catholic. In recent decades, more people have joined the growing number of independent charismatic and evangelical churches. The Anglican presence in South America, meanwhile, is confined to a good-sized province in Brazil and the tiny province of the Southern Cone. Four dioceses in Ecuador, Colombia, and Venezuela are still formally part of the American Episcopal Church, and remain dependent upon it for a large portion of their financing. But deep in the remote regions of a beautiful continent, I found that Anglicanism might, at last, be beginning to take root.

The village of San Francisco de Telan is high in the Andes. As I looked down from its heights, I saw a winding river flowing past a farming community in the valley below. The little group of seminary students I was traveling with had left that farming community an hour earlier and begun our journey up the mountain on a narrow dirt road. The green valley where we began gradually gave way to dusty fields and small villages like San Francisco, where a few hardy souls tried to make a go of farming. Stepping out of the van, I immediately gasped for breath and my head began throbbing with an elevation-induced headache. No one in the village could tell me just how high we were, but the lowest guess I heard was 12,500 feet. Quito, where we had spent the first few nights of this trip to Ecuador had been one thing. There, I needed to stop at the top of the staircase to catch my breath.

But here the few extra thousand feet made everything much more difficult. It was windy and cold. I zipped up my jacket and looked around.

We were parked in the center of the village. On one side was a store and school. Facing it was a community center. In between was what we had come to see: the church. It was perched on the edge of the village square. Its thick thatch roof hung down over the sides of its mud-brick walls. It was not exactly shabby-looking, but it was not new either. I asked how old it was and no one could remember a time when it had not been there, exactly as it was now. The church had been used and used well by many previous generations in San Francisco.

Our guides in this place were two church leaders. One, Padre Eulogio, is a former Catholic priest who had recently been received by the Diocese of Central Ecuador. The other, Luis Alberto, also a former Catholic priest, was in the process of having his orders received. Between the two of them, they share responsibility for San Francisco and more than twenty other similar villages. It was Saturday evening and Eulogio was here to conduct Mass. With only the two of them and so many villages to care for, services happen whenever the priests are able to make it to a village, whether it be Sunday or not.

The Quichua, an indigenous Andean people, have lived in villages like San Francisco for generations and learned to survive at great altitudes.* With the arrival of colonists and, later, independence, many Quichua moved down the mountains in search of employment on the large farms of *mestizo* landowners. Only in the last few decades has agrarian reform allowed some to own land for themselves. Even then it is not the best land. Like so many other indigenous peoples around the world, the lot of the Quichua is now largely poverty, poor health, and a paucity of opportunities. In San Francisco, while some people spoke Spanish, the language of conversation was still largely Quichua.

The people of San Francisco did have at least one thing in common with other Ecuadorians. Like *mestizos* in towns and cities, they had been, by and large, Roman Catholic. Catholic missionaries evangelized the region and oversaw the construction of churches like the one in San Francisco. But not long before our visit, leaders in San Francisco and other surrounding villages approached the Episcopal Church

---

* For simplicity's sake, I refer to the people in San Francisco as Quichua (spelled Quechua in other Andean countries), a broad term for a language group composed of many diverse peoples. In fact, the people in this region of Ecuador are Puruhá.

and expressed an interest in joining. They said they were not getting the sort of pastoral attention they needed. The Episcopal Church appealed to them because of its familiar sacramental tradition.

When Eulogio told us this story before we set out for San Francisco, it was hard not to see it as a feather in the cap of the Episcopal Church. Our visit to San Francisco came only a few months after Pope Benedict announced the creation of an ordinariate—a special grouping within the Catholic Church—to receive disaffected Anglicans. When we heard about San Francisco, more than a few Episcopalians in my group smiled at the thought that the movement between churches might be going both ways. From the perspective of the body of Christ, of course, our thoughts betrayed an embarrassing denominational chauvinism. After all, the important thing was that the good news of Jesus Christ be preached in San Francisco, not the denomination that the people belonged to. Still, it is always gratifying to find unreported stories that challenge dominant narratives.

But as Eulogio continued to tell us about the ongoing transition, it was clear the scale of the challenges overwhelmed any brief fillip of pride the news gave us. The Diocese of Central Ecuador is small and institutionally weak compared to the many Catholic dioceses in the country. The news of the transition had, predictably, proven distinctly unpleasant to other Catholics. The local Catholic bishop tempered communication with the Episcopal bishop and denounced Eulogio and Luis Alberto for following—or leading, according to the Catholic bishop—their people into another fold. Again, from the perspective of the body of Christ, this was not welcome news.

But even if the Catholics had blessed the departure of these people, there were many more problems. The first was language. As part of the American Episcopal Church, the church in Ecuador uses the 1979 Book of Common Prayer. That prayer book has been translated into Spanish but not Quichua. Particularly for the older people in San Francisco, to take part in a Spanish-language service is as foreign to them as a Xhosa-language service was to me in Mthatha. Aside from Eulogio and Luis Alberto, the Episcopal Church does not have Quichua-speaking clergy to lead services or begin translation work.

In fact, the church does not have many clergy at all. At the time of my visit, there were fewer than fifteen clergy in the Diocese of Central Ecuador and they were concentrated in the urban area around Quito.

The people in San Francisco may have been dissatisfied with the pastoral attention they received from the Catholics, but Eulogio and Luis Alberto cannot adequately cover all the villages either. Eulogio and Luis Alberto are talented, smart, and hard-working clergy. But they are also doing multiple services a day in different communities, separated by long drives on bumpy dirt roads high in the mountains. It reminded me of rural clergy in England traveling between multipoint benefices. It is a taxing and straining job, and it is not clear that it is a sustainable model of ministry in the Andes any more than in rural Cambridgeshire.

But on the day of our visit, these concerns were secondary. Eulogio greeted the village leaders who came to meet him. People soon began to trickle in for the service: older women in felt bowler hats and colorful knit ponchos, men in baseball hats and jeans. It was only a trickle, though, and it was clear that it would take some time before everyone was gathered. The challenges of travel in the mountains meant there was no set schedule for the visits by the clergy. They came when they could. That did not necessarily mean the congregation was ready when they did.

I poked my head in the church. There were a handful of rough wooden benches. Low-hanging rafters forced me to duck my head to get through the door and stay bent once I was in the church. In the corner there were two guitars. I wandered over to check them out. Luis Alberto, who had come into the church after me, motioned for me to try them out if I wanted to. It was as good a way as any to pass the time until the service began. I strummed a chord and began fiddling with the tuning pegs. When Luis Alberto saw that I seemed to know what I was doing, he picked up the other one, began tuning it, and motioned for me to sit down.

He played first, strumming and singing a Quichua song. His voice was clear and loud and his chords broad and deep. I watched his fingers and strummed along, mimicking the chords though always a beat behind. When he finished, he gave me an expectant look. I knew the drill. It did not matter that we had a limited common vocabulary. This was a jam session, just like any I had ever been a part of. Racking my brain, I started playing the first thing that came to mind: "When the Saints Go Marching In," a song I had sung with preschool children at the community center I worked at in Mthatha. Luis Alberto watched the chords my fingers were making and played along. His English was better than either my Spanish or Quichua, so he began to sing along in a rough approximation of the lyrics. When the song was over, I returned his expectant look. He launched into another Quichua song and this time I recognized the tune. Simon and Garfunkel recorded it as "El Condor Pasa (If I Could)" on their "Bridge Over Troubled Water" album, but the tune is originally an Andean folk tune. This time I could not only play but hum along as well.

Our impromptu jam session continued through several more songs. Eulogio came in and started setting up for the Eucharist. As it came around to be my turn to play again, I realized I was running out of songs. Grasping for something to play, I reached for a dependable, albeit non-Christian, standby, Chuck Berry's "Johnny B. Goode." Luis Alberto looked surprised when I began strumming the twelve-bar blues but quickly picked up the rhythm. Sitting there, in the mud-brick church at 12,500 feet in the Andes, I realized my headache had disappeared and I apparently had more than enough air in my lungs to sing. I found myself wishing I knew how to play Bob Marley's, "Jammin':" "We're jammin', we're jammin', we're jammin' in the name of the Lord."

⌘

I was in Ecuador with a group of students from Yale and Harvard, on a midyear trip to learn more about the church in Latin America, its ministry, and the way it was responding to the changing world around it. Chris Morck, an American missionary who had been working with the diocese for several years, was our host. A few days before our visit to San Francisco, we were in Quito, Ecuador's capital, and met with Julián Guamán, a Quichua theologian. His job was to try to help us wrap our minds around a different way of thinking about how the world works. It was a tough task.

For his people, Guamán told us, thinking is not linear, like in the West, but a spiral. "In linear thought, you always have a goal and are always working toward that goal. In spiral thinking, you are always coming back to a similar place." This way of thinking has several implications for how one approaches the world. "In indigenous thinking," he told us, "extremes are dangerous. Just feeling is bad. Just thinking is bad." The key was to connect extremes and not go too far in one direction. If you or your descendants are going to come back to a similar place as you have been before, you want to be careful to preserve what you have. Indigenous thought has another important aspect. "Everything is relational. The individual doesn't exist except in relation to others. In our language, the verb is the most important part, not the subject. That's why indigenous people struggle to speak Spanish." When European missionaries arrived, however, the differences between Western thought and indigenous Andean thought were collapsed with little regard for—or even awareness of—the fact that there are different ways of looking at the world. Guamán told us his work now focused on how mission from the Euro-Atlantic world and the appropriation of Christianity had changed how indigenous people think. He also told us about the relative weakness of the Catholic Church among his people, particularly in urban areas. They were looking for other ways of expressing their religious faith than what they had known, as well as new ways of understanding their changed circumstances in an urban, nontraditional environment. What they were finding was evangelicalism, taught by missionaries from conservative Protestant denominations in the United States. Nearly sixty percent of his people, he estimated, were joining these new churches.

People in our group responded positively to his message. When some comments seemed to romanticize a way of life about which we knew very little, Guamán cautioned us. "You can't adopt indigenous concepts wholesale and Christianize them divorced from their context." Instead, he told us, our job was to do what many missionaries had failed to do: "Recognize that in other peoples there is the seed of the word."

Our group continued to talk through these ideas after Guamán left. Then, shortly before the visit to San Francisco, we had a chance to hear more about indigenous thought when Luis Alberto talked to us about his ministry. When missionaries first arrived, Luis Alberto said, they divided communities. Some people accepted the new teachings. Others rejected them. The Quichua had a strong indigenous religious tradition, and many people did not want to lose that. So they took their religion underground and hid it from the missionaries. Some put up a facade of Catholicism while also maintaining their indigenous practices. As portions of the Bible came to be translated into Quichua, however, the people made an interesting discovery.

"It turned out we believed in the same Lord," Luis Alberto told us. "We just knew him by a different name. We discovered that the gospel itself isn't bad. But the way it was delivered to us was." Quichua people, along with many other South Americans, became even more interested in Christianity as liberation theology took hold of the continent in the second half of the twentieth century. Reading the Bible in small groups—the so-called "base communities"—and reflecting on the ways in which it applied to their daily lives had helped many people come to Christ. Despite opposition from the church hierarchy, liberation theology continues to survive and shape religious life in Ecuador and throughout the continent.

Reading the Bible in his own language with others like him had shaped Luis Alberto's approach to Christianity. His ministry was centered on a verse from the Gospel of John: "I have come that they may have life and have it more abundantly." "This is what we need to teach people," Luis Alberto said, "abundant life. That is what God wants for them. But for abundant life, people need their own land, good health, and education. These are all things that have to do with abundant life." Given the history of his people in their mountain villages, land was particularly important. "A people that does not have land does not have life," he said.

The other biblical passage that guided Luis Alberto in his work was the temptation of Christ at the outset of his ministry. The devil challenges Jesus to turn stone into bread, presents him with all the kingdoms of the world, and dares him to jump off the top of the temple. For Luis Alberto, the importance of the passage was in its interpretation. "Bread is at the foundation of our economic life," he said. "Jesus realizes he can't save the world by economic power alone. Rejecting the kingdoms of the world means you can't save the world by politics alone. Turning down the offer to jump off the temple means you can't save the world by religion alone. The church needs to speak to all aspects of a person's life." That was how people would begin to realize abundant life. Sometimes, however, the church had not understood this and focused only on particular aspects of life. In order for the church to be truly itself, Luis Alberto said, it first needs to understand what full life is so that it can then explain that to other people. "Jesus Christ does not divide people," he said. "But mission and economic power can."

We asked him what he thought of a group of students from the United States coming to his country to learn about his people, given the difficult relations in the past with outsiders. Did any role remain for global mission? "Missionaries should convert themselves to the indigenous way," he responded. "Then mission can be a way to strengthen communities and support us in our struggle for full life. For us, there is no other way."

⌒〰〰〰⌒

To see people like Eulogio and Luis Alberto travel up and down mountains to preach the gospel of full life was inspiring. But the story in the rest of the Diocese of Central Ecuador is more discouraging. For the last several years, the diocese has been riven by conflict, split over power, authority, and control. Priests have been inhibited and prevented from exercising their ministry. A group of people appealed the election of a new bishop all the way to the floor of the Episcopal Church's General Convention in 2009. It is a sad, if too familiar, story in the church. To have a small diocese rocked and split by such deep divisions is nothing but disappointing.

In this context, the Quichua congregations in places like San Francisco pose a challenge to the diocese. As always with the church in the Global South, measuring church membership in these villages is difficult. But it is clear there are at least several thousand people in the Andes interested in becoming Episcopalian. The entire Diocese of Central Ecuador before its split had only a few thousand members, mostly in urban areas. If and when these new communities become formal parishes of the diocese, the nature of the diocese could change dramatically. A largely *mestizo* diocese could easily become a largely indigenous one. Or some combination of the two could emerge. Or something else entirely could happen. One question that was being asked at the time of my visit was just how seriously the people in these villages want to be Episcopalian, as opposed to just generally Christian. If the Episcopal Church cannot provide the pastoral attention necessary, some of the villages might continue with their journey and evolve into some sort of a-denominational church that more fully depends on a traditional spirituality. At the time of my visit, the full implications of events in villages like San Francisco had barely begun to sink in.

Eulogio and Luis Alberto are responding as best they can. Before heading up the mountain to San Francisco, we spent the afternoon at a workshop on pastoral care, held in the farming town in the valley below the mountains. Representatives from many of the nearby villages trekked down the mountains to learn about the ways in which they could care for and support one another. The teaching was in Quichua, of course, but just seeing everyone assembled was a proud-to-be-Anglican moment. Subsistence farming is a difficult existence that does not allow many breaks for relaxation or education. To see such a large group of villagers gathered in one place was enough to give me hope that their experiment with the Episcopal Church might endure.

Back in Quito, there were signs of hope as well. On our first day, we had visited Comité del Pueblo, a neighborhood that had begun forty years earlier when landless people began to take over some large tracts owned by a few wealthy landowners. Our destination was Cristo Liberador, an Episcopal church built of concrete blocks painted a rather unappealing blue, surrounded by an ugly chain-link fence, and bordering a dusty road. On the drive over, we passed several Catholic churches that were varying degrees of magnificent. As if we needed it, Cristo Liberador was a reminder that being Episcopalian in such a Catholic country is often like being the poor little brother. Nothing is ever quite as nice.

Inside the church, there were only a few wooden benches for pews. The rest of the space was filled with white plastic chairs. (This, I was learning on my travels, is the universal Anglican seating device.) We were there for a weekday service of Morning Prayer, attended by three dozen elderly residents of the neighborhood. There was a clear dignity and solemnity to the service. These men and women may have been in the poor little brother church, but that did not mean they were not devout and prayerful. They greeted us warmly after the service and welcomed us upstairs to tea. We climbed a rickety set of steps and squished around a too-small table in a back room of the church, the Harvard students scrunched up against the short indigenous woman wearing a traditional poncho, the Yale students pressed close to the quiet men with only a handful of teeth remaining. It was, for me, another moment in which I felt a measure of pride at sharing a faith with these sister and brother Anglicans. They did not have much, their church was small, and it stood out from the dominant religious culture of the neighborhood, city, and country. Yet still they gathered a few days a week for Morning Prayer and tea and funded it all through their own pledges and contributions to the church. As I sat there and tried out my best Spanish with the women next to me, I was reminded of something I had once been told: Wherever you go in the world, you can probably find a few Anglicans. There may not be many, but they will be there and they will be doing the work of the Lord.

༒

"Johnny B. Goode" was the last number Luis Alberto and I had time for before the congregation began filing into the church in San Francisco. As they did, I thought of something Luis Alberto had said when we spoke with him before coming up the mountain. The key to full life, he had told us, was being in a community. "I want to be in the community to engage myself in daily community life," he said. "The only way I can transform the world is in daily encounter with the other." This service would definitely be our encounter with the other for the day. The contrast in the social position of the members of my group—relatively wealthy, mobile, and educated at some of the most elite institutions in the world—and the people coming into the church was stark. There were a dozen of us gringos and forty or fifty Quichua in ponchos and felt hats. We barely had a language in common, let alone an economic background or similar set of life experiences.

The Eucharist service was from the same Book of Common Prayer with which I had been raised and was deeply familiar to me. Though the service was in Spanish, Eulogio translated large chunks of it into Quichua on the fly. As I shook hands and exchanged the peace with my fellow congregants, I had a feeling I remembered from St. Andrew's in Mthatha: we seemed to have barely anything in common, but in this moment of the peace we could still recognize one another as fellow Christians. When the Eucharist was celebrated, the sacrament we shared was the same sacrament that Christians around the world share.

On the way back down the mountain after we had shared a second, nonsacramental meal with the people of San Francisco, I thought about the people in the communities we were driving through. Their story was so striking—of an indigenous faith, of the enculturation of the gospel, of a movement into the Episcopal Church—that I knew it needed to be told more broadly. But I also knew I was not the one to share it: the people in these communities needed to tell their story for themselves. I thought back to a conversation earlier in the week in Quito with Nilton Giese, a Lutheran pastor who was serving as the general secretary of the Latin American Council of Churches. He told us about the work of his organization and what it means to be an ecumenical organization in a region that is still so dominated by the Catholic Church. He stressed the interrelatedness of people around the world, especially Christians. "We are no longer two separate realities," he said. "We need to understand better where we are coming from." He paused. "The problem is that Latin Americans don't generally speak a lot when they meet Americans. The Americans are so busy talking, we just listen. We Latin Americans don't have all the answers, but we also don't think all the answers are coming from you in the north."

He paused again and looked at us pointedly. "Latin Americans don't usually do what I did today." We looked at him, puzzled. "That is, I spoke to you. How can you create more opportunities for our voices to be heard?"

Driving down the mountain from that little church in San Francisco, his question rang through my head. How can these voices be heard?

CHAPTER 9

A Prospering Church?

*Diocese of Owerri, Church of Nigeria
(Anglican Communion)*

There is something thrilling about being driven to church in convoy.

Bishop Cyril Okorocha of Owerri is paying a pastoral visit to Christ Church, one of the oldest and largest churches in his diocese. The archdeacon in charge of the parish has driven over to the Bishop's Bourne in his own car. He has brought with him two lay people, one driving a van with "Christ Church Anglican, Owerri" stenciled on the side. Bishop Cyril, immaculate in his purple cassock, climbs into the backseat of his waiting silver Toyota Corolla sedan. I scramble in alongside, not wanting to be left behind. The two vehicles from Christ Church lead the way out the front gate of the Bourne with the Corolla directly behind. The guard on duty is a former sergeant in the Biafran rebel army and he salutes our little convoy as we pass by, an affectation he alone adopts toward the bishop. The only thing missing, I think, is flashing lights on the roof of the car.

Whatever illusions of grandeur I may have had upon leaving vanish as soon as we turn on to one of Owerri's main streets. Motorized tricycle taxis dart in and out, disrupting our procession. Potholes deep enough to swallow the car pockmark the road. The bishop's driver negotiates them slowly. The driver of the van does not. Our convoy is soon split up as they pull far ahead of us.

Christ Church is in the middle of Owerri's market, the oldest and most cramped part of town. Even on this Sunday morning, the stalls are bustling with activity. A few blocks short of the church, I hear trumpets playing and drums beating and see a small band approaching us—three trumpets, four drums.

"Is that for us?" I ask Bishop Cyril.

His look at me says, "Of course," but he does not respond. He is too busy screwing together his collapsible crozier and putting on a stole over his cassock. "Stay here," he tells me, and steps out.

For the next four blocks, Bishop Cyril strides down the center of the street, waving and smiling at all he sees. Children, and not a few adults, approach him for a blessing. For these few minutes, all the attention in this section of the market is focused on Bishop Cyril. He soaks it in with a big smile on his face while people in the market exult that the bishop—their bishop—has paid them a visit.

In a few minutes, Cyril is inside Christ Church's expansive compound. I am still in the Corolla, a few feet behind. Directly in front of us is the church, a long, low building. European missionaries built its original section, but it has been expanded several times since. Around the back, I catch a glimpse of the church's three-story school. Through the open windows of the church, I can see a packed sanctuary. Outside, there are even more people: choir members in green robes, more lay leaders, children from the neighborhood—all crowd around Cyril, looking for a blessing, looking to be touched, looking for a short moment in the swirl of attention that surrounds him.

Cyril barely breaks his stride. He moves to the front entrance of the church and, hardly missing a beat, begins the procession down Christ Church's center aisle, marching just behind the crucifer. I am under strict orders to stay close to Cyril, so, seeing no other option, I get out of the car and plunge into the procession with the choir. The music is thumping loudly. The choir members are dancing as they make their way down the long aisle. I do my best to sway along with them. But I am overwhelmed by all the people. Christ Church has three aisles and there are people crammed into every pew, plastic chair, and windowsill. I am surrounded by an intense swirl of colors—purple, green, yellow, magenta, cyan, on the clothing of the women as well as the men. All of them are singing and swaying just as much as the choir is. I am a solitary white face dressed in drab earth tones in the midst of a multicolored, high-energy, and deeply joyous moment of worship.

Reaching the front, Cyril takes the microphone that is handed to him. Holding his crozier and the microphone in one hand, he dances and sways with the rest of the congregation, his free hand waving in the air, cassock swishing at his feet.

The music ends—pauses, really—for a moment and Cyril greets the congregation.

"Praise the Lord!" he shouts.

"Hallelujah!" the people respond.

For the next fifteen minutes, Cyril leads his people in an informal, high-energy, praise and worship session. There is more singing in Igbo and English, more dancing, more swaying, more clapping, and more loud music. The energy level that spiked when Cyril stepped out of the car four blocks from the church has not faded a bit.

With a final, loud "Amen!" Cyril retires to the sacristy to vest while the people in the congregation sit down for a moment to catch their breath and prepare for the service. This, after all, was only the warm-up.

Say what you will about Anglicans in Nigeria, but this cannot be denied: they are having fun.

⁙

I was connected to Bishop Cyril through his chaplain, a young priest who was sent to Cambridge to study at the same time I was at West-cott House. It was a fortuitous connection. Cyril Okorocha first made his name as an evangelist in the revival that followed the end of the Biafran War in the early 1970s. He studied abroad and worked for a time for the Anglican Communion Office in London. His diocese, Owerri, is an historic one in the church, and in the heartland of the Igbo people. This is the former Biafra, which suffered so grievously in the civil war of the late 1960s and is now close to the center of the country's oil-fueled growth. One thing led to another and before long I had an invitation to Owerri. Although I knew from my diverse experiences in Uganda, Sudan, and South Africa not to be fooled into thinking there was such a thing as the "African church," when I let myself think about what I would encounter in Owerri, my perceptions were shaped by what I had experienced elsewhere. Just a few days in Owerri, however, showed me what a mistake this was.

The sheer scale of programs and projects in Owerri was over-whelming—schools, clinics, social services, a newspaper, and more. During my visit, Cyril cut the ribbon on the diocese's new medical clinic, a two-story building with several large windows and a small balcony on the second floor. The senior medical officer showed me the rooms for HIV counseling, patient consulting, and group educa-tion sessions; the fully functioning lab with several impressive-looking machines; and, of course, the requisite generator and water tower just outside to make up for the poor quality of government-provided ser-vices. The clinic had been built entirely with Nigerian money.

The new clinic was not far from the diocesan conference center, a sixty-bed facility that could accommodate a whole range of events, both church- and non-church-related, and generate income for wom-en's ministries in the diocese. Next door was the diocesan printing press, a hot and crowded operation with two presses printing pro-grams for upcoming diocesan meetings, essays and addresses by Cyril himself, and a number of other products for individual clients.

The press, in turn, was not far from the offices of the diocesan newspaper, *The Christian Voice*, the weekly sixteen-page publication that covers local church news, as well as news from nearby dioceses and around the country. Leafing through past issues, I was struck by the amount of news there was about Anglicans around the world. The issues I looked at had articles about Anglicans being persecuted by the Mugabe regime in Zimbabwe. When the American church appeared, it was not often in a positive light. A few editorials and articles were reprinted from the website of David Virtue, a virulent source of con-servative Anglican polemic. This is what Anglicans in Owerri relied on for their church news. In my visits around the diocese, I saw recent issues of *The Christian Voice* on many coffee tables.

Not far from the newspaper's offices was the lead church for the archdeaconery. The congregation had outgrown the building, however, so the building was being enlarged. Since the congregation needed a place to meet while the work was underway, the old building was still standing. New walls were under construction on either side. The enlarged church would eventually enclose the old one, at which point the old one would be demolished. The new walls were half again as tall as the old. I saw children walking past the construction site, headed home from the archdeaconery's school.

In just these few acres of land, the amount of church-related activity was incredible—conference center, newspaper, clinic, print-ing press, church, school. There was more going on here than in the entirety of many American dioceses. True, this was a particularly active part of the diocese with a handful of diocesan-wide ministries based here. But there were other plots like this scattered around the city. The lead church in every archdeaconery—of which there were at least nine in the diocese—had a school attached to it. On land on the edge of the city, the diocese was building a new boarding school with a three-story dormitory and a three-story classroom block using money raised entirely within the diocese. I asked the archdeacon who chaired the diocesan construction committee how many projects were currently underway. He groaned. "I can't keep track of them all sometimes."

The activity of church organizations on weekdays was matched by the activity on Sundays, as I saw at Christ Church. Cyril told me that when he first became bishop, he had confirmed seven hundred people in a service that lasted until one in the morning. He now limited services to "only" two hundred confirmands each. "Confirmation is important," he said. "Many young people here belong to secret gangs and cults for a time. When they are confirmed, they are saying they no longer want to belong to those. It's a big step for them." He told me about one young man who, during the examination portion of the confirmation, had danced around uncontrollably. The congregation believed he was fighting with a spirit that was possessing him. When he was confirmed, he immediately calmed down and was now a leading member of the youth wing of his congregation. I thought back to my own confirmation, and the casual approach so many of us had taken to the rite.

It was not just in confirmation that the diocese responded to the needs of its young people. A few days after the ribbon cutting at the clinic, I went to a graduation ceremony presided over by Cyril's wife, Eunice. Eight young women had completed a course in sewing overseen and paid for by the diocesan women's ministries. Now, on this graduation day, they were being given a sewing machine and a small loan to start their own business. First, though, some of last year's graduates stood up to testify to the significance of the program. "I now help feed my family, pay the school fees for my siblings, and am self-reliant. I don't have to ask my parents for money," said one, before handing Eunice money to repay what she had been lent at this ceremony the year prior. Another mentioned how the money she earned making dresses with her sewing machine helped pay her mother's hospital bills during a recent illness. She, too, had money to repay Eunice.

The ceremony dragged on, as these sorts of things are wont to do. In between the prayers over the sewing machines, the distribution of money, the admonition from Cyril to the young women to read Proverbs 1:10—"My child, if sinners entice you, do not consent"—I thought of my work when I lived in Mthatha. In the community center there, I had struggled to start a microcredit program that aimed to do similar sorts of things: help women start businesses and then use the money they repaid to lend to more women. My program sputtered, laid low by a variety of factors, my cultural ineptitude among them. In Owerri, while it was true that some young women had not repaid the money, the program, by and large, seemed to be succeeding. What was the point of someone like me facilitating such a program, when people in the local church seemed to be doing a fine job?

Nor was ministry in the Diocese of Owerri confined merely to young people. My time in Owerri coincided with the annual conference of the Anglican Christian Fathers' Fellowship, an organization Cyril started when he became bishop as a kind of parallel to the Mothers' Union and as a way to involve men in the church. There were branches in every parish in the diocese and the idea was gradually spreading to nearby dioceses. The conference was held at St. Titus, a church nearly as large in size as the cathedral in Juba, Sudan, and yet one that in Owerri was merely the lead church in a peripheral archdeaconery. When we arrived, there were six or eight hundred men in the pews, patiently listening to speech after speech. In many ways, the conference proceeded like any other large meeting I had been to in sub-Saharan Africa: too-long speeches to an audience that moved first from engaged to disinterested and then from disinterested to somnolent.

Yet the conversation sparked my interest. Speaker after speaker lamented the ways in which fathers were failing to raise their children in the faith and not modeling regular attendance at church. The result, the speakers said, is that children are being influenced by Pentecostal churches and leaving the Anglican Church. This was the cause of great consternation for the fathers present. Toward the end of the session, the priest facilitating it concluded: "We need fathers to raise Christ-centered children who can bring light to all parts of society. We are not meeting our responsibility."

Cyril's keynote address was on the conference's second day. It was a three-hour stem-winder of an address, interrupted—distressingly—by celebratory cannon shots from a wedding party in the neighborhood, and featuring discursive sections on Igbo cosmology and the parenting strategies of Abraham, Moses, and Eli. The main theme—though at three hours, there were many themes—came back to the issues raised the day before. Fathers are supposed to raise their children in the ways of godliness, Cyril said, but Anglican fathers in Owerri and elsewhere needed to do a better job.

The picture of the "African church" that was emerging from my visit to Owerri was of a confident and expansive organization, reaching out to those it encountered and playing a central role in the lives of its people. If I needed any further confirmation of this view, it came on a day trip I made with Cyril to the diocesan synod in Awka, a diocese based in a major market town two hours from Owerri. The new bishop was a protégé of Cyril's and Cyril was there to lend his support and encouragement. Located right in the middle of the sprawling and low-slung market, Awka's Cathedral Church of St. Faith dominates the center of the city. Its sanctuary can accommodate at least 1,500 worshippers and is routinely full for several services on Sunday. To the side are meeting rooms and diocesan offices. In the part of the synod we attended, delegates considered and approved plans for a multimillion dollar diocesan conference and retreat center that will dwarf Owerri's. Completion was still several years off, but the project was generating excitement and enthusiasm that indicated that raising the funds would be possible.

Immediately next to St. Faith's is the cathedral it replaced, a relic from the era when British missionaries controlled the church. No doubt, it was impressive when it was built. But now, standing next to St. Faith's, it is a small building, puny, really, in the shadow of its successor. The paint is peeling on the outside walls. When I poked my head inside, a chicken was pecking its way across the floor of the now-empty church.

As a metaphor for the church in Nigeria, one can do worse than the two cathedrals. Across Nigeria, the Anglican Church is a vibrant, growing, and lively institution that is firmly in control of its own future. The missionary, colonial past? That's for the chickens.

If I was finding much to be impressed with in Owerri, I was also finding aspects of the church's life that raised disquiet within me. The loud
and rocking service at Christ Church was a good place to start.

The service's energy level, music selections, and sheer exuberance
were good indications of the influence that Pentecostal and charismatic styles of worship have had on Anglicanism in Nigeria. One
of the fastest growing religious phenomena in the world, Christian
or otherwise, is Pentecostalism. In Africa, Nigeria is, in many ways,
its seedbed. Beginning with the Biafran civil war and intensifying
in Nigeria's economic crises of the 1980s, Pentecostal churches have
exploded with growth across the country, presenting a challenge—in
worship style, belief, and, I was to learn, theology—to the forms of
church inherited from the mission forebears.

The sermon that Sunday at Christ Church was an hour long,
not in itself noteworthy. What was noteworthy—and disquieting—
was the content. The preacher was a visiting bishop, whom Cyril had
invited for the weekend. The first half of his sermon was on the first
few verses of the book of Joshua, in which God reaffirms the gift of
the Promised Land. The bishop referenced the death of Moses, with
which the passage begins: "Your past represents the biblical Moses.
This morning I see little Joshuas sitting in this congregation, thinking about the challenges they will face in the future. Is anyone here a
Joshua?" he asked, his voice rising. "God knows there are challenges
ahead of you. That is why he is making you a Joshua. Today, heaven
is laying a hand on you to do wonders in your life and family. Someone will arise this morning. There is a family that has been living
in crisis that will come out of that crisis this morning." Each pronouncement was greeted with loud "Amens" and "Hallelujahs" from
the congregation. Citing problems like a lack of money and sickness,
he continued, "Somebody is going to cross over this morning! You
will go over that Jordan!" He was shouting now and members of the
congregation were rising to their feet. "Your future will be greater
than your past! As from today, anywhere you put the soles of your
feet, he will give it to you! Jesus is calling you with more power than
he called Joshua!"

As I sat in my pew, squirming a bit more with each passing declaration, I realized what I was listening to: the prosperity gospel.
The prosperity gospel is closely associated with the newer forms of

Pentecostalism that have emerged in recent decades and teaches that success—financial or otherwise—comes with one's decision to follow Christ. Therefore, if one is not successful, the—fallacious—line of thinking goes, there must be something deficient about one's theology or faithfulness. Jesus rewards those who are faithful. Therefore, those who look successful and have the trappings of wealth must be faithful. It is a syllogism that is as simple as it is heterodox.

On the ride home from Christ Church, I looked with new eyes at the churches we were passing. There was "River of Life International Ministries: The Church of Fire," "Charismatic Renewal Ministries International," and, more simply, "The International Praise Church," along with several other places with similar names. Owerri was crawling with Pentecostal churches. Some were quite large and, on this Sunday afternoon, still had crowds outside, some as large as there had been at Christ Church. I recognized the names on one or two churches as nationwide Pentecostal denominations that had started a few decades earlier and now had branches across the country.

I asked Cyril about the sermon that morning and shared with him my thought that it seemed to be influenced by the prosperity gospel. He sighed. "The prosperity gospel is a virus that is taking over our church. Our Anglican church is becoming 'Anglocostal.'" It was a frank admission. In the competitive Nigerian religious marketplace, the Anglican Church sees the growing Pentecostal churches as a threat and is blurring its distinctiveness to become more Pentecostal in style and substance. The offering envelope at Christ Church had Malachi 3:10 printed on its cover: "Bring the full tithe into the storehouse . . . and thus put me to the test, says the LORD of hosts; see if I will not open the windows of heaven for you and pour down for you an overflowing blessing." The influence was also clear in the many services I attended in Owerri: loosely structured, free-flowing worship was the norm, no matter what the prayer book mandated. At lunch after the service at Christ Church, I had asked the archdeacon in charge of the congregation how he planned worship. I mentioned I noticed him using several spontaneous prayers. Was that common, or did he use a predetermined liturgy?

"There is not very much liturgy," he replied. "Usually we use extemporaneous prayers." Then he hastily added, "But it is still within the"— he paused, looking for the right phrase—"ambit of Anglicanism." The conversation moved on, leaving my follow-up question unasked: who or what determines what is in that ambit and what is not?

༄

My visit to Owerri came just a few weeks before the diocese's annual ordination service. In the month before the scheduled date, the ordinands—more than twenty-five men—gather with their families in the diocesan conference center for a final, intense period of formation. Not all of them will be ordained priest or deacon in a few weeks. Many will spend several years as consecrated church teachers, an advanced lay role that allows the diocese time to assess the candidate's suitability for ordained ministry. What does unite them, however, is their education. In his time as bishop, Cyril has mandated that all candidates for ordination have a postsecondary degree. Nigerians are, on the whole, well-educated and there are several universities in Owerri itself. Still, the fact that the diocese can set such a high standard and have no shortage of candidates is one more marker distinguishing the church here from a place like Sudan. When Cyril told me of this policy, I thought of the students at Bishop Gwynne College, who were fortunate to have a high-school diploma.

On the day I visited, the ordinands were discussing mutuality in ministry. The archdeacon in charge of the lesson was a gentle-looking man who helped the class think about how priests can work together in parishes and also work alongside their lay people. The session was just ending when we arrived and Cyril introduced me and asked me to say a few words. I explained my interest in exploring what unity looks like when the body of Christ spans the globe and acknowledged—though they needed no reminder of this—that there have been differences between our two churches in recent years. A few of the ordinands asked questions—but the exchange was polite and restrained. I was still too new to be anything more than an unknown quantity, a guest to be shown hospitality, not yet a friend to be meaningfully engaged. As the questions petered out, the archdeacon who had been teaching the lesson had a point he wanted to make. "There are many cultural differences between our two churches," he said, though whether homosexuality counted as one of them I was not sure. "What matters, though, is Romans 14:19." He quoted it from memory. "Let us then pursue what makes for peace and for mutual upbuilding."

The archdeacon's name was Paul and he was in charge of Owerri's cathedral, the Cathedral of the Transfiguration of Our Lord. Not long after the session with the ordinands, Paul invited me to accompany him to a neighboring diocese for a meeting. It was a beautiful drive through the rolling eastern Nigerian landscape. The two-lane road took us through market towns and small villages of subsistence farmers. Scores of churches lined the road, both Anglican and not, and I made a note of their names as we passed by. In the sixty-mile drive, we passed through four Anglican dioceses.

Paul is the sort of man who, when he walks into a home, immediately says, "May peace be upon this home and its inhabitants." His earnestness is a function of his genuine Christian devotion. His father was an archdeacon in Owerri before him and Paul has long anticipated this ministry. He is the farthest thing from a demagogue, and our conversation in the car meandered through a range of topics as we explored the differences between our churches. We talked about how silly it is to call bishops "my Lord," as I had heard people call Cyril. We talked about the church's obsession with hierarchy, and the vast number of archdeacons and canons in the diocese, far more than any English diocese where the titles originated. Indeed, in Owerri as in many other Nigerian dioceses, archdeacons were effectively equivalent to area deans in the Church of England. Paul was intrigued when I told him how some churches are trying to do a better job emphasizing the ministry of all the baptized.

The conversation turned to the lesson with the ordinands. I mentioned how much I appreciated his comments about peace and mutual upbuilding. He acknowledged the comment but had some questions for me. He had heard that some priests in the United States are gay. "What would these—" he paused, looking for the right word, "brothers, I guess you would call them." He started again. "What would these Christian brothers of yours say if I asked them how they could be homosexual and train for ordination?" I told him how seminary classmates of mine who are gay tell me they believe God created them to be that way. He paused to digest this information. After a few moments he spoke again. "In every culture, there is something to be converted by the gospel. In Nigeria, it is our lying, cheating, and pervasive corruption." He paused again, reflective. "What is it that needs to be converted in America?" It was an honest question, asked genuinely, and

I realized it was not one to which I had ever given serious thought. I stumbled, looking for an answer. I mentioned American culture's obsessive drive to sexualize human interaction, though I made clear I did not think same-sex relationships fall in this category. He nodded thoughtfully and, thankfully, did not press his question.

We talked some more about the differences and divisions between the churches. It was clear we disagreed, but it was also clear that this disagreement did not change the respect and affection either of us was developing for the other. I told him I was interested in figuring out what role there was for people like me in a place like Owerri. The old mission era was gone, but there was no new model yet. "That's a good question to be asking," he said. "I think we need to be stressing mutuality more in the church. Everyone has to show up ready to give and receive something." It reminded him of a sermon he preached to his congregation after the 2010 Lausanne Conference of evangelical Christians. "The statement from that conference calls on Christians to live a life of 'humility, integrity, and simplicity.' If thousands of Christians can agree on that," he said, "surely there is something we can learn from it."

Paul's emphasis on the Lausanne statement was commendable and I had no doubt that they were values he lived in his life. But there were practices I had seen in the church that made me wonder if everyone shared his commitment. At the end of Cyril's keynote address at the Anglican Christian Fathers' Fellowship, there had been a time for the "appreciation." Envelopes were distributed, a big bucket placed in the chancel, and men came up and put their envelopes full of money in the bucket. With one exception, it was not all that different than what I remembered at the stewardship Sunday at St. John's in Northampton. The exception was that as they approached the bucket, each man took the microphone, said their name, gave a little speech thanking the bishop, and announced how much they were giving. (The money went to the ACFF and not the bishop.) After each announcement, there was applause, its volume dependent on the size of the gift. As the appreciation dragged on—there were several hundred people in attendance—the master of ceremonies intervened: "No more speeches, please, we don't have time. Just tell us how much and put it in the bucket."

To pass the time while the appreciation continued, I flipped through the copy of the new Nigerian prayer book I had been given a few days earlier. At the back is printed the Jerusalem Declaration, the manifesto that came out of the meeting of the Global Anglican Futures Conference in Jerusalem in 2008, the meeting Nigerian bishops attended in lieu of the Lambeth Conference. My eye was drawn to the declaration's second point: "The Bible is to be translated, read, preached, taught and obeyed in its plain and canonical sense, respectful of the Church's historic and consensual teaching." Looking up from the Jerusalem Declaration to the appreciation that was still going on, Jesus' instruction in the Sermon on the Mount came to mind: "When you give alms, do not let your left hand know what your right hand is doing so that your alms may be done in secret, and your father who sees in secret will reward you" (Matthew 6:3–4). No matter how I tried to square it, the appreciation seemed in direct contravention of Jesus' teaching. There was nothing secret about this appreciation. In fact, publicity was its purpose. Moreover, it seemed impossible to reconcile the desire to read and obey the Bible in its "plain" sense with what I was seeing in front of me.

As we left the conference that afternoon, I asked several priests about the practice of appreciation. Each said it was commonplace. I mentioned the teaching in the Sermon on the Mount. All were familiar with the passage, but each shrugged and said, "It's our culture. It's how we give." With one priest, I pressed the conversation a little further. Leaving aside Jesus' teaching, I told him, I did not think public giving was necessarily wrong. Perhaps it encouraged people to give more. Perhaps, in a culture where corruption is rampant, it encouraged transparency in the church's financial affairs. I was certainly open, I said, to the idea that we could modify how we understood Jesus' teachings in order to accommodate both this aspect of Nigerian culture and the way in which giving has evolved in the church. He nodded, satisfied with the solution.

But I pressed on. If I could show leniency in scriptural interpretation on this point, would he be willing to show the same leniency on the American church's interpretation of same-sex relationships? The American church has made changes to respond to the culture it finds itself in. The priest shrugged. What I was saying sounded reasonable to him, he said. "But being opposed to homosexuality has become a test of whether you believe the Bible or not," he said.

"Why?" I asked. "Why homosexuality and not, say, public giving?"

He shrugged again. "I don't know," he said. "It's just the way it is. If you want to be a faithful Christian and do well in the church, you can't be in favor of homosexuality even a little bit." He walked away, ending the conversation.

⊙﹏⊙

At just over two weeks, my time in Owerri was brief but intense. I had seen diocesan and church programs that, as an American Episcopalian, I wished we had in our church. I had met thoughtful, reasonable Anglicans who genuinely wanted to learn more about how the American church could have a gay bishop. But the most astounding aspect of Nigerian Anglicanism, I came to believe, was the influence of Pentecostalism. It was necessary to understand this relationship in order to begin to understand the Nigerian hierarchy's opposition to the American church.

Prosperity gospel thinking has pervaded the Nigerian church in such a way that a church's perceived success—measured in size, membership, and finances—is connected to its fidelity to the gospel. Stories of the decline of the American church are well known in Nigeria; on multiple occasions I was asked about a church in the Midwest that apparently had closed and been turned into a mosque. I knew nothing of it, but it seemed to be common knowledge in Owerri. Following this line of thinking—as deep-set as it is fallacious—it is easy to conclude that the decline of the American church means it is no longer faithful to the gospel. Ample "evidence" for this was provided by the election of a gay bishop.

But there is something deeper at work as well. The rapid growth of Pentecostal churches clearly frightens Anglicans. One young priest I talked to told me of his concern for the future of the church. In the past, he said, the "big men" in society belonged to the historic denominations, especially the Anglican Church, and the church had been supported by their tithes. But more and more, he said, the next generation of societal leaders was joining Pentecostal churches. With the survival of the church clearly in mind, he said, "The next twenty years will be very significant for the Anglican church in Nigeria." It seems unlikely that as well-entrenched an institution as Nigeria's Anglican Church could vanish in a generation. But its status and position in society could be significantly affected. And so, Anglican leaders keep an eye on Pentecostals the way a business watches its competitors.

In a context like this, the ordination of Gene Robinson comes as a discomfiting shock. Pentecostals and others could tar Anglicans as the "gay church," poaching its members and their tithes. One of the most confusing things about the Nigerian hierarchy's recent actions has been their refusal even to engage in dialogue with other Anglicans about their differing views. The 2008 Lambeth Conference was designed to enable precisely this sort of dialogue to occur—and the Nigerian House of Bishops boycotted it. In a religious environment like Nigeria's, however, the willingness to dialogue—and consequent implication that one might be wrong in one's views—is seen as a sign of weakness. And so to protect their position at home, Nigerian church leaders withdraw from Communion institutions. The conversation goes nowhere.

It was hard, as I reflected on my time in Owerri, to know the best way forward. For the American church, its cultural context mandates a greater openness to gay people in all levels of the church. For the Nigerian church, however, the context mandates directly the opposite. It is the definition of an impasse.

CHAPTER 10

Seeking Security

Diocese of Umuahia, Church of Nigeria
(Anglican Communion)

For the most part, as I traveled, I struggled to find opportunities to interact with women. In Owerri, I was shooed out of a kitchen when I poked my head in to thank the women who cooked dinner. But at Trinity Theological College in Umuahia, I had a rare chance for sustained conversation with women. And it did not go at all as I imagined.

Umuahia is the capital of Abia State, the neighbor to Owerri's Imo State. I was there only for a few days. My host was Oliver, a professor at Trinity whom I had been connected to through a mutual friend and who was eager for me to learn about theological education in Nigeria. He was intent on having me hold a "forum" with the students at Trinity. But since my visit was on the day before the end-of-year graduation, students were difficult to round up. Their wives, however, were at the seminary for a week-long, pregraduation training on what to expect as a clergy wife and were just finishing a meeting in the college's chapel. Oliver introduced me, stood me in front of the fifty-odd women, and told me to start talking.

I briefly introduced myself: I was studying for ministry, I came from the American church, and I was interested in what Jesus' prayer for unity might mean when Jesus' followers are spread around the world. Eager to learn more about them, I asked them what sort of challenges they expected to face when their husbands were assigned to parishes. The question was greeted with silence. I wondered if they were used to having guest speakers ask them questions. Tentatively, though, one woman raised her hand and broke the ice. "I am concerned about working with older women. The pastor's wife is supposed to be in charge of women's ministries, but other women are older than me and have more experience." Some women murmured their assent and started contributing their own thoughts. They were worried they did not have enough resources for ministry. They were concerned about how to deal with syncretism and how to handle people who wanted to belong to secret cults as well as the church.

Feeling comfortable that the conversation was off to a good start, I began talking more about my interest in unity. Everyone nodded. Unity was important; after all, Jesus had prayed for it. I paused and looked around, deciding if I should push the conversation further. I was a guest and did not want to offend the sensibilities of people I barely knew so soon after my arrival. Still, there was a pretty obvious elephant in the room. I decided to mention it.

"We Anglicans are having trouble with unity right now," I said. "Bishops in our two churches do not have very good relations." There were murmurs of assent to this. They knew what I was talking about. I decided to bring it out in the open. "What is it that divides us?" I asked.

The response was swift. "You have gay bishops."

"Does anyone know anything else about the American church?" I asked, looking to see if their knowledge was more than what dominated the headlines. There were many answers.

"Some of your priests smoke!"

"And drink alcohol!"

"Your women do not wear anything on their heads in church."

"And some of the women wear trousers."

These were true differences between our churches, I acknowledged, and we talked about some of what gave rise to them. But the women wanted to bring the conversation back to the question of homosexuality. "How can you ordain a gay man as bishop when the Bible says it is an abomination?" one woman asked directly. As I had at Bishop Gwynne College, with Paul in Owerri, and with many others, I began to talk about other ways of reading the Bible and my own experience. I told them about seminary classmates who told me they are gay and how they believed God created them in this way. As I said this, there was a rumbling among the women. "Not true." "Not possible." "No, no, no," I heard them say.

I barely had a chance to finish answering the first question before more questions started coming. Everyone wanted to ask—no, tell—me how the American church could do something that was so clearly condemned by the Bible. I patiently tried to answer each question, but it was difficult when so many women wanted to know the exact same thing. The tension peaked when one woman stood up and said, "Please tell me this yes or no right now: are you gay?" When I said I was not, there was a palpable sense of relief in the room. Still, the thought behind the question seemed to be that there were two sides to the issue. Either you were opposed to homosexuality or you were homosexual yourself. The idea that I could explain the view that one could be gay and Christian without being gay myself did not seem to be understood.

The conversation was never overtly hostile. But it was tense. And it certainly was not friendly in the way similar conversations in Sudan had been, or even the conversations I had with Paul and others in Owerri. It was clear why: I had no relationship with these women. They did not know me and I did not know them. I had appeared from nowhere, been handed a microphone, and started talking. I did not see the sense of going all the way to Nigeria only to paper over differences between our churches. That was why I had moved the conversation in this direction in the first place. But it was equally clear that this was not the right way to broach such a difficult subject. Relationships actually matter. Because Paul and the students at Bishop Gwynne knew me and I them, we knew that the other's views on homosexuality were not the only or even most salient feature of the other's faith.

As it was, the women and I were soon out of time. I concluded the conversation by saying that my goal was to help them understand how Americans had reached the decision we did. But, I added, I did think we could disagree on this question and still be in unity. After all, Christians disagree on plenty of other questions. There were some negative looks when I said this, as though such a thing could never be possible. But there were also glimmers on a few faces that indicated perhaps some people found sense in what I was saying. At any rate, the conversation had not soured relationships too far. The women still insisted on having a group photograph with me to commemorate my visit; whether they would remember the visit as ignominious or not was unclear.

Later, I browsed through the library at Trinity. There were well over 1500 books, far more than at Bishop Gwynne College in Juba.

But many were faded with age and falling apart in the tropical heat. Few seemed to have been published more recently than the mid-1980s. As I leafed through a volume on biblical scholarship, I wondered where the theology on sexuality-related issues was a quarter century or more ago. Given that, were the disagreements the women and I had such a surprise?

⟨⟩

Prior to my arrival in Nigeria, I thought a basic fact of Anglicanism was that few Anglicans attach much importance to membership in a global Communion. I knew clergy in the United States and England who were only aware in a fuzzy sort of way that such a thing as the Anglican Communion existed. But in Umuahia and Owerri, things were different. The official name of the Anglican province in Nigeria is "Church of Nigeria (Anglican Communion)." To my knowledge, no other province uses the phrase "Anglican Communion" in its title. I asked repeatedly about the importance of identifying oneself as part of the Communion. No one could give me a good answer. "It's always been that way" was the most frequent answer.

But one student at Trinity College had a different answer. "For Nigerians, it is important that we belong to something bigger and more important. So we like to know that we belong to the Anglican Communion because it means that we have international connections." The comment made intuitive sense. Unlike the Euro-Atlantic world, where being Christian can be seen as old-fashioned, quaint, and retrograde, belonging to a church in many parts of sub-Saharan Africa is seen as an advanced, forward-thinking move, in which one leaves behind one's traditional ways for what is newer, better, and more cosmopolitan. The knowledge that becoming Anglican in Nigeria involved becoming part of an international communion would be a fillip for the church. I thought of the names of the Pentecostal churches I saw in my travels. Many of them had phrases like "international" or "worldwide" in their title. I pointed this out to the student. "Yes," he said, "but they don't have real connections like we do. They just want people to think they do." In a context like this, in which genuine international connections are an important marker for the church, the consecration of Gene Robinson provoked outrage. International connections are supposed to be a source of strength for the church, not embarrassment.

As the women at Trinity College demonstrated, the Nigerian Anglicans I was meeting were well-versed in the current debates about the Anglican Communion. Owerri's diocesan newspaper, as I had seen, routinely carried articles about global Anglicanism. More than that, there were books about Anglicanism. Owerri's diocesan printing press was only one of several in the region. Many were run by independent publishers who made a living by publishing pamphlets and books for whomever could afford it. For an extra fee, the author could get an ISBN number for his book, ensuring it was properly registered and giving it an extra stamp of authenticity. In markets and in shops, I saw countless titles for sale, spanning a huge range of topics from diet to relationship to religion and many more. I found a very good commentary on 1 Corinthians by a leader of a Baptist denomination. There was another book about "postbaptismal sin." In the Nigerian church, there are clear behavioral expectations for Christians, which, naturally, people fail to meet. This book sought to explain what grace was and how it applied to a person's life in Christ. Leafing through it, I was reminded of an earlier African theological debate, in the fourth and fifth centuries, sparked by a group known as the Donatists, in which many of these same questions were at stake. Some of these books were serious works with extensive footnotes. Others were little more than pamphlets, riddled with typos and layout mistakes, though no one seemed to mind. All were relatively inexpensive, which made them available to a wide audience. When I visited clergy in their homes, I was often struck by just how full their shelves were. Full bookshelves are not unfamiliar to an American or British priest, of course, but I thought of the clergy who were training at Bishop Gwynne College. There, they owned a Bible and not much else.

Several priests I met in Owerri had authored books of their own and insisted on giving me copies. The titles were wide-ranging: *Purity & Power*; *The Mission of the Church in the 21st Century*; *Where Is the Lord God of Elijah?: A Prophetic Outcry for Revival*, and many others. Even though they were often only slim paperbacks, by the time I arrived in Umuahia, my luggage was straining under the weight. There, Oliver, my host, insisted on giving me copies of his book. For his dissertation, he had interpreted the household codes in Ephesians and Colossians in light of Igbo culture to see the ways in which those teachings on gender relations challenged Igbo culture and the ways in which the culture challenged the teachings. His conclusions were surprisingly liberative for a part of the Bible I had only ever heard associated with repression. I did my best to read as many of these books as I could. It was a gift to read theology produced by Africans for other Africans. One mark of a truly autonomous church is the ability to "self-theologize," that is, to take the good news of Jesus Christ and apply it to one's own context. These Nigerians did not need outsiders to tell them what to believe. In books like these, they were figuring it out for themselves.

I paid particular attention to the books about Anglicanism. There were titles like *Rediscovering Anglican Spirituality* and *The Fundamentals of Anglicanism*. Many were apologetic works, designed to make the church more attractive in a competitive religious environment. The problem was a lot of them were, well, wrong. It was not that there were interpretations of difficult issues that I disagreed with—that was to be expected—but rather that they were full of factual mistakes. One book detailed the history of the creation of the Anglican Consultative Council, one of the four Instruments of Communion, in a way that was almost comically incorrect. Another recalled the debate over homosexuality at the 1998 Lambeth Conference of bishops. Referring to the passage of a resolution that rejected "homosexual practice as incompatible with Scripture," it claimed this resolution "silenced the suicidal mission of the United States of America and Canadian dictators and saved the Church from the greatest religious scandal and betrayal of the Christian faith of the century." In doing so, it referred to Lambeth as the Communion's "highest policy making body." As the events following Lambeth 1998 made clear, bishops at Lambeth—to the chagrin of many—do not set policy for all Anglicans everywhere.

A few factual errors are one thing. These books still represented an exciting movement in theology. But as I kept coming across these books and seeing how much they circulated among clergy and lay people, I had a larger concern. It seemed possible that Nigerian Anglicans were creating their own narrative about global Anglicanism, one that differed substantially from the narrative I learned in the United States. Two different narratives based on two different sets of facts could, in turn, lead to two different assessments of the current situation and diagnoses of possible paths forward. For instance, if Nigerians believed that Lambeth was the "highest policy making body," then the 1998 resolution on homosexuality could be seen as the final word on the topic. If that was true, then it might make sense to conclude that the American church needed external oversight in the form of missionary bishops consecrated in Nigeria and sent to the United States. Meanwhile, Americans were busy telling themselves—accurately, I believed—that the Lambeth resolution had no such juridicial force.

If Anglicans cannot even agree on a particular set of facts, then reaching a consensus on the nature of the problem and possible ways forward becomes even more difficult. Rather than genuinely international and cross-cultural academic and ecclesial dialogue, the result could be two groups of people in their own echo chambers, each convinced their own position is right because the facts on which they base their argument are so clearly uncontested. As I thought about it more, I wondered if this was not a situation Anglicans might have to deal with in the future, but one we are dealing with right now.

Oliver, my host in Umuahia, was deeply concerned for my safety. Trinity College is on the edge of town, and on a trip into town to see a church-run school, Oliver made sure two seminarians rode in the car with us, "just in case anything happens." (It was never clear to me what the seminarians would do if we were accosted.) I was in Umuahia about three months after national elections that had left this part of the country unstable and its people frightened. Discontent with politicians had led many young men to join gangs. They roamed the region kidnapping people and holding them for ransom on almost a daily basis. "These gangs say that they are just doing what the politicians do—cheating and stealing to get ahead," Oliver said. When we visited a distant, rural part of the diocese, Oliver cut short our visit and sped home to be back before dusk. I appreciated the concern, but I wondered if it was not too much. I regretted that there were places it was deemed unsafe to visit. I asked Oliver if it was all really necessary. "Two weeks ago," he replied, "a young girl was raped and murdered not far from Trinity's main entrance." I thought of his own young children. Everyone was on edge, and rightly so.

In Owerri, there had been this same undercurrent of concern and fear. In contrast to Juba or Gulu, where I wandered relatively freely around town, I was kept on a short leash. Cyril would not let me go anywhere without a priest wearing at least a collar and preferably a cassock. At one point during our visit to the cathedral in Awka, I wandered out the front door to take a picture of the whole building without telling anyone. It was as if the Queen of England had gone missing, such were the alarms my absence set off. When Solomon, Cyril's driver, tracked me down—I had been absent for all of three minutes—and brought me back, Cyril reprimanded me and told me that Awka's market, abutting the cathedral grounds, is a dangerous place, known for its kidnappings and crime. Anything could have happened to me. Solomon did not let me move more than a few steps from him for the rest of the visit. Later, I accompanied Cyril to a funeral he conducted for a distinguished lay member of the diocese. Not knowing the family, I told Cyril I would sit in the back row of the large church and watch. "You'll sit here," he said, and pointed to the front row near the family. "You don't know who can get you when you sit on the edges of a big church service. You'll be safe here." Before the recent elections, Cyril and Eunice used to go jogging around their neighborhood each morning. But there had been so many kidnappings in the area, they now walked a short loop around the diocesan compound instead.

In the time I was in Nigeria, tensions heightened even further. Boko Haram, an Islamist extremist group based in the northern part of the country, bombed the national police headquarters in Abuja, Nigeria's capital. That put Christians on edge. One Sunday morning before church rumors flew that Boko Haram had tried but failed to bomb a church in Enugu, the capital of the state north of Umuahia. I never found out if there was any truth to the rumor, but it had done its job—people were concerned and afraid.

To an extent, these insecurities are a feature of life in many parts of the developing world. But judging by how people spoke of them, they seemed much closer at hand in Umuahia and Owerri. No one had much confidence in the police. Who would? Their main job, it seemed, was to set up roadblocks around town to extract bribes from passing drivers. "The politicians are busy enriching themselves from the state," one priest told me as we drove through a checkpoint, waved through because of his cassock. "But they"—he indicated the police—"treat us like animals." Public institutions, in general, are weak. Power generation in Nigeria brings new meaning to the word sporadic. As a result, a generator is a necessary feature of every household. At Oliver's home in Umuahia, he had fruit trees and chickens in his yard. In Owerri, Cyril did too, along with a fishpond. "We have become self-sustaining here," Cyril said as he showed me his compound. "We have to be. The government doesn't help us."

The weakness of societal institutions, I thought, went some way toward explaining the outsized role of the church. People came to church looking for the security, confidence, and certainty they could not find elsewhere in society. They wanted to hear that God would take care of them when others would not. Government could not improve their lives, but God would shower them with blessings. These views were reflected in the theology I heard and the way it was preached: confident, declarative, forthright. I thought of the English and American theologians who extol the virtues of ambiguity, uncertainty, and vulnerability in theology. But there was none of that wishy-washiness here. Strength ruled the day. Indeed, this likely was a further factor contributing to the boycott of Lambeth 2008 by Nigerian bishops. The conference was designed around a particular form of dialogue designed to prompt an honest exchange of views across boundaries of difference. But in Nigeria, such a task would be anathema for many church leaders. Christianity is not about entertaining the possibility that one might be wrong. It is about being right—and propounding those views with all one's might.

More important than church politics, however, the pervasive concern and instability is frustrating for another reason. The contrast between Nigerians and their government is stark. The latter, it is clear, is corrupt, weak, and incompetent. The scores of Nigerians I met were educated, creative, and hard-working. Yet rather than taking these talents and putting them to work building a hopeful future, Nigerians are in a constant defensive crouch. Rather than being a tool to ensure their future prosperity, they saw the government as something to be managed, avoided, and overcome. Before my visit, I had read about Nigeria's wasted potential. In the talented church members I met who lived in daily fear of the unknown, I saw it.

⁂

Charting a path for the church in such an environment is not easy. But there were signs that it was happening. In Owerri, I had attended a preaching conference at the diocesan conference center. More than one hundred clergy from several dioceses in the region had come together for a week to learn more about "expository preaching." It was run by the Langham Foundation of Nigeria, an offshoot of the influential evangelical organization founded by John Stott. The conference facilitators deplored the prosperity gospel. "We are turning the Bible into entertainment and that is why we have so many Christians who are not deep in the faith," one told a plenary session. "The root of the prosperity gospel is to say that the Bible is all about me, me, me. We want to say the Bible is about God, God, God. It's not that we are against prosperity. But we don't think the reason Jesus Christ came to earth was to bring prosperity. He came to save mankind from sin." The speaker insisted that as preachers prepared sermons, they first had to determine what the text meant in its original context before they applied it to the contemporary world. "It's them then, before us now," he said, a line that became his refrain. He encouraged them to ask questions as they read the Bible. "Where does this passage fit into the wider story of God's dealing with his people? Does the text support or undermine a particular social order? If it undermines, how can it undermine a social order in our own time?" It was good stuff, and I was grateful to see that not all Christians in Nigeria were embracing prosperity thinking. But I also knew this was a drop in the ocean. Preachers needed time and resources for this kind of scholarship. There were lots of books in Nigeria, it was true, but not many of them would be useful in helping priests answer these kinds of questions.

As the conference continued, I was tempted to ask how these principles might apply to passages like Leviticus 18:22 or Romans 1:27 that are the foundation of a biblical argument to condemn homosexuality. But the priests here came from many dioceses and I had little relationship with them. It did not seem right to hijack a conference at which I was a guest (and for which I had had the registration fee waived) to discuss what was most interesting to me. I kept quiet during the plenary sessions and chatted with conference participants during breaks. Amara, one of the young students providing behind-the-scenes support for the conference, was about to graduate from one of the universities in Owerri. He was a leader in the local chapter of the Nigeria Fellowship of Evangelical Students, an evangelical campus organization. We bonded over my past membership in InterVarsity, which belongs to the same international umbrella organization as NIFES. Amara told me about the social problems in Nigeria and the need for people in his generation to do a better job than the current generation. "We Nigerians are religious," he said, "but our faith isn't showing in how we run the country. Our fathers have failed us. We cannot fail ourselves or our children." He was animated about the subject and guardedly hopeful about the country's future. We talked a little about what the gospel is and how it could apply to the societies in which we lived. Amara said more people needed to practice biblical leadership, and actually do what the Bible said, rather than say they believe it and then ignore it. I mentioned how I thought biblical teachings about interdependence and the strength that comes from diversity were important for American culture to relearn.

This brought the conversation around to our different churches. I asked him what he knew about the American church. He paused, collecting his thoughts. "We know there are some in the church who obey Scripture and some who do not," he said. "As a result, we've sent bishops to be with those who obey Scripture and have not turned it upside down to suit them." Before I could respond, he continued: "I can disagree with you, but that doesn't mean I should cut myself off from you. That wouldn't help the matter. Even the early church had lots of disagreements, but they still came together to propagate the gospel."

I told him I agreed with him on that point. But Amara was one of the few people of my generation with whom I had had an extended conversation in Nigeria so I tried a different tack. "Do you think women can be priests?" I asked. Though I had seen women in many leadership roles in various church services and diocesan ministries, the Church of Nigeria does not yet ordain women.

He looked away, abashed. "I think women can preach and lead worship . . . ," he tailed off, unwilling to state clearly that he opposed women's ordination. "I am coming from my own context," he said apologetically, trying to explain his opposition.

"Me too," I said. "We can't help it. It's all we know."

He seemed encouraged by that. "I think it's wrong for a woman to be a priest. The men wouldn't listen to her."

"I disagree," I said. "I think women can be priests."

Amara sat there in silence. He smiled uncomfortably at me, as if he wanted to agree.

I continued: "But can we disagree on this question and still be in unity?"

"Yes!" said Amara forcefully, as if there was no doubt in his mind. "We have different contexts," as if that could explain our differences and clear up the lingering discomfort he was clearly feeling.

"So why can't we say the same thing about homosexuality?" I asked.

He paused, thoughtfully. "I'm not sure," he said. "But it's just the way it is."

As I prepared to leave eastern Nigeria, this was the thought that gnawed at me. Despite the openness I had found in people like Paul, the archdeacon in Owerri, who genuinely wanted to learn more about my church, for many Nigerian Christians opposition to homosexuality has taken on totemic significance. One has no choice but to be opposed to it if one wants to be seen as a faithful Christian. In this context, reaching a point where Nigerians and I could agree our views on homosexuality were not a relationship-defining issue seemed almost impossible.

Then again, perhaps there was hope. Later that same day during a break in the preaching conference, I sat next to Eugene, an older priest not far from retirement. He had fought for the Biafran rebel army and then had a career as a secondary school teacher. Eight years earlier, shortly before his retirement, he was ordained. His ecclesial ambitions were no greater than faithfully pastoring his congregation. We sat together and amiably reflected on the divisions in the Communion. As our conversation came to an end, he said, "These problems have hurt our association in the last few years. But flexing our muscles left and right does not solve any of our problems. I don't think we need to be in a hurry. With the passage of time, we can come to a greater understanding of each other." He looked at me, concluding his remarks: "You need to learn more about Nigeria and we need to learn more about you. After all," he said, "we are all Anglicans."

That was the most hopeful message I could take away from eastern Nigeria. Anglicans actually do need to learn more about one another, about the theology each is producing, about the context each ministers in. Such efforts to do so have, to date, been minimal, frustrated by numerous obstacles. But at the local level in Nigeria, I was finding numerous conversation partners. It was in this mutual learning, I thought, that Anglicans could begin to find a way beyond the impasse.

CHAPTER 11

Off the Beaten Path

Diocese of Yola, Church of Nigeria (Anglican Communion)

St. Luke's, Waciri, is not an easy parish to get to.

The journey starts on the paved road leading out of Yola, the capital of Adamawa State in northeastern Nigeria and see city of the eponymous diocese. Trucks trundle down it, headed for the border with Cameroon. It is a well-maintained road. The driver of the little red car that is taking Yohana, a priest in the diocese, and me to Waciri does not have to swerve much to avoid potholes. After fifteen minutes, we leave the tarmac and turn on to a dirt road. The main obstacle here is the herds of cows and goats that wander freely in search of pasture, with little concern for either the road or our car. These herds are the livelihood of the Hausa people, the dominant people group in northern Nigeria. We see several small groups of Hausa walking amid the herds, boys flicking switches to keep the animals in line, women carrying what seems like an entire kitchen on their head. When they see us coming, the boys clear most of the animals off the road. Despite the obstacles, it is a smooth ride, passing through large villages and rural countryside.

After an hour on this secondary road, we come to a fork. We take the one that is distinctly the less-traveled-by. Pitted, rutted, and eroded, our new route barely qualifies as a road. In fact, it is probably better to call it a glorified motorcycle track since that is the vehicle most commonly sighted here. In forty-five minutes we travel only a handful of miles, across streams, through gullies, and up steep banks before arriving in the village of Mani. Here the road ends. It is obvious why. All around are steep, forested hills.

These are the Koma Hills and they have a measure of fame in Nigeria. In the early 1980s, as the story goes, the governor of the state was flying overhead and noticed people below him, living in what to that point had been thought an uninhabited area. When others went to investigate, they found whole communities of people who practiced subsistence agriculture, hunted with bows and arrows, and wore clothing made of leaves—if they wore anything at all. It is this last fact, no doubt, that garnered the people so much attention and led to a Christian presence in the area. In the quarter century since their "discovery," several churches and Christian organizations, all Nigerian-led, have arrived in the Koma area determined to—as they themselves describe it—"civilize" the Koma people. Some Koma have come down from the hills and live in Mani where there is a church-run school.

Our host that day in Mani is Samson, the priest who oversees the Anglican congregation in Mani along with the congregations in the surrounding villages higher in the hills. Samson speaks Hausa but not English, so in order to talk with him, Yohana, the priest from Yola, translates for me. The three of us walk around the church in Mani, a small building built of bare cinder block with a dirt floor. There are cutaways for the windows, but they lack frames or glass. Staring through the hole in the wall, I can see the green plain stretching back the way we came. It is dotted with mud huts and green fields.

Our trip had originally been planned for two days prior, but there were torrential rains that day and we worried about getting stuck on the road to Mani. Mani lacks cell phone reception so we assumed Samson would understand that the rain forestalled our journey. Sadly, that had not happened. "All the people from all the villages in the hills came down to see the American visitor on Saturday," he tells me. "We were waiting all day for you to show up. They were very eager to welcome you here." I ask if there is a way we can visit one of the villages. There is some discussion between Yohana and Samson. Eventually, they decide Waciri is close enough for a visit.

The three of us hop onto Samson's motorbike and head off through the village toward the hills. If before we were on a glorified motorcycle track, now we are on a mere footpath. There are more washed-out gullies and streams to navigate. Yohana and I frequently have to get off the motorbike and walk because the little machine cannot handle our weight on this terrain. The track ends at the foot of a major hill. "Now," says Samson, "we walk." Yohana and I had left Yola in the predawn semidarkness, but it is now midmorning and the sun is high in the sky. Forty minutes, straight up hill, we walk. Pretty soon, I am rationing every drop of water I brought with me from Yola. At last, we crest a rise and there is the village of Waciri. Perched on top of the hill, there are some crops just beginning to sprout through the ground. Turning around, there is a beautiful view to the valley below, which we had just bounced across by car and motorbike. Above us the hills continue to rise, toward more villages and, soon enough, the border with Cameroon.

It is pretty, but there is no thinking this is an easy life. The village is made up of mud huts with thatch roofs. Each seems particularly precarious, as if one good rain—perhaps like the one two days earlier—could wash it right away. In the field, men and women are bent over their tools, hoeing acres of land by hand. The remit of the government does not stretch this far. There is no school, no clinic. Clean water is hard to find. The children's bellies are large from a lack of protein in their diet. Inadequate diets also mean that a few of the older people have large goiters at their throat. I knew poverty and precariousness from my work in Mthatha, but I had never seen anything this comprehensive, pervasive, or remote.

Standing in the middle of the village is a building larger than any other. It is white, with a tin roof and a few holes cut in the walls for light. Inside, the seating is a series of rounded and hardened mud benches a few inches off the ground. This, Samson tells me, is St. Luke's, the church in the village. Word begins to spread through the village that a visitor has arrived. The few who can take a break from their work began to gather, sitting in the back of the church and resisting my attempts to engage with them. Waciri is remote. There is no familiarity with or knowledge of a person like me from such a radically different background. I ask Samson when the last time a foreign visitor was here. "About six years ago a woman from England tried to come," he says. "But she couldn't make it up the hill." Other than that, he can't remember anyone.

When there is a critical mass of people on the benches, Samson quiets them down and turns to me, expectantly. I begin with my usual opening. "My name is Jesse and I'm from the church in the United States. Does anyone know who Jesse is in the Bible?" It takes a minute for the message to get through. Yohana translates my English into Hausa and Samson translates the Hausa into Koma, the local language. After the translation works its way through, I turn to the congregation and wait for a response. To my surprise, no one knows who Jesse is. In every other group I visited in Nigeria, at least someone knew Jesse was the father of King David. Beginning this way, I had learned, was an easy way for people to remember my name and not struggle with its pronunciation.

Samson turns to me apologetically: "They do not know the Bible well. It hasn't been translated into Koma and none of them can read Hausa. They only know what we can teach them." I ask them instead to tell me about their life together. This sparks some interest. About fifty people come to church on Sunday, they say. As Samson is the only priest for all the surrounding villages, it is usually a young lay pastor who leads the services. The lay pastor teaches from his Bible, translating into Koma as he does, and they play music together. They take out their instruments and show me a drum with a cow-hide covering as well as something resembling a xylophone made out of cow horns and mahogany boards. Pretty soon, there is an impromptu demonstration of their musical talent. I bang away on the xylophone as best as I can.

The music breaks the ice and it turns out they have questions for me. What kind of food do I eat? Cow? Maize? I struggle to explain how food can be processed and turned into little packages. This produces not the slightest glimmer of comprehension. I rummage in my backpack for a granola bar and show them the packaging. Seeing their still confused looks, I open it, break it, and give bits of it to them, feeling ever so slightly like I am distributing consecrated host. They chew on it with puzzled looks, as if not quite believing it is food.

Our backgrounds are so different and we have so little in common that for once I am truly at a loss for words. Most of the questions I have been asking elsewhere in Nigeria seem wildly inappropriate. Only a few people here are aware that St. Luke's is part of something called the Anglican Church. No one has ever heard of the Anglican Communion. They are simply people who gather in this place to praise God in the way they know how and learn about God's word. They are Christian. They are the church.

If we are going to make it back to Yola before dark, we have to leave soon. But before I leave, I want to make sure my small congregation knows who Jesse was. The message takes time to work through the double translation, but I tell them how Jesse had a son named David. David was the youngest son, and his father almost forgot about him. But God specifically selected David and made him king. This, I tell them, is part of God's pattern of taking people whom the rest of the world has forgotten and making them important in God's eyes. In fact, if David were alive today, he might be in a place like Waciri tending his sheep.

St. Luke's, Waciri, is not the largest church in the diocese. It does not have the nicest building. Its people are not the richest or most educated members of the diocese. But God built a whole church out of apostles who were not exactly leading lights in society. And it is exactly far-flung places like this, I tell them, where God is present and at work. Out of such as these is the kingdom of heaven made.

⟡

The visit to Waciri came at the end of two weeks as the guest of Marcus Ibrahim, bishop of Yola. Marcus and I met when he spent time at a seminary in Connecticut some months earlier and I immediately liked him. He was in his mid-forties, short, rotund, and full of enough energy to power a small ship. At a diocesan committee meeting, a lay leader told me people liked their bishop. "He keeps bouncing," he said. "And we hope he keeps bouncing, bouncing, and bouncing in the Lord."

I was particularly eager to visit Yola because it is in Nigeria's north. Southern Nigeria, as I learned in Owerri and Umuahia, is overwhelmingly Christian and, thanks to oil money and other resources, somewhat prosperous and well-populated. The north, I knew, has a Muslim majority, and is poorer, less populated, and farther from the country's levers of power. In fact, it is discontent caused by this inequity that has contributed to the rise of Boko Haram, the group that had blown up the police station in Abuja. Compared to the lush and rolling green of the southeast, Yola seemed brown and dusty. Northern Nigeria is on the edges of the Sahel, the dry region that runs in a band across Africa just south of the Sahara.

In Owerri, Cyril and Eunice were generous in their hospitality but never smothering. Things were different in Yola. When we sat down to dinner the first night, Marcus immediately hopped up and turned the TV to CNN. "I know you Americans like CNN," he said. I demurred and told him he could turn it off. "Oh no," he said. "You're just saying that. I know you like it." Actually, I thought, I would rather talk with you than watch Piers Morgan interview Barry Manilow. But I kept the thought to myself and tried to tune the television out. Marcus's wife, Leah, was also hopping up and down, making sure there was plenty of food on the table and that I liked the kind of juice she had put out. If I did not, she made clear there were plenty of others to choose from. I sensed something was not quite right. Marcus and Leah were being too welcoming, too hospitable, too interested in making sure every last detail was exactly right. I was being suffocated by the hospitality. I praised their welcome, hoping they would tone it down just a bit. "Jesse," said Marcus, "you are the first visitor from another country to this diocese in sixteen years and the first since I have been bishop. We want to make sure everything is exactly right!"

There was nothing to do but learn to receive the hospitality Marcus, Leah, and others showed me, even if that meant watching CNN and shoveling forkful after forkful of food into my mouth. This latter task was not hard. I am easily pleased when it comes to food and I kept complimenting Leah on her cooking: "It's perfect!" I'd say. Or, "This is terrific!" Given their relatively young age, I related to Marcus and Leah in a way I had not with Cyril and Eunice, who were of my parents' generation. Before long, mealtimes became quite a lot of fun. Marcus began to tease me. "You are always saying, 'Perfect!' 'Terrific!'" Pretty soon, he answered for me every time Leah asked how the food was. "Perfect!" "Terrific!" I laughed with them but asked why they noticed those words in particular. Marcus stopped giggling and was serious. "Jesse," he said. "Many people from your country come to Nigeria and do not like what they see. We're glad you like what we can give you."

On my first Sunday in Yola, Marcus was scheduled to preside at the weekly service at the chapel on the grounds of the state government buildings. In Adamawa State, the governor is Muslim and the deputy governor Christian. As we pulled into the chapel parking lot, I noticed a minaret and crescent moon on top of a building some ways behind the chapel. The distance was telling; throughout my time in Yola I had little interaction with Muslims and learned little about the church's relation with Islam. It is a delicate interfaith balance in northern Nigeria—and across the country. The chapel was overseen by a short, tough, and large Pentecostal pastor. Marcus introduced me before being taken away to vest. Leah and I took seats amid the cabinet ministers and other—Christian—leaders of the state. It had been clear on the drive over that Marcus was nervous. He was only invited to the chapel once or twice a year. It was an opportunity to address the key players in state government, who, in turn, favored him with their patronage from time to time. It certainly did not damage his image to be on good terms with the deputy governor.

It happened that two days earlier, the state of New York had approved same-sex marriage, something I learned from CNN. If I had missed it, I would have learned of it in the bulletin for the morning's service. There was a message from the chaplain lamenting New York's decision, adding that the "perversion of the world has distorted God's concept of marriage." The notice concluded with a warning: "This is a sign of the last days and as Christians we need to be cautious of these times." New York's decision may have contributed to Marcus's nervousness. At the very least, it was on his mind. He began his sermon by acknowledging that some Anglicans in the United States supported same-sex marriage but assured the congregation it would not be allowed in Yola. He dwelt on the topic at length, becoming increasingly animated. He concluded the lengthy opening section of his sermon by stating emphatically, "I am a true Nigerian!" Opposition to homosexuality, it seemed, was part and parcel of Nigerian identity.

During the announcements at the end of the service, Marcus introduced me and said I was an American who was "brave enough" to come to Nigeria when other bishops and priests from the United States would not. The chaplain asked me to stand in my pew and, from the chancel, prayed for me: "We send you as a missionary to your country to quench this fountain of sin that has welled up in your society, this menace that threatens your country. We pray for righteousness to spring up in your land and for true followers to gather around you." I wanted to stop him, to let him know that while there was sin and menace in my country, we probably differed as to what we thought it was. But there was no chance for me to speak. Anyway, contradicting the chaplain in front of half the state cabinet did not seem a wise idea.

Standing outside the chapel after the service let out, I exchanged greetings with congregants and thanked them for their welcome. As

I waited for Marcus, I was reminded of something Americans can easily forget: the rest of the world is watching us—all the time. This fact does not change the rightness or wrongness of any actions. But it might mean sparing a thought and a prayer from time to time for how our actions affect our sisters and brothers around the world, who spend lengthy sermon minutes on the actions of their fellow believers. At the same time, the chaplain's assumption that only Americans who subscribed to a particular set of beliefs would bother to visit Nigeria disturbed me. At what point had one's beliefs on the single issue of homosexuality become the shorthand test for fidelity to biblical orthodoxy? It was a question that continued to trouble me.

⁂

If Owerri was the large, well-established, blue-chip corporation of dioceses, Yola was the scrappy start-up. There were lots of opportunities for growth and plenty of different projects and programs to be started in response to needs in the community. Marcus took me out to see a plot of land where the diocese hoped to start an agricultural project as a way to raise funds for building churches in new neighborhoods in Yola. The diocese was also making slow progress on a new office block that would have space to rent out to businesses. The overriding goal was to raise revenue to pay clergy better, train them, and start more programs.

A major focus of the diocese's work was education. The weakness of the government in Nigeria means it has essentially abdicated any role in schools. When he became bishop, Marcus started the Anglican Junior Seminary Yola, a secondary school. When I visited, there were about sixty students at AJSY, and they met in an old house that had been donated by a family in the diocese. The language of instruction is English, unlike many of the Islamic-run schools in the area, and the school admits boys and girls equally, making AJSY one of the few institutions in the state that educates girls in English. I was asked to speak to an assembly, and was impressed by how articulate and interesting the students were. They had very good and challenging questions for me and were promising young Nigerians. It was clear, however, that the house was too small. The assembly met while crammed into what I imagined was the main living space, with students standing against walls or sitting on the ground with their knees scrunched up against their chests to make space for the people around them.

Marcus took me out to see the spacious piece of land the diocese purchased on the edge of Yola to build a new school. Progress was coming, but it was slow. In the two years prior to my visit, the diocese raised the funds necessary for three classroom blocks, which have enough space for double the number of students currently enrolled. But delays in building the dormitory meant the school was not yet able to open. The builders had completed the dorm's foundation, but then the money ran out. Marcus and I walked across the foundation, and he pointed to where the individual rooms and communal spaces would be. He was bubbling over with excitement about the possibilities of the school, sketching in the dirt ideas for expansion once this initial site was up and running.

All the money for the construction had come from Nigerians, some from donors who lived outside the diocese, but much from members of the diocese. At a diocesan council meeting I attended, the conversation centered on raising funds for the four hundred bags of cement necessary to finish the dorm. Each bag cost about fifteen dollars. Council members brainstormed ways to raise the money: Ask each deanery to contribute a set amount? Approach the richer members of congregations? Eventually, they settled on assigning each congregation a specific number of bags of cement to provide based on the congregation's size and average offering in the past year. It was not clear, however, that congregations had the wherewithal to provide what was being asked.

"Have you looked for any international support?" I asked Marcus when we were at the school site. Off the top of my head, I could think of several organizations that were interested in funding projects exactly like this one.

"We have," Marcus said, in a tone that combined disappointment, frustration, and regret. "But no one will help us. They think because of the problems in the Anglican Communion that they can't work with us in Nigeria."

I was not surprised. The narrative of disunity and fracture in the Anglican Communion is strong. "Well, there are things we are supposed to disagree about . . . ," I said, tailing off. We looked at each other and laughed. If Nigeria was supposed to be closed territory to American Episcopalians, the friendship that Marcus and I were fast developing was proof that that belief was wrong.

"Look," Marcus said. "I want to build this school. Children need to be educated. Girls need to be educated. That's not happening in Yola. Anglicans can work together on this." We let the words hang in the air. We both knew that. But how could other people come to know?

"What about GAFCON?" I asked. "Didn't you all go to Jerusalem in 2008 for a reason? Won't those conservative Anglicans support you?"

Marcus shook his head. "They come to Nigeria, but they never leave Abuja and Lagos. They only want to talk to the archbishop and the big dioceses. You're the only one who has ever come to Yola."

The sun was setting. We stood on the foundation and looked back at the future AJSY together. The empty classroom blocks and the dormitory foundation, as well as the students crammed into classrooms in an old house, represented the real-life lost opportunities that result from the narrative of disunity in the Anglican Communion, a narrative that has been propagated by some of its most senior members. Marcus and I were testament to the utter wrongness of that narrative. But our story would never seize headlines or lead to special meetings of Anglican leaders. As we headed back to the car, my steps were heavy with deep, profound sorrow.

Education was not the only thing Marcus had been working on since becoming bishop. He was particularly proud of his cathedral. In his time as bishop, the congregation had raised money to add fans, reroof the building, and acquire a bigger generator to power the praise band's instruments when the power cut out. Now, they were raising money to add air conditioning. "Is something wrong with the fans?" I asked. I thought about AJSY and the other projects Marcus had in mind. How had air conditioning for the cathedral become a top priority?

We were just turning on to the street that led to his house. At the corner was a large building under construction. When finished, it was clear it would have two stories and a large seating area inside. Marcus pointed to it as he turned the corner and said it was going to be a Pentecostal church. "These Pentecostals have everything," he said. "When this one is complete, I'm sure he'll have air conditioning. If we don't, our members will start going there instead."

The competition with Pentecostal churches was as constant a threat in Yola as it was in Owerri. A few days later, I accompanied Marcus to Mubi, several hours north of Yola and the other major city in the diocese. A growing congregation there sought Marcus's advice as to whether their next construction project should be to enlarge their church building or construct a new vicarage. Marcus let them talk the issue out among themselves, but it was clear he was firmly on the side of enlarging the church. "When you build a modern church with air conditioning, even the Pentecostal pastors will be coming here," he said. Referring to a new Pentecostal church down the street, he noted, "If you give that pastor two or three or five years, he will be opening branches all over. Build a bigger church on this land. Then even the Pentecostals will respect us." Despite what I was learning about the importance of size and strength for the Nigerian church, it was still easy to shake my head at this. Didn't they know that bigger was not necessarily better and that there were more important things than an air-conditioned sanctuary? Then one Sunday I was invited to preach—and I realized just how real the threat was.

I had been invited to a church plant in Bachure, a new neighborhood on the outskirts of Yola. Joseph, an ordinand in the diocese, and his wife, who spent most of her time managing the diocesan finances, oversaw the plant, their second such project. A previous church plant had grown into a full congregation and was handed over to a priest, at which point Joseph was sent to seminary. Joseph was home on break during my visit and invited me to join them.

As we pulled off the main street and into Bachure on Sunday morning, I realized Anglicans were not the only church around. At the junction of the two roads, there was a veritable forest of signs advertising churches in the neighborhood: "Church of Christ," "Christ Embassy Church," and "Apostolic Church of Nigeria," not to be confused with "Christ Apostolic Church." And there in the forest was ours: "Anglican Church of Bachure." In the short drive from the forest of signs to our church, we passed two other churches. One consisted simply of plastic chairs under a yellow canopy. The other, Christ Gospel Ministry, had an actual building made of cinder blocks. Their service had already begun.

As a church plant, the Anglican Church of Bachure did not have a building—yet. The congregation had first met in a woman's living room. They had grown, however, and now met in a temporary shelter made of metal poles that supported a wood frame and a tin roof. Grass mats served as partial walls. Just a few days earlier, I had joined Marcus at the foundation-laying of the new church building. The congregation had raised enough money to begin construction, though not nearly enough to complete it. As a result, the church that Sunday morning looked more like a construction zone than a church. Since the foundation-laying, workers had built walls in the shape of a church to a level about three bricks above the ground. We crossed over that and entered the temporary shelter, which was still standing in the middle of what would be the nave. There were a few pews inside and a small plastic pulpit.

I started poking around the church, familiarizing myself with where I would sit and where I would preach. As I did, I realized we would not be alone. Christ Gospel Ministry was less than one hundred feet from the pulpit. Since Christ Gospel Ministry had a band, a sound system, and the electricity to power both, every single word of their service was audible in our sanctuary. Joseph and his family carried on with their preparations as if nothing was amiss. Nothing was. This was how Sunday mornings went in Bachure. By nine o'clock, starting time for the service, we had seven people in church: Joseph, his wife, their four children, and me. We began anyway. Joseph's wife led us in song. His older son read a Bible passage. Joseph led us in the weekly Bible study set by the national church office in Abuja. Slowly, people began to trickle in. When it was time for me to preach, the congregation had reached fourteen. I stepped to the pulpit—and realized just how hard it was going to be to say anything.

Every word from Christ Gospel Ministry was still audible. The rest of our little congregation seemed to be able to tune it out so I tried to do the same, though as Christ Gospel Ministry had just then launched into a loud praise number, it was nearly impossible, complicated by the echo of their sound system—pray-pray-pray-se-se-se the-the-the Lor-Lor-Lor-d-d-d. More significantly, I could not stop thinking about the forest of signs we passed on the way in. If people did not like what they heard in this congregation, there was no reason they could not just go to one of those other churches—and take their offering with them. Fundraising for the new church building was lagging, I knew. Joseph had mentioned they had money to buy bricks to bring the wall to shoulder height. After that—finishing the wall, adding a roof—they were praying more donors would step forward. In order for that to happen, however, the congregation had to keep growing. It was a catch-22. If the church had good music and a comfortable, enclosed building, people would come. But in order to get that building, the congregation needed more members. To get to that point, these members needed to stay in the congregation. If they did not like my sermon, well, they might be too polite to walk out in the middle of the service, but they might not come back next Sunday or show up for the midweek service. As I stood at the pulpit, I realized there was a much closer connection between the quality of my preaching and pastoral leadership and the congregation's success than I had ever experienced elsewhere. It was a free market of religion. If you can't perform, you're finished.

The appeal of the prosperity gospel suddenly became clear. If I stood there and told people that if they put money in the offering plate God would bless them, not only would I have the money to build the church, I would begin to look like a success to others around me. My mind went back to my visit to Mubi with Marcus. On our way home, we stopped in at another congregation, one with a new pastor. He was eager to show Marcus the work he was doing on the building—new paint on the walls, expanded seating in the balcony. Marcus was full of approval. The new priest was paying his assessments to the diocese and still had money left over to improve the condition of the church. That, in turn, was attracting more people and more money. In this context, the sermon I had prepared seemed completely out of keeping with what the congregation was expecting—and maybe even looking for. I struggled through it regardless. It was a disjointed effort, but people listened respectfully. I hoped I had not dealt a death knell to Joseph's hopes for the church. He and his wife were experienced at this sort of thing. Surely they could cover for whatever mistakes I was making.

From one perspective, the competition between Pentecostals and mission denominations in Nigeria is fascinating. That so many different denominations would want to start churches in a place like Bachure testifies to the growing importance of Christianity across the country. Being on the front lines of that competition—hearing another service while trying to conduct my own—brought to life just how significant it is. But from the perspective of the unity of the body of Christ, the competition is devastating. Does one neighborhood need so many churches? And why do the Anglicans have to be present when another church is already well established? These questions, though, did not seem to be on the radar screen of people like Marcus or Joseph. What matters is a growing Anglican church. Bigger is better. Prestige is its own end.

The prosperity gospel was on full display the Sunday I attended the main service at the cathedral. The curate was preaching on Luke 6:38—or rather, a portion of it: "Give, and it will be given to you." There was no mention of any of the surrounding verses about judgment and forgiveness. Preaching on a portion of a single verse allowed him to rail on about the importance of tithing and how it would lead to prosperity in return. "He has promised you as an individual that you will overflow!" he thundered. "Amens" abounded in the congregation. I was disappointed by the sermon, but it was what I had come to expect. Still, when I went to a baptism a bit later on, I was surprised to find that the children were named Prosper, Destiny, and Victory. Prosperity thinking affects all facets of life.

Following the service in the cathedral, I sought shade under a tree in the churchyard. A young woman in her early twenties came striding directly over to me with a determined look on her face. She introduced herself and said she had a few questions for me. I was delighted to be speaking so directly to a woman: "Go for it," I said.

"What did you think of the service today?" she began.

Looking to emphasize the positive, I told her I thought the praise band was good. I particularly liked the part of the service where a young family with their new baby was welcomed back to church, two weeks after the birth.

"Did you notice any differences in our service compared to yours?" she asked.

"Sure," I said. "It's longer than what I'm used to, the music was different, and there were some differences in the liturgy. We do communion every Sunday, for instance."

"Is that all?" she asked, somewhat disbelieving.

"Well," I said, not sure how much criticism I was ready to get into on this hot day in the churchyard. "The preaching is different too."

"Now we are getting to what I want to talk about," she said. "What do you preach about in America?"

"Here," I said, "the sermons seem to be about what God can do for you. On a good day in the United States, it is about our response to God's love for us."

"Exactly!" she said. "In Nigeria, everyone is preaching prosperity. The result is that lots of people go to church, but no one changes their life. No one is preaching the way of the cross." Before I could ask her more, she abruptly shifted gears. "I hear in America a man can marry a man. Is that true?"

"In some parts of the country, that is true."

"In Deuteronomy, it says it is an abomination for a man to lie with a man."

"Actually, no," I said. "That's Leviticus: chapter 18, verse 22."

"Yes, thank you," she said, flustered for a minute. Then she paused. "You read the Bible." The tone was one of surprise and a bit of wonder that someone from an allegedly apostate church would know the Bible.

"Yes," I said, "every word."

"So do you believe homosexuality is OK?" she said, curious now.

I started to give her the outlines of an answer, explaining how many Christians in the United States believe the witness of the Bible on this question is complex. She was listening intently. Just as she started to ask me to clarify a point, her father called to her and told her it was time to go. She looked torn but turned to leave. "We *have* to continue this conversation," she said emphatically as we parted.

Sadly, we never were able to continue the conversation. But as I prepared to leave Nigeria, her comments struck me as the most important thing I had heard. Yes, the conversation *had* to continue, not just between me and her but between Americans and Nigerians more generally, and Anglicans around the world. I was finding plenty of people interested in genuine and meaningful relationship, but I knew I was only scratching the surface. The conversation *has* to continue.

CHAPTER 12

Out of "Our" Control

Protestant Christianity in China

The young Christian woman who served as my tour guide around Nanjing was named Maple. With a name like that, not to mention the T-shirt with a big red maple leaf she wore—the gift of some Canadian friends—it was hard for me not to like her. She had recently graduated from college, was articulate in English, and had an endless enthusiasm to show off her city to the small group of Yale students with whom I was visiting China. She was also eager to tell me about her faith. She had been raised in a household that practiced a Chinese variant of Buddhism and come to Nanjing some years earlier for college. It was then she first heard about Christianity. People talked about it at school. It was an idea in the air among her friends. A few were already Christian. They invited her to Bible studies and church services. She went along, looking to learn more.

The pastor of the church her friends took her to was an American man, Pastor Tim. Tim and his wife were from Tennessee. Several years earlier, they had felt called to mission work in China. Although neither was ordained in any denomination, they sold their belongings and moved to Nanjing. I never met Pastor Tim, but as Maple told me about him and described her faith, it was easy to form a picture of him as an evangelical—perhaps one of the many Southern Baptists active in China—who interpreted the Bible in a way that placed almost exclusive emphasis on personal conversion and individual salvation; in other words, not Anglican.

After Maple had been attending church for some time, Pastor Tim asked her if she would like to be baptized. "What does that mean?" she asked.

Pastor Tim explained that baptism would mark her conversion to Christianity. She would die with Christ to her sin and be raised again to new life. It was frightening to hear this, Maple told me. Did he mean die for real? And what about new life? Would it hurt? Maple agonized about the decision for several months as she sought to understand just what baptism meant. As I listened to her, I thought of the early church and the ways its rites were a source of tension with non-Christians in the Roman Empire precisely because they were not understood. In China, a similarly non-Christian environment, Maple's ignorance about baptism is simply part of what the church encounters as it grows.

Eventually, after reading the Bible, talking with friends who had been baptized, and praying, Maple's fears were allayed and she was baptized. "When I went under the water," she told me, "it was the most incredible feeling. I came out feeling like an entirely new person." She now celebrates May 17, the day of her baptism, as her birthday. "It is," she said, "the day I was born again and raised to new life." Her new life of baptism now centers on the church. Between worship services, Bible studies, and fellowship groups, she is at church at least five days a week, and is always thinking about ways to invite new friends to church with her. She eats, sleeps, and breathes her Christian community. I asked about her family: Are they Christian? "Not yet," she replied, though the determined look on her face told me they were in her sights.

⟨⟩

It is difficult to know the number of Christians in China, but it is clear that as China's economy has taken flight in recent decades, the church has begun to grow dramatically. More and more people are pouring into churches, whether those sanctioned by the government or those that are not. This I knew personally, even prior to my visit. A classmate and friend at Yale, Tian, was a former professor at one of Beijing's universities. Tian was born in northeastern China in the 1960s, grew up in the teeth of Mao's disastrous Cultural Revolution, and came of age during—and participated in—the demonstrations in Tiananman Square in 1989. Like many others involved in Tiananmen, including some of its senior leaders, she became attracted to Christianity as it became clear that the hopes of the movement were not to be realized. In Tian's case, she was introduced to Christianity and was baptized when she studied in Hong Kong in the mid-1990s. It was the Anglican Church there that had nurtured her faith. Buoyed by that experience, she returned to Beijing eager to tell others about her new faith. But she attracted the attention of the authorities as it became clear that students who were visiting her regularly were becoming Christian.

For Tian, it is no accident that China's rapid economic progress and the church's growth have gone hand-in-hand. "We have no values," she told me. "Too many of my students are committing suicide." Although there were new opportunities for material progress in China, many Chinese she knew were lost in crippling feelings of isolation and alienation. In our last conversation before I left for China, Tian told me, "There is such great spiritual need." As my group from Yale visited local churches around the country, the truth of Tian's comments was obvious in over-flowing services in rural communities, seminary students eager to return home to preach what they were learning, and the enthusiasm of Maple and others like her. From the perspective of the Anglican Communion, however, the Chinese church poses a unique challenge.

Several generations of Anglican missionaries worked in China in the nineteenth and early twentieth centuries. When the Communists triumphed in China's civil war, they authorized five religions— Buddhism, Islam, Taoism, Catholicism, and Protestant Christianity. The effect of the policy was that all the Protestant mission denominations active in China were amalgamated into a single organization, overseen by the Three-Self Patriotic Movement and the China Christian Council, the dual official Protestant bodies. (Three-Self refers to the vision articulated by Anglican mission executive Henry Venn that the goal of mission should be to create churches that are self-governing, self-supporting, and self-propagating.) Catholics, meanwhile, came under the direction of the Chinese Catholic Patriotic Association. Denominationalism, the Communists taught, was a relic of a bygone imperial era. In the halcyon days of Communist rule, there was no need for denominations. Nor was there any need for missionaries. Those that remained in the country during the war were expelled.

Despite this official sanction, Christians were heavily persecuted at times, and the church suffered, particularly during the Cultural Revolution. Not until the opening of China that began in the 1980s did Christianity truly begin to take root. As it did, four kinds of churches began to flourish: the official and sanctioned Protestant and Catholic churches on the one hand and parallel, unsanctioned churches, on the other. These latter are often called "house churches," though many have long since outgrown houses and worship in larger locations. The extent to which these house churches are tolerated depends on the mood of the government and the profile the house churches keep. Our visit to China coincided with a period of intense repression of the unofficial churches, and my hopes of visiting Tian's friends in her old congregation were dashed when it became clear that to do so would draw unwanted attention to them.

In the midst of all this change, Anglicanism sort of fell through the cracks. Anglicanism needs bishops—"the historic episcopate locally adapted" of the Chicago-Lambeth Quadrilateral—but the Protestant churches in China do not have bishops. What bishops there are in China are Catholic and their appointment is a matter of continued controversy between Beijing and Rome. Ding Guangxun—known to Westerners as K. H. Ting—was ordained an Anglican bishop in the 1940s before the reorganization of the country's religious landscape. He kept his orders but tied himself to the official Protestant bodies and played a significant role in the redevelopment of the church and its theology in the 1980s. Until his death in 2012, he remained an elder statesman of the official church. What stature he had in the church—and it was significant to the end—was due to his personal authority and gravitas, not his orders, Anglican or otherwise.

For the last many decades, Anglican mission has largely depended on the presence of both a sending and a receiving bishop. Diocese-to-diocese connections are at the heart of inter-Anglican relations. If an Anglican wanted to work in China, it was not clear who would receive him. In the past, Anglicans ordained missionary bishops to build up the church in places of the world where it did not yet exist. It is how the American West was evangelized, for instance, and there had been missionary bishops for China. But it does not take much to imagine the outrage from the Chinese government at the consecration of a missionary bishop for China: "We have a church, thank you very much, and we have bishops. We have no need for yours!"

The result is tragic: in one of the world's fastest growing churches, Anglicanism is barely represented.

A week before meeting Maple, the group of students I was traveling with found ourselves outside a shapeless white building in the middle of Beijing's university district. The building looked little different than any of the other squat towers on the street, all thrown up in recent decades in China's mad rush to growth. The distinguishing feature of the building was the four large Chinese characters along the top. Directly below them, in smaller letters, was the English translation: "Christian Church." But the real indication that this building was a church was that on this Sunday morning in May, a line of people began at the two sets of double doors, spilled down the steps, and stretched around the corner. As we joined the queue, I was reminded of waiting to be admitted to a concert hall or a movie theater before an important performance.

Just before ten o'clock, one set of doors opened and the congregation of the previous service began to spill out. A few minutes later, the ushers opened our set of doors and the line began to move forward. Inside, the sanctuary reminded me of an evangelical megachurch of suburban America: rows of seating facing a stagelike chancel with a podium and a screen to project what is happening on the stage to people in the back. The auditorium—nave—of this church could seat at least a thousand. In a few minutes it was close to full. Before long, people were standing in the aisles.

This service—one of six to take place in the church on this day— was in Mandarin, and it began when a robed choir processed down the aisle and took their seats behind the podium. Two clergy followed, both vested, one a woman and one a man. Different people approached the podium to read from the Bible and at one point we joined in saying a psalm. Interspersed with the readings were hymns, the tunes of two of which I recognized as old standards of any Anglican hymnal. At the appropriate time, the female clergy member took to the podium and delivered a half-hour-long sermon. Following the sermon, a children's choir came forward for a special performance. Parents crowded around taking pictures while the choir director tried to get her young charges to sing and sway to the music. They did, just not in the same direction or on the same beat. Overall, the service leaves me with an Anglican "feeling": Anglicanism may be formally absent in China but this liturgy is not unfamiliar.

The service ends just more than an hour after it began and the earlier scene repeats itself. One congregation files out and is replaced by another, though our group remains in place. The new service is in English and its congregation looks different than the earlier one. Whereas in the first, our group stood out as the only obviously non-Chinese people, at least a tenth of the new congregation is American or European expatriates. More significantly, the new congregation is younger. Given the number of universities in the area, it is unsurprising that the young woman who sits next to me tells me in halting English that she is in the second year of her studies. She started coming to church when her friends invited her. They come to the English service, she says, partly because the music is better, but mostly so they can practice their English.

The worship in the new service is different as well. Rather than a robed choir, a praise band comes on stage. There are two or three guitar players, a drummer, and about six singers, all led by a young American on guitar. Rather than hymns, the service begins with praise choruses, the lyrics of which are projected on the screen behind the stage. Some are familiar to me from InterVarsity. After twenty minutes of music, we sit down for one or two readings from the Bible, followed by the sermon. The preacher this time is a man, Pastor Wu, and he is not vested. Rather, he is wearing a natty suit and tie and is at home behind the podium. His sermon notes are on an iPad, but he does not need to reference them often. The congregation listens with rapt attention as Wu holds forth in flawless English on mothers in general and the Canaanite mother in Matthew 15 in particular. (It is then I remember that it is Mother's Day.) In her challenge to Jesus—"Yes, Lord, yet even the dogs eat the crumbs that fall from their masters' table"—the Canaanite woman broke down barriers between herself and Jesus. "Do you have any barriers between you and Jesus?" Wu asks. "Today, let us learn from this mother and go to the Lord. We must be as persistent as she was and as humble as she was in her relationship with the Lord." This liturgy has Anglican echoes as well, but it is the Anglicanism of Holy Trinity in Cambridge. It is a service designed for easy consumption by new Christians. They do not need to know much—when to sit or stand or kneel—except what is projected on the screen in front.

Following the sermon, a table is brought out and set with items for the Eucharist. The congregation remains standing while Wu prays over the elements using a modified form of St. Paul's teaching on the

Eucharist in 1 Corinthians 11. As he concludes the prayer, Wu looks up and makes a request that nearly knocks me over: "If you are not baptized, please sit down." It is a direction that is theologically sound and, I believe, pastorally sensitive. Still, I can think of no situation in which any American Episcopal priest I know would say those words. In places like St. John's in Northampton, the watchwords are inclusivity and welcome. Those words are increasingly interpreted to mean that the Eucharist should be given to all who attend a service, regardless of baptism. Even as the shock of what Wu has said sinks in, at least a third of the congregation—many of whom are sitting toward the front—promptly sits down without complaint. The ushers bring us the elements and I reach over the young college student sitting next to me to receive a small cup of wine that tastes more like cough syrup. She watches patiently, but does not receive herself.

All that is left after communion is a few final praise choruses. The young American leading the music takes it upon himself to offer a few words of reflection. He waxes on about the importance of giving oneself to Jesus, emphasizes the importance of a one-time conversion to Christ, wonders aloud what it would be like to be Jewish, and on several occasions gets tangled in his words and loses his train of thought. I recognize this from my days in InterVarsity—it is a praise sermon, the moment the music leader gets to shine. But particularly in contrast to the polished performance of Wu, it is cringe-worthy. His theology is weak and he is embarrassing himself. A few in my group cannot help but begin to snicker.

As we leave the church, past another long line of people waiting to get in to the next service, I wonder who should be laughing at whom. It is easy for a bunch of Yale-educated students—almost all of us from liberal, mainline denominations—to giggle at the weaknesses of evangelicalism, which we rarely encounter. Yet no matter the shortcomings of the young musician's theology, his praise sermons are having more influence—for good or ill—on one of the largest congregations in Beijing than we can ever hope to. Maple's Pastor Tim, too, was an example of this. I did not doubt the young musician and Pastor Tim were well-meaning and devout, but I also did not think their theology was laying the groundwork for a sustained and sustaining life of faith.

When mainline, Euro-Atlantic Christians pay attention to the church around the world, it seems it is often in either hand-wringing fear or contemptuous derision of the world church's alleged conservatism. But in conversations with Christians from a variety of backgrounds in China, I found them as open to conversation, discussion, and changing their minds as anyone else. In this, they were not much different than the Nigerians or Sudanese I had spoken with. The conservatism of the Global South church seems more a reflection of its influences than anything else. The Chinese church is not fated to be conservative. But its primary teachers to date have been.

The key challenge in a growing church is not necessarily baptizing people but helping them grow in their new faith. Catechesis is as important as conversion. This is a need the church in China feels acutely, as I heard repeatedly. Naturally, the bulk of this teaching will come from the Chinese themselves as they continue to develop a Christian theology most appropriate to their context. But this does not mean there is no role for people from mainline denominations in the Euro-Atlantic world. In a culture like China's that is driven by the obsessive need for ever more economic growth, a theology that stresses the sufficient abundance of God, for instance, could be prophetic. Yet the retreat of liberal, Euro-Atlantic Christianity from the church in the Global South—measured in dollars, personnel, and engagement—in recent decades effectively amounts to ceding the playing field to others.

As we walked out of the church that Sunday morning in Beijing, I asked myself: Is a praise sermon a cause for mirth, smugly complacent in our sense of theological superiority? Or is it a goad to deeper involvement and engagement with our sisters and brothers in Christ around the world? By this point in my travels, one thing had become clear: when it comes to the world church, comfortable complacency is what the mainline liberal church seems to do best.

꧁꧂

Far from Nanjing and Beijing is Yunnan Province in China's southwest. Yunnan's capital, Kunming, is more than 1500 miles from Beijing, and there is a mountain range that separates the province from much of the rest of the country. "The mountains are tall and the emperor is far away," it is said in Yunnan, an indication of the region's relative independence in Chinese history. Yunnan borders Laos, Vietnam, and Myanmar, giving it some of the greatest ethnic diversity of any province in China. The distance from Beijing also means there is a relative—by comparison—degree of freedom about religion that is lacking elsewhere.

At the time of my visit, Kunming was the home of some of the few Anglicans at work in China. Doug, Elaine, and their children had been working in Yunnan for over a decade under the auspices of Anglican Frontier Missions, a mission-sending organization that emphasizes "unreached peoples" and proclaims itself unencumbered by the need for a receiving bishop. Doug and Elaine were "tent-making" missionaries: that is, like St. Paul, they provided much of their own financial support for their work in Kunming. Doug's work in the timber industry got the family the visa and some of the financing they needed to stay in Kunming. Then, they looked for ways to support the local church.

In Kunming, that took the form of working with groups of local Christians, leading Bible studies, and otherwise supporting new Christians. I told Maple's story to Doug and expressed my admiration at her dedication to church. Doug knew the story well, particularly the eagerness and enthusiasm that came with conversion. But there was another part of the story, he told me: burnout. New Christians like Maple might be in church five days a week for the first few years after converting. Soon enough, though, the experience begins to wear on them, their attendance becomes more sporadic, and eventually they may stop going to church altogether.

"This is where I've found I can be most helpful," Doug said. "Anglican spirituality is a big help." It is refreshing, he said, to share the Daily Office with someone for the first time, for instance. "Several women came to me and said that the missionaries were always telling them what to think and believe. 'OK,' I said, 'I won't tell you what to believe but let's read the Bible together.' So we read the Gospel of John and Hebrews together because that's what they had first been taught from." Most of all, Doug says, he wants to show the Christians he meets that there is more to their faith than one's "personal relationship with Jesus Christ." For burned-out Christians, he wants them to learn about grace. "I want them to know that nothing they can do can earn the love of God."

Doug's work had also connected him to a Bible college deep in Yunnan's hinterland. To get there, we flew an hour to Mangshi, a small but bustling town whose major attraction was the giant new Buddhist temple at the top of a hill on the edge of town. From

Mangshi, it was a five-hour bus ride over winding mountain roads to the town of Yingjiang, not far from the border with Myanmar. Yingjiang is the economic hub for a deeply rural and agricultural region. Our journey there had taken us past fields of rice paddies, tended by farmers with hoes and a few with plows pulled by cattle. Stepping off the bus, it felt like another world from urban Kunming, let alone Beijing.

We are met by Pastor Mi, who immediately strikes me as overworked, frazzled, and completely dedicated. There are Christians in 220 of the villages around Yingjiang, Mi tells us. He is one of eight ordained pastors that share responsibility for the area. Not only is the scale of the work around Yingjiang immense, its complexity is staggering. The people in the 220 villages represent a wide array of ethnic groups. The Lisu, long one of the marginalized ethnic groups in the region, have been Christian for generations. A British missionary, James Fraser, spent many years in Yunnan in the early twentieth century, and the Lisu responded to his preaching. For Mi, the connection is obvious: "Christianity has a special appeal to people in need or people who are struggling. That is why the Lisu have been Christian for so long." In Lisu villages, the challenge is finding qualified leaders for the churches.

The challenge is different for the Dai, another large ethnic group in the region. Unlike the Lisu, the Dai have long held power and influence. "Those who have money and power, it is difficult for them to convert," Mi said. He cited Jesus' teaching about the rich man and the eye of a needle. "People who have a lot of money are very prideful." I asked if his congregations were made up primarily of upper-class or lower-class people. "Very few rich people here are Christian," he said. "There are two," he said with the air of someone who knows the source of his major stewardship support.

But there is a larger challenge with the Dai. "There is a saying: 'To be Dai is to be Buddhist,'" Mi said. "To become Christian is to relinquish everything it is to be Dai." Nonetheless, some Dai have been converting to Christianity. That, in turn, Mi said, put a burden on the churches that welcomed Dai converts. They had to become the home and community for people who left behind the foundation of their identity. But some Lisu Christians struggle with this welcome, preferring to interact only with other Lisu. "Where there are Christians from many ethnicities, like here," Mi said, "we have to teach that the church is like the creation of a new ethnic group." It is not an easy message for some people to hear.

The main focus of the church's efforts, however, is the Han, China's dominant ethnic group. In the past, almost no Han lived in Yunnan. Now, as China's relentless growth has created more and more opportunities—and the central government has sought to spread its influence as far as possible—Han make up half the population of Yingjiang. "For the Han, they want to earn a lot of money. So when they become Christian, they have to wrestle with having money and what it means to be a servant." The church is very small among the Han, Mi said. But ten years ago it was nonexistent, so this counted as progress. Overall, as a result of significant growth in the last decade, Mi estimated ten percent of the people in the Yingjiang region are Christian.

Mi took us out to the Bible college on the edge of town. Its facilities are basic—cinder-block dorms, utilitarian classrooms—but Mi made sure to emphasize the importance of this school. There is a seminary in Kunming, Mi noted, but it only takes thirty students a year. Anyway, as I now knew, Kunming may be in the same province, but it is a world away. "We need training, training, training," Mi said emphatically. "We need more training centers, more qualified people to teach and instruct believers." They could accommodate two hundred students a year at this school, he said, training them in Bible, preaching, and evangelism in a three-month course before sending them out to be leaders of village churches. "I can evangelize by myself," said Mi, "but I'm only one person. If we have more people working with the Spirit, then we can spread further." That growth seems likely. The area around Yingjiang lies on the path of a proposed oil and gas pipeline connecting Myanmar with China. The plans have unsettled people, who wonder how it will affect their lives and what changes the government will introduce in its quest for development. The unsettledness has created an opening for the church. "When we evangelize," Mi said, "we talk about how Jesus can give you hope and peace in difficult times. Jesus can be a rock."

As we drank tea with Mi, I thought of Eulogio and Luis Alberto in the Andes in Ecuador. The people were coming and the church was growing, but the leadership simply did not have the resources to keep up. But why? Why is the church growing so quickly here? Mi shrugged when I asked him. "This is the time that God is working. We don't know why. It is just happening." He thought a moment. "God is moving. We are trying to stay out of God's way."

⌒◌◌◌◌⌒

The next morning is Sunday and Doug and I ride with Mi in his van out of Yingjiang through a pouring rain. Before long, we have turned off the main, paved road, and begin to climb up a dirt road. The land around us is obviously fertile and there are coffee plants, the cash crop for the area's farmers, on either side of the road. I ask Mi if the village has both an official and unofficial church. It does not. In a place this remote, the government cannot be bothered. They are all Christians together. After half an hour climbing the dirt road, we arrive at a Lisu village, the first that Mi is visiting this morning. "Short drive this morning," Mi says as he parks. On many Sundays, he has to drive longer than half an hour and on worse roads than what we have just encountered. The church itself is a small building with cinder blocks and a thatch roof.

Despite Mi's presence, the barefoot lay pastor—who trained at the Bible college in Yingjiang—leads the service. It is clear from the energy with which he directs the choir that he is trying his hardest to make everything the best it possibly can be. It is not unlike a priest in an Episcopal congregation preparing for a visit from the bishop. The rain, which is dripping through the old thatch, does not dampen the congregation's enthusiasm for worship. They sing loudly and well. Mi preaches on 3 John, the first time I can remember hearing a sermon on that book of the Bible.

Even though Mi has more congregations in other villages to visit, we stay afterward for a meal with the leaders of the congregation. Mi sits with them and advises them on the situations they encounter in their ministry. Doug strikes up a conversation with one of the men, Zhou. The two have a lot in common, it turns out. Zhou is preparing to move to a different part of Yunnan about twelve hours away and become a missionary among the Han people. He is motivated by Jesus' Great Commission to go to "all the nations"—"all the ethnic groups," if the Greek is translated properly—and especially to the Han, who for him constitute an unreached people. Before he can leave, however, Zhou still needs to figure out the logistics. He will need to find work and need a place to live. Still, he imagines he can support himself and his family for about $4,000 a year. I do not know how much it costs for Doug and his family to live in Kunming, but I do know the Episcopal Church spent four or five times that on me when I lived in Mthatha. Zhou's ministry is a bargain.

The more Zhou talks, the more sense his plans make. He already speaks Mandarin. Although he is Lisu, he knows the complex cultural dynamics of Yunnan pretty well—he was raised in them, after all— and his period of adjustment to life in a new part of the province will be less severe than it is for someone coming from farther away, like the United States. He is much better value than any Euro-Atlantic missionary, who, no matter how hard we may try, cannot—and are not allowed to—shake certain expectations about living standards, health insurance, and furloughs. In studying mission, I had learned about south-to-south mission, that is, Christians from the Global South traveling to other parts of the Global South as missionaries. In Yunnan, in addition to Americans like Doug and Elaine and a whole host of Southern Baptists, there were missionaries of various stripes from Malaysia, Singapore, and Taiwan. But with Zhou, it was about as close as you could get: one person, motivated to share the good news of Jesus Christ with others not that far away.

Sitting in the little house in a village perched on a mountainside planted with coffee beans, I looked out at the pouring rain. A thought that had first been planted in my head when I saw Bishop Nelson talking with the missionary bishop's children in Gulu and had grown when I saw the ministry of the church in a place like Owerri, finally crystallized: the gospel is out of "our" control. For too long, white, educated Euro-Atlantic men like Doug and me have convinced ourselves that the growth and spread of Christianity is the result of our hard work, and that we can control the church, the message of the Bible, and maybe even God. Zhou was proof that those views were erroneous, and grievously so. I praised God for him and his family's ministry. It is not that there is no role for Westerners. But dominance and control—in whatever subtle forms they are now manifest—cannot be the goal. The sooner we accept this realization, the sooner we will be able to move forward as a truly global body of Christ.

CHAPTER 13

An Exilic Church

Abyei, Diocese of Aweil, Episcopal Church of the Sudan

I had always known, of course, that people like Atholo Bol exist in the world. Stories of armed conflict and displaced people are a depressing staple of news reports. But I came face-to-face with a refugee from armed conflict when I sat down next to the seventy-year-old grandmother on a makeshift cot she had set up outside a church-run primary school now serving as a refugee camp. We were in Agok, a small market town in the disputed Abyei region between Sudan and South Sudan. Six weeks before my visit, militias allied with the northern government launched surprise attacks across the region. Coming as they did shortly before South Sudan's independence, the attacks were seen as part of an effort by the north to destabilize the south. No matter the motive, Bol, like thousands of others, fled her home, seeking refuge on the far side of the Kiir River, south of which the militias were reluctant to go. The mother of five and grandmother of nine spent three days walking across the countryside before finally arriving in Agok. Since the attacks she had been living in a classroom, subsisting on the limited international food aid that had made it to Agok. "What happened this year completely wiped out what I had," she told me. "There is nothing left to live off."

Bol's story was not unique. As I moved around the different classrooms, I heard variations of her tale. Abraham Ajak was a young man now staying with his family in the school. Agok was overwhelmed. "Many people have lost their life," he told me, "but not by the gun— by disease, by hunger, by drinking water that is not safe. Every family here is grieving." In the week since the attacks, Agok had swelled in size. Tens of thousands of refugees crammed into huts with extended family members or built new ones with plastic sheets donated by aid agencies. Food, shelter, and medication were in short supply.

As I wandered around, it was hard to believe that just a week earlier, ten months after my first trip to Bishop Gwynne College, I had been in Juba for a second visit that coincided with the celebration of South Sudan's formal independence. The independence celebration was boisterous and cathartic. Many people told me, "I never thought I would live to see this day." It was said with such emotion I knew they meant it literally—and were thinking about the friends and family members who had not survived the war. At a thanksgiving service the next day in Juba's All Saints Cathedral, the bishop leading the service told the congregation, "Let us sing our new national anthem." He paused. "Our new national anthem," he said again, with wonder in his voice. "Let us sing our new national anthem!" he proclaimed with joy as the women in the congregation began ululating and the men shouting as if in disbelief that South Sudan should have something as basic as a national anthem. The subsequent rendition—which we all, South Sudanese and foreigners alike, sang from lyrics projected on the cathedral wall—brought me closer to tears than any tug-at-your-heart-strings version of any anthem I had ever heard.

But now in Agok, it was clear how much work remained to be done to make that independence meaningful. Abyei is the place where the Arab north and African south meet; it has long been an uneasy relationship. The adjective I most heard used to describe Abyei is "well-watered." The area's fertility, in an otherwise arid region, makes it a target. The Kiir River—known as the Bahr el-Arab to northern Sudanese—has created the abundant and verdant grasslands that make Abyei an attractive place to water cattle and grow crops. Dinka settled here, but traditionally reached agreements with the pastoralist Misseriya farther north to graze their herds during parts of the year. To hear some Dinka describe it, this worked. "When it was our grandfathers, it was OK between us," Chirillo told me. He was a lay leader in the Episcopal church in Abyei, who fled during the attacks. "But when the politicians in Khartoum realized there was oil in Abyei, then they wanted to make war. It is the politicians who caused this war. They are using the Misseriya to take our land." Indeed, there is evidence to support this. A time-honored tactic of the Khartoum government is to arm militias and send them south against Khartoum's enemies. Such a strategy led to widespread famine and displacement during the civil war, and only continued after the signing of the Comprehensive Peace Agreement in 2005. Similar attacks in 2008 displaced thousands.

The conflict in Abyei pits the mostly Christian Dinka against the Muslim Misseriya, but it is more a conflict over the region's resources than it is about religion. The resources at stake are more than just oil, which is more abundant elsewhere along the border between the two countries than it is in Abyei. (Shortly after the 2011 Abyei attacks, northern forces attacked two other border regions, Blue Nile and South Kordofan. Those conflicts continue unabated at the time of this writing.) In addition to the good grazing land and water, northern-ers are said to have their eye on gum arabic, used in candies and soft drinks in the West. I had heard of "blood diamonds" before visiting Abyei. Now I wondered if we should be talking about "blood M&Ms" as well. The 2005 peace agreement called for a referendum to deter-mine if residents of Abyei wanted to be part of the north or south. But the referendum never happened amid mutual suspicion and disputes over who should be allowed to vote. A hastily reached agreement, con-cluded just before my visit, called for the demilitarization of Abyei and the deployment of Ethiopian peacekeepers under the auspices of the United Nations. But no one in Abyei seemed to trust the UN very much after an existing detachment of peacekeepers stood by during the recent attacks. The Ethiopians began to deploy in Abyei during my visit, but the response of the refugees was telling: few left, or seemed to be making preparations to return.

But there is one organization the refugees do trust—the church. The school where Atholo Bol and others were staying was run by the Episcopal church in Agok. When the attacks happened, the students moved outside under the trees and refugees took over the classrooms. The church compound became a center of activity for people search-ing for information on missing family members and looking for news about relief supplies. Anglicanism is relatively new to Abyei. During the mission period, the region fell in the area the colonial govern-ment reserved for Catholics. But like many other Dinka communities, missionaries struggled to interest the residents in the gospel they preached. It was not until the 1990s, as more and more Dinka turned to Christianity during the civil war, that a handful of enterprising young Dinka Episcopalians, recently converted, returned to Abyei and began to preach the gospel again. This time, people listened, and the results were clear in the compound where I was standing. At the worship services I attended in the mud brick and thatch church, the congregation flowed out the door.

Refugees were looking to the church for more than spiritual nurture. In it, they found their basic humanity recognized. Abraham, the young man displaced during the attacks, told me, "The church sees Abyei not as a land of resources but as a land of people, people who have lives, who have rights to live peacefully like others and not be threatened like animals." Moreover, the refugees were looking to the church in hope for the future. Barnabas, an older refugee who had fled with his family during the attacks, said, "The role of the church is to speak out to the international community to give an accurate report of what is happening here. It is the church that will say what they have seen with their own eyes."

⟨✦⟩

It was precisely the church doing what Barnabas described—speaking out to the international community—that led to my visit to Agok. After the May attacks, the Episcopal Church of the Sudan appealed to international partners for aid and support. The church quickly found donors who were willing to fund relief supplies to be delivered to Abyei. But in South Sudan, finding funding is merely one step in a long process. Currency shortages and international sanctions meant it took five weeks for the money to be transferred to the church's accounts. The independence celebrations—and numerous holidays and bank closures that entailed—were a further delay. Finally, two days after independence, the church had a team ready to go: Bishop Abraham Nhial, whose diocese includes the church in Abyei; John Sebit, the director of ECS's relief and development arm; Peter Deng, who worked for ECS in Juba; and, somewhat out of place, me, from whom nothing was expected other than that I tell others about what I saw.

The four of us flew to Wau, capital of Western Bahr el Ghazal State and a town with a market large enough to support the kind of purchases we needed to make but close enough to Agok that we could get them there. When we got off the plane, I was surprised at who was there to greet us. It was Zechariah, a former classmate of mine at

Bishop Gwynne College. On that visit, I knew him only slightly. He was friendly and welcoming to me like everyone else, but he struggled with English. It was hard to spend too much time with him without becoming frustrated. I knew he was from Abyei and I wanted to learn more from him, but it was easy to gravitate to other students whose English was better.

Zechariah, nonetheless, made an impression. He is tall, even by the standards of the Dinka. His height accentuates his thin arms and legs, giving him a kind of gangly and awkward appearance. This was not helped by the fact that when I attended class with him, he was perpetually disorganized. The impression he made was a comical one. It was immediately apparent in Wau, however, that Zechariah was an entirely different person. He was happy to see me, but he rarely laughed. His English had improved and I was able to hear his story without much difficulty. The attacks in Abyei had come as he was preparing for his end-of-the-year exams at BGC. "It made me sick to hear about it," he said. "I lay in my bed and could not move. I did not know where my family was or what had happened to them." BGC's principal told him he could go home, but the journey would have taken days and Zechariah wanted credit for finishing the year at school. He rallied to finish his exams, helped by a phone call with his family in which he learned that while they were in Agok, all had survived.

As one of the senior priests in Abyei, the provincial staff in Juba had asked Zechariah to help them organize the relief supplies they hoped to be able to deliver. So Zechariah had waited, first in Juba, then in Wau, for the money to work its way through the banks and for the four of us to arrive. In Wau with him were two other priests from Abyei, Nathaniel and Santino. They were ministering to refugees who had fled even further than Agok and were now clustered around towns like Wau. Zechariah, Nathaniel, and Santino had done reconnaissance for us, and their plan was straightforward. Purchase the goods needed in Agok from the traders in the Wau market. Hire a truck. Transport those goods the hundred or so miles to Agok and deliver them. In theory, the plan seemed airtight. In practice, it was not.

The money the church had to spend came from international donor agencies with tight purchasing guidelines. John—wisely—wanted to do nothing that would jeopardize his relations with them. As a result, the first morning in Wau was spent finding three quotations for each of the twenty or so items we wanted to purchase. Peter, whose Arabic was best, bargained with the traders for some astronomical amount of corn meal—twenty tonnes, say—and then, when they had reached a mutually agreeable price, made a note of it, thanked the trader, and moved on to find another. In the context of a South Sudanese market, it seemed more than a little foolish.

Meanwhile, Santino and Zechariah went looking for a truck. The market had many for hire, but it was not as simple as taking the first one that was available. The two of them had to gauge which driver was the most reliable and which truck was both least likely to break down and large enough to carry the amount of material we were planning to purchase. This last criterion proved unexpectedly challenging. Though the trucks were rated for large capacities—up to thirty tonnes, about what we estimated everything would weigh—drivers were reluctant to take a full load. The rainy season was coming and the roads were deteriorating. More weight meant more chance of getting stuck in a muddy, impassable road.

When the group reconvened in the middle of the day, there was a new set of questions: How did the quotations Peter gathered change how much we could buy? Even if we did spend all the money we had, would we be able to fit all the resulting purchases in a single truck? How much did everything weigh? The math quickly became complicated and the simple chart we used to keep the budget became covered in cross-outs and marginal notes before it was scrapped altogether in favor of a new draft. I looked at Zechariah as he poured over the details. "I never learned anything about disaster relief in seminary," I said. "Did you?" He shook his head. "It might actually be something useful," I said. He smiled briefly and turned back to his work.

I left the group to their work in the afternoon and went to find Bishop Abraham. He had stayed behind at the headquarters of the Diocese of Wau, our hosts, and was meeting with people from Abyei who had fled this far. I did not envy him the task. When I arrived, he invited me to sit with him and the family he was talking to. The mother, a young woman probably about my age, was missing her left arm below the elbow. Abraham gave me a brief synopsis of her story. "When the Misseriya attacked, she was so startled that she fell in her cooking fire. Her arm was burned badly. She made it to the hospital in Wau, but they could only amputate it." The woman was trying to cradle a young boy in her lap, but he was limp and lethargic and kept slipping out of her grasp. "Their son is very sick, probably with malaria, but there is no medication for him." The look on the face of the husband told of exhaustion, despair, and deep, intense defeat. Abraham looked at me: "Do you have anything to say to them?"

I paused, lost for words. The previous term at seminary I had taken a course titled "Pastoral Care with Displaced Communities." Surely there was something there that could help me? But the look on the father's face haunted me, preventing me from thinking of anything else. "I, I, I . . . ," I stammered, wishing I had stayed in the market. I paused again. "No," I finally said, wanting to sink into the ground. Abraham came to my rescue by leading us in prayer. When he was finished, we said goodbye to the family, but not before he arranged for the boy to get malaria medication. I took that as my opportunity to retreat to the room we were sharing and think about what future a woman with one arm would have in a subsistence culture. Not much, was the answer.

⌒⫘⫘⌒

The group in the market had more success with their tasks than I did with mine. It took time for traders to come up with several tonnes of beans or a couple hundred mosquito nets, but they did. Peter prevailed on them to accept the rate he had negotiated earlier, though some were reluctant to do so. A truck had been found, but the driver was unwilling to take all we planned to purchase. Abraham leaned on a friend in an international relief organization for the loan of a small truck to carry the rest. Loading twenty tonnes of corn meal is not something that can be done in an instant, particularly in the absence of a forklift or pallets. As a result, Zechariah, Peter, and I spent Friday morning sitting outside a warehouse on the edge of the market watching as three young men loaded four hundred fifty-kilogram bags of corn meal into our truck. It was tedious, but necessary.

Part of the tediousness, I realized, came from the contrast between what we were doing and what I had said I would be doing. When I wrote grant applications for this second trip to Sudan, I told prospective funders that I was interested in seeing the priests I had met at Bishop Gwynne College in their home dioceses so I could "learn about what mission and ministry looked like in their local contexts."

Now, as I sat outside the warehouse, I wondered if I was doing what I had said I would. Where were the overflowing church services? Why was I thinking so much about logistics? Almost as soon as I asked the questions, I realized the answers. This *was* mission and ministry. Zechariah was a priest and he was dead set on getting these supplies to his people. Despite the obstacles—the need for three quotations, the challenges of the truck, the difficulty of getting the money to Wau— this whole endeavor was the church's gospel-centric response to the situation in Abyei. I was reminded of something John had said during a planning meeting when we first arrived in Wau. "We are the church," he said emphatically. "We are always on the ground, even after all the other organizations have left." This trip constituted only a small part of the church's work in and for Abyei.

We finally left for Agok in the late afternoon on Friday, forty-eight hours after arriving in Wau. Zechariah and Peter rode with the truck. The rest of us crammed into the cab of a pick-up truck we hired in the market, driven by a young man—I was not sure he was out of his teens—named Jackson. Abraham's diocese is one of the newest in the Episcopal Church of the Sudan, created to keep up with the church's growth, and he does not yet have a reliable vehicle. I thought of Nigerian bishops and their four-wheel-drive SUVs. In South Sudan, such episcopal vehicles are few and far between.

The first part of the trip was hopeful. We made good time passing through one dusty village after another. All were more or less the same. There were mud huts with tall thatch roofs, sometimes built on stilts to keep the animals—domesticated and not—out. Where there were schools, they were often made of grass walls or had walls of sticks. In between the village centers there were large open fields, planted with sorghum. Occasionally, we saw herds of cattle being tended by young boys. Few of the people we passed were fully clothed, not from cultural sensibilities so much as from lack of resources. Except for the occasional shop we passed, there was no electricity. The line of jerry cans we saw waiting at wells indicated how hard people had to work just to stay clean and hydrated. This was South Sudan, the world's newest nation: beautiful but almost desperately poor.

Our late start meant we had to break up the journey. We spent the night in a little village called Wunrock. "We're more than halfway there," Jackson promised. "It's two and a half hours to Agok tomorrow." But the road north from Wunrock was markedly worse than what we had traveled on the day before. The nature of the area was changing as well. There were fewer villages—in fact, before long, I could see none at all—and the vegetation was growing taller and more lush. "This is Abyei," Nathaniel told me, gesturing around. There were also more signs of the Sudan People's Liberation Army, the rebel army that is now the military of South Sudan. A few trucks bearing soldiers passed us in the opposite direction. At one or two points, we passed a line of soldiers marching somewhere. They waved to us but otherwise let us be.

Before long, we reached a junction, a rare occurrence in a place with so few roads. It was the turn to Agok and it had a new obstacle. There was a wooden stick across the road and a group of soldiers standing nearby. Off to the side, we saw their camp: a few huts with more soldiers resting under the trees. "The road is closed," Nathaniel said, puzzled. Jackson rolled to a stop in front of the barricade and began speaking to the soldiers. Nathaniel translated for me. "They say the road is very bad and muddy so they have closed it. We cannot get through this way."

"Is there any other way around?" I asked him.

"There is," he said, "but the road goes right along the Kiir River that is the dividing line between north and south right now. The soldiers are saying they will not let anyone on that road. Anything that goes on that road, they are shooting on sight."

Jackson kept talking to the soldiers. Eventually, one of them shrugged and lowered the barrier. "I told him I could make it through," he said to us over his shoulder.

The road that lay in front of us reminded me of a sight I had seen growing up in New England: an unplowed street that several cars had already tried—and failed—to make their way down. But instead of snow, this road had mud. There were several deep tire ruts filled with pools of water. The soft road had simply been unable to bear the load of previous vehicles that passed through, collapsing underneath and leaving the scars we saw before us. In other places, the road had lost any claim to be called dirt. It was simply mud, through and through, inviting us, tempting us, daring us to try to cross it. I looked at Bishop Abraham. This was his diocese, and he wanted to visit his people. In anticipation of our arrival in Agok, Abraham was wearing the dark suit and purple shirt his people expected of their bishop. Nathaniel wanted to get home as well. There were two trucks on the road behind us with loads of supplies. Abraham gripped the roll handle. So did I. Jackson slowly rolled the car forward, looking for the best path.

We made it 150 feet from the barrier before we sunk into a tire track from which there was no escape. Jackson gunned the engine forward and then in reverse but only succeeded in sending up plumes of mud. We piled out of the truck, gingerly picking our way to somewhat dry land. Behind us, we could hear the soldiers at the barricade laughing. It was not as if we had not been warned. No one seemed to expect or want any help from Abraham and me so we stood at a distance and watched as Jackson and the rest of our group tried to free the truck. They rocked it forward and backward. When that failed, they tried diverting the water in the hole we were in to another puddle. They looked by the side of the road for pieces of wood or anything that would give us traction. There was lots of tall grass and a few bushes but almost no dead branches of any size that could serve the purpose. In the meantime, the truck sunk further into the mud.

In search of shade, Abraham and I made our way back to the barricade and the soldiers' outpost. Clearly, it was unusual for them to have not only a bishop but also a white person—a *khawaja* in Sudanese parlance—in their camp so they gave us chairs. We sat and watched the life of this little outpost. Under one tree, one man was repairing the springs on a wire-frame bed. Behind us, the sole woman in camp was preparing the midday meal. In between our feet wandered a few chickens. It was not much different from a Sudanese home, which I imagined it was not long ago. There was one difference, though. Here and there wandered the soldiers who constituted the outpost: young, thin, and dressed in whatever haphazard collection of military clothing they had been given. Each had a semiautomatic weapon dangling off his shoulder. Parked nearby was a single Toyota pick-up truck. In the truck bed, a machine gun was mounted with plenty of ammunition lying ready. Independence may have come to South Sudan, but that was no reason to slacken one's posture toward the north.

Our deliverance came in the form of a convoy of four trucks that rolled up an hour after we got stuck. Out of the first truck came a man who, it was clear from the way he walked and the way he carried himself, was in command. He was as surprised as anyone to find a bishop and a *khawaja* in the outpost. Before long, though, he and Abraham were laughing like old friends. The commander shouted orders to his men. Two trucks drove to where our truck was still spinning fruitlessly in the mud.

"He is going to give us an escort on that other road they closed," Abraham told me. "His cousin is a friend of mine."

Soon enough, we were driving north again, this time as the middle truck in a five vehicle convoy. Ahead of us and behind us were two trucks, each mounted with machine guns and carrying about a dozen soldiers perched on the edge of the truck bed. I am, at best, uncomfortable around guns. Here, at the center of one of the world's potential flashpoints, I was surrounded by them. I resolved to take my cues from Abraham, who was holding the roll bar as if nothing had changed. Plus, the soldiers had shown energy and enthusiasm when the commander issued his orders. It was not every day they got to escort a bishop and a *khawaja*. I tried not to think about the fact that most of them were not yet twenty. Besides, what other option did we have?

Our speed picked up a bit once we turned down a new road. Nathaniel leaned over to me. "This is the road they have closed. If there is another attack, this is where it will begin." Before long, the trucks ahead of us stopped in the middle of the road and motioned for us to do the same. I looked around. We were in the middle of what had once been a market. No buildings now remained, just charred circles where huts had once been, and a wall that had survived the onslaught. In a few places, I could make out the remains of market stands where women once sold their wares.

The road forked here. We were parked on the right fork, the road that led, I presumed, to Agok. Along the left fork, which led through the market, the road was littered with spent bullet shells. I wandered off to the side of the road to get a better look at one of the destroyed huts. It was only then I realized there was a loose circle of soldiers around me. It tightened quickly and prevented me from moving very far from the center of the road. "Stay in the middle," the commander told me. "We don't know where the mines are."

The road ended abruptly in a sight I had never seen before. "This is the bridge they destroyed," the commander said and pointed. The span over the river had probably been two hundred feet long. Now it lay along the riverbed thirty feet below us and broken into several sections. The thick metal shone in the sun. "In 2008 when they attacked, they came this far but left the bridge alone," the commander said. "Now they have destroyed it." Independence had changed the stakes. The north was intent on undermining the new south however they could. I looked down at the Kiir River, a place so contested the sides cannot agree on a single name. The water flowed slowly down the wide river. Nathaniel told me it was home to hippos and alligators, but none were in evidence. This was the source of the region's life, the very richness that made the area so contested. There was little life to be seen, however. I could think only of death.

Abraham was standing at the edge of the bank, looking across the river to the north. "That is part of my diocese," he said, pointing to the other side of the river. He looked down at the bridge in the riverbed. "How am I supposed to get there now?"

⟨∾∿∿⟩

We became stuck once more on the journey from the bridge to Agok, but this time Abraham helped push. His dark suit and purple shirt got splattered with mud, but we set ourselves free reasonably quickly. Given the obstacles we encountered both in Wau and en route, when we arrived in Agok, Abraham decided to compress what he hoped would be nearly a week in Agok into just three days. One of the trucks of relief supplies had broken down along the way, and then found a different route to Agok. They finally arrived just as we were preparing to leave. Abraham spent his time meeting with clergy, who were in the difficult position of ministering to their people while also dealing with the displacement of their own families. I sat with Samuel, a priest. "In this situation, the role of the church must be to go into the community, to preach, to remind them that God created you and loves you," he said. But it was clear it was not an easy task, and that he was only barely holding things together. "Sometimes all I can do is kneel in front of God and ask how we can suffer like this."

Abraham presided at an overflowing worship service in the church. He preached on a portion of Jeremiah 29. He began with a well-known verse in the chapter, "For surely I know the plans I have for you, says the LORD, plans for your welfare and not for harm, to give you a future with hope." I knew this verse well, but barely knew its context. Jeremiah was preaching to Israelites in exiles in Babylon. The passage ends, "I will restore your fortunes . . . and I will bring you back to the place from which I sent you into exile." Here, in Agok, I was seeing what exile looked like. Abraham invited me to speak. I took the megaphone which was all the church had for amplification and stumbled through something about being one body. When one part of the body suffers, all suffer. "Christians around the world share in your suffering," I said, "because we are all part of one body." I hoped it was true, but I also knew it was easy for church members in the United States and elsewhere to flip past the news of the latest African tragedy.

Mostly, I wandered around the church compound, still a bit dazed at where I was, how I had come here, and what I was seeing. I watched as children scratched out their A-B-Cs in the dirt under the tree. Later, I watched them play, jumping rope and chasing a tattered soccer ball around the yard. Mostly, I wondered what the future held. The Ethiopian peacekeepers were deploying, but few people trusted them. More seriously, the rhetoric I heard indicated a return to the traditional sharing of the region was not possible. A handful of people thought that if Khartoum stopped interfering, the Misseriya and Dinka could return to coexistence. But most disagreed. "If a person allows themselves to be pushed to attack," Barnabas, the older refugee, said, "it shows what is in their heart. We can't trust them anymore." Samuel, the priest, agreed. "I don't think peace is possible. We want there to be a border and we want them to be in their own land." That elided the point. The reason there was conflict was that whose land was whose was disputed.

These were some of the more pleasant comments I heard. Disparaging comments about "Arabs"—the catch-all term for northerners—were frequent. Before long, I was despairing about the future. There was no progress on a meaningful referendum. Few people I spoke to had much good to say about the Misseriya or saw how the two groups could coexist. "Intractable" and "insoluble" barely seemed sufficient adjectives to describe the conflict. I thought about St. Paul's teaching in 2 Corinthians 5 about the "ministry of reconciliation" that comes to us through Christ's death and resurrection. But how does reconciliation begin in a place like Abyei? The lines between the groups were deeply drawn, and there seemed little willingness to reach out to the other.

But then a young woman named Awel changed my mind. Like so many others, the young mother—she could not have been much past twenty—fled south with her two children during the attacks and had been living in a classroom ever since. She was part of a group of women I was speaking with one evening. I put my despair at the seeming intractability of the conflict to them: "How can there be peace in Abyei?" There were a few of the unhelpful and unrealistic answers I was familiar with. The most common was, "When the Arabs leave."

But then Awel spoke from the edge of the group. "I am praying for them," she said. It caught me off guard.

"For whom?" I asked.

"The Arabs," she replied. "I am praying for the Misseriya."

Other women had answers to the question they wanted to share and jumped in before I had a chance to ask Awel more. She drifted away from the conversation before I could catch her.

Still, as I looked over my notes that evening, praying for the Misseriya seemed to be one possibility for peace in a place where there are too few. What would happen if we took Jesus' commandment seriously—"Love your enemies . . . pray for those who abuse you"?

Maybe, if a few others join Awel, we will find out in Abyei.

CHAPTER 14

"There Is Always Something New to Learn from the Bible"

Diocese of Aweil, Episcopal Church of the Sudan

Bishop Abraham and I returned to Wau from Abyei worn out from the journey. But Abraham had been away from his diocese on a two-month trip in the United States to raise awareness about the situation in South Sudan and he was eager to get home. Soon enough, we were back on the road, this time headed northwest from Wau to Aweil, capital of Northern Bahr el Ghazal State and see city of one of the Episcopal Church of the Sudan's newest dioceses. The road was unpaved and bumpy but blessedly free of mud. The scenery was much the same as the previous journey. We passed through several small villages along the side of the road, often little more than a collection of mud huts with a small shop that sold a few items.

For Abraham, the drive was full of memories. Like John, the student I had met at Bishop Gwynne College, Abraham was raised in a village not far from Aweil but had to flee his home when he was still a child, joining thousands of other children who walked into exile in Ethiopia in the late 1980s. The region was in the middle of a series of famines brought about by the violence and disruption of the civil war. He had traversed the region we were now driving through on foot, hiding from militias allied with the northern government and a southern rebel army looking to recruit new members to its ranks. After several years in Ethiopia, a sudden change of regime there meant Abraham and tens of thousands of others were forced to flee back into

Sudan. From there, they eventually made their way into Kenya and a refugee camp called Kakuma, which became their home for nearly a decade. Abraham and his friends were, in the terms of international nongovernmental organizations, "unaccompanied minors." But the rest of the world knew them—if they paid attention at all—as something else: the Lost Boys of Sudan.

Abraham had made only brief reference to his story in my presence, mostly in a joking matter. One night in Wau before we left for Abyei, our group was discussing if we should walk or take a motorcycle taxi to dinner. "I'll walk," Abraham said. "I walked from here"—he pointed to the ground beneath his feet—"to Ethiopia. This is not far." Needless to say, we walked to that meal. But on the ride to Aweil he began to tell me more of his story. His life encapsulated much of the recent history of his new nation.

In nearly fifteen years in exile, two things happened to Abraham and the other Lost Boys that likely would not have happened had they stayed in Aweil. First, they were educated. Along with many other refugees, Abraham learned to read, write, and speak English in schools run both by Sudanese and by refugee agencies in Ethiopia and Kenya. There were few schools in Aweil when he was growing up. In any event, young boys such as Abraham were needed to tend herds in cattle camps and not many were sent to school. The other change was as striking: after decades of Dinka indifference to Christianity, the Lost Boys were swept into the conversion of their people to Christianity. When European missionaries were expelled from Sudan in 1964, there was only a handful of Dinka converts. The second civil war, which began in 1983, was especially catastrophic for the Dinka. Yet by the mid-1990s, it became clear that something was changing in Dinka religion. No longer did the Dinka practice their traditional religion. They were Christian, some in the Roman Catholic Church but many in ECS. Congregations in Kakuma swelled in size. Baptism and confirmation services could take an entire day—and sometimes longer—to ensure all who wanted to participate had an opportunity.

Abraham became an integral part of this change. Baptized in Ethiopia, he was confirmed and ordained in Kakuma. When the American government resettled some of the Lost Boys in the United States, Abraham moved to Atlanta where he worked several jobs while pursuing a degree at a local university. From there, he moved to Trinity

School for Ministry, an Episcopal seminary outside Pittsburgh. Upon his graduation—he was just over thirty years old—he found to his surprise that he had been nominated to be bishop of the new diocese that ECS was creating in his home region. This decision alone was significant. During the mission era, Aweil and Wau were part of the region the government allocated to the Roman Catholics. To this day, both towns have large and imposing Catholic churches, a legacy of this history. As in Abyei, the Episcopal presence among Dinka in Aweil dates to the civil war. As refugees returned home, some as soldiers in the Sudan People's Liberation Army, they began to share the gospel they had learned in refugee camps with their family and friends. Now, fewer than two years prior to my visit, that work had borne fruit in the creation of the Diocese of Aweil.

Just as we crossed the river into Aweil, the road turned to pavement—brand new, by the look of it. "Bashir paved this last year," Abraham told me, referring to Omar al-Bashir, the president of Sudan. "He was trying to get people to vote against independence in the referendum." Under the terms of the peace treaty that ended the civil war between north and south, unity was to be "made attractive," in part, by spending resources on development in the south. But for these few miles of pavement, that had manifestly failed to happen in Aweil. The quality of the road was good and would not have been out of place in any American city. That was about the only familiar aspect of what I was seeing, however. On each side of the road stretching into the distance were low-slung huts, some made of brick, others of sticks. Most of the roofs were thatch. There was nothing more than a single story. This was Aweil, a state capital that looked like nothing more than a larger version of some of the villages we had passed through that morning. We pulled off the road next to a small, square brick building, about twelve feet on a side. "This is my house," Abraham gestured. "We're here."

The only way I knew this was our destination was the crowd of clergy who were there to welcome us. Abraham's return from his travels as well as the presence of a *khawaja* visitor meant many of the clergy of the diocese had turned out. The crowd swept us into a cinder-block building not far away. The floor was hard-pressed dirt. At one end was a slight raised area on which stood a lectern. Behind the lectern on a wall was a small cross. The windows were open holes in the wall, and a pigeon was flying around inside. Looking around, I saw three plastic chairs, but no other seating. It took me a moment, but I realized this was the cathedral. When the church plant in Bachure outside Yola was complete, it would be larger than this. Abraham and I were led up to the lectern. Some children from the nearby school sang their delight at having the bishop back home. Several of the senior clergy made blessedly short speeches about the significance of our arrival. Before long, the children were dismissed and Abraham and I headed for his house to catch our breath after the long and bumpy ride.

The twelve-foot-square building that served as his house had two rooms. The one on the right was where the school principal and his wife lived. The one on the left was ours. I poked my head inside. There were two single wire-frame beds set about three feet apart on a sandy floor. My bag had already been placed on one. We were here. This was the headquarters of the Diocese of Aweil.

I stepped back outside to look around more. I heard noise from children coming from three low-slung buildings made entirely of grass that centered on a dusty square not far from the cathedral. This, I presumed, was the cathedral school, no different than anything else I had seen on the drive from Wau. I did not have long to take in the scene, however. Four students I had studied with at Bishop Gwynne College were among the clergy who welcomed us, and they quickly came over to greet me. They were eager to show off the diocesan compound. The cathedral in particular was a point of pride. "It is the only cinder-block church in the diocese," said George, one of my former colleagues. "Samaritan's Purse"—an aid organization started by Billy Graham's son, Franklin—"gave us money to build it when they learned we wanted to be a diocese. Bishop Abraham was enthroned here last year."

I asked what the other churches in the diocese were like.

"Most of them are made out of sticks and grass, like the homes," said George. "In my church, we meet under a tree. Someday we might have a building like this one but right now we don't have the money."

In the context of what I had seen of Aweil and the surrounding region, the cinder-block cathedral was impressive. Its walls were not going to wash away in the next rain storm and its tin roof did not look like it would leak. It had a permanence that other structures lacked. Still, to hear George use the word "enthrone" in reference to a building like this was jarring. There was no throne. Aside from the few plastic chairs, there were no seats at all.

As George showed me around, I thought back to Owerri and the large schools and churches I had seen there. Any of the outlying churches in Owerri would have been better cathedrals than what Aweil had here. Compared to what Abraham had—and shared—the houses of some bishops in Nigeria were veritable mansions. The idea of the "African church" as a convenient term to generalize about the experiences of Christians on an entire continent finally died for me. It was a term without merit. The distance between Aweil and Owerri was greater than that between Owerri and the cathedral close at Canterbury.

A few months before my visit to Aweil, Abraham and I spoke on the phone to iron out details. He had a request of me. "When you are here, can you teach my clergy?" he asked.

I paused. Why would a bishop want a seminarian with two years of theological education to teach his clergy? Some of the priests had been ordained for twenty years or more and served during the worst of the civil war. Abraham sensed my hesitation. "Most of my clergy have no training at all. They are eager to learn anything. Will you teach them?"

"Is there anything in particular you would like me to teach?" I asked.

"Anything!" he said emphatically. "They need to learn."

It was hard to say no. "Sure!" I said, and promptly forgot the request.

On the drive to Abyei, however, Abraham reminded me of what I had agreed to do. "The clergy will be ready for you when we arrive," he said. So it was not just the bishop's return from his two months in the United States that brought out the crowd of clergy to welcome us to Aweil; they had come because I was to conduct a clergy conference for them.

I knew from my time at Bishop Gwynne College that the civil war had prevented much clergy training from taking place. The students at BGC were ones of exceptional promise who were studying subjects they should have learned before ordination. But now I was to lead a conference for fifty priests, only a handful of whom would ever have the opportunity to study outside Aweil. There were four women in the group, about half of Aweil's complement of female clergy. For them, the challenges of managing a household and serving as a priest meant it was even harder to seek education elsewhere. What I vaguely knew about clergy conferences at home involved someone with a wealth of knowledge and credentials speaking about a topic of some weight and substance. In Aweil, I realized, my two years of seminary education—no matter how insufficient I thought it was—made me that person.

The conference I put together centered on the theology of the church. What is the church? Who is in the church? For what purpose does the church exist? These seemed appropriate questions in a context where the church is being called upon to play an outsized role in society. Beginning the morning after our arrival in the dirt-floor cathedral, I taught. And taught. And taught. I started in Matthew 18, one of the few places Jesus uses the word "church" and built out from there, talking about the church as a community of reconciliation, whose members live into the "ministry of reconciliation" Paul describes in 2 Corinthians 5. We talked about the first apostles who built the church, imperfect people who nonetheless opened themselves to the power of the Holy Spirit and performed great deeds testifying to the resurrection of Jesus Christ. We discussed what it meant to be the body of Christ and the ways in which diversity nourishes that body.

As I taught, I realized several things simultaneously. First, the clergy were rapt with attention. They listened to what I had to say and asked good and probing questions of me. When I divided them into small groups to study Bible passages more closely, I heard the discussion continuing in each one. Second, no matter that I had found the idea of it intimidating, this clergy conference was proving to be the best method I could think of to build relationships. When it comes to encountering another Christian and learning about his or her life, there is no substitute for sitting together around a Bible passage and speaking about how it is interpreted in our context.

This led to my third realization. I knew from the questions I was being asked that some of what I was saying was gently challenging beliefs these priests held. This was most apparent when I started talking about reconciliation in an interfaith context. As my experience in Abyei had demonstrated, the cleavages between southerners and northern "Arabs" are deep. To suggest, as I did, that reconciliation might involve Muslims provoked passionate debate. What I realized, however, is that the only reason I was getting such an engaged hearing was that what I was saying was rooted in particular passages of the Bible. The extent to which I could root my teaching in the Bible was the extent to which it was received.

The fourth realization came from the third. While my teaching was provoking challenge, everyone wanted to engage with me and learn from me—and their questions were challenging some of my assumptions. No one wanted to end the conversation. Everything I was teaching was in the broad mainstream of the theology of the Episcopal Church in which I was raised. I thought of the alleged conservatism of the "African church." I thought again about Maple and her Pastor Tim in Nanjing and the need for theological education throughout the world church. Here in Aweil we had different views of course, but we also had hugely different contexts. None of that obscured the recognition that each of us had something to learn from the other. I asked myself again: Is the church in the developing world conservative because it is fated to be that way? Or is it because its major influences—the people who care enough to invest their time and talent in sisters and brothers around the world—are that way?

After I concluded in the late afternoon and was gathering my things together, a priest approached me. The look on his face was one of great emotion, combined with deep gratitude. "I was ordained twenty-two years ago when I lived in exile in Khartoum," he told me. "I have always wanted to learn more about the Bible but there has never been the opportunity. Today, however, you have shown me that there is always something new to learn from the Bible. Thank you." It was hard not to be exhilarated by a comment like that. I returned to Abraham's room exhausted but satisfied. But as I kicked off my shoes and lay back on my bed, relieved to be off my feet, I had another thought: Why was I doing this teaching? Where were the seminary professors, cathedral deans, and rectors of cardinal parishes to lead clergy conferences in places like Aweil? Why did clergy here have to rely on a seminarian with an incomplete education to teach them? In the brief time I had spent with the bishop of Wau, he had asked me to help him open a Bible school for his clergy. "My clergy need to learn," he told me then. I agreed with the sentiment but told him I could not help at the time. Who could?

Abraham came in and sat down on his bed. "I hear it went well," he said. I nodded. "So I told them you'll be doing a second day of teaching tomorrow." I sighed and rolled away from him, too tired to respond.

Nonetheless, we continued the next morning, talking about Christian leadership and how it differs from other models of leadership in the world. Again, the conversation was rich and probing as we

gathered around Bible texts together and thought through their implications. At the end of the day I told them I would be leaving soon. I
asked them what sorts of things they would like to learn that would be
the most helpful to them in their ministry. The answers came quickly:
church administration! Pastoral counseling! Stewardship and how to
get people to tithe! Their concerns were practical and somewhat distant from what I had focused on. But they were equally subjects rooted
in biblical theology and could be taught as such. These were sensible
concerns, the kind of things that are of central importance in making
a church function. I revised my thought from the previous day. Aweil
did not need mere cathedral deans or seminary professors as instruc-
tors. A few good lay people would do just fine.

⌒⟋⟋⟍⟍⌒

The exigencies of air travel in South Sudan meant I had to leave Aweil
and return to Juba only three nights after I arrived, or risk being stuck
in Aweil for another week. Though I wanted to visit the church under
a tree that my BGC colleague George led, it was not going to be possible given the size of the diocese and the challenge of traveling around
it. But there was one visit I could make.

Paul was one of the quietest students at BGC and I had not
known him well when I was there. Like Abraham, John, and several
other clergy in Aweil, he was one of the Lost Boys, baptized in Ethiopia and ordained a deacon in Kakuma. He had not been resettled in
the United States, however. Instead, in 2002, when the end of the civil
war was in sight, he returned home. At the time, Aweil was a garrison
town of the northern army and it was not safe for a young Dinka man
to live there. He lived in a village in the bush, worked with the church,
and tried to return to a life he had left when he was ten years old.

When the war ended, Paul went to live in a new community on the
edge of Aweil, called, appropriately, New Site. New Site consisted primarily of former refugees returning home and former villagers who had
moved to Aweil. After my last teaching session, Paul and I set out on
foot across town, passing through the endless series of huts that make
up neighborhoods in Aweil. There were a few pumps and wells scattered throughout our walk, each with a long line of yellow plastic jerry
cans and crowds of girls and women waiting patiently for their turn at
the pump. Children ran around us. They were dressed in clothing cast

off by Westerners, donated to thrift stores, sold to traders, repackaged, and sent on to markets in the Global South. In the distance, we could see the compound of the various United Nations agencies at work in the region. A few tall light poles stood in the compound's middle, an indication of something it had that none of these neighborhoods did: electricity. Aside from the UN compound, the plastic products, and the T-shirts advertising road races or family reunions in the United States, there was little in the scene to suggest we were in the modern era. Life here was not terribly different than it might have been several generations earlier. New Site, Paul's neighborhood, was like any of the others we passed through. Children chased after one another, women cooked meals over charcoal fires, and a few men went past on bicycles.

Before we left, Abraham had told me Paul's church was one of the largest in the diocese. I had been in Aweil long enough to know I should not let this comment shape any expectations. But when Paul stopped me in front of a large lean-to structure, I was not immediately sure why. A roof of tarps and sticks sat on top of several large branches that served as columns. There were no walls. Underneath, a few large branches were arranged as benches. The roof was about five feet above the ground. I ducked to get underneath. "This is my church," Paul said. My mind went to the large archdeaconery churches I had seen in Owerri. This was its equivalent in Aweil, a structure in which I could barely stand and which, I estimated, could comfortably seat one hundred people.

"How many people come on Sunday?" I asked.

"Three hundred," he said.

It was uncomfortable crouching in the church so we stepped back outside and Paul pointed out a large tree not far away. "We began under that tree when the war ended and it was safe to come here." He pointed in the other direction to a site that was under construction. "This is our new church. We hope to move in there soon." We walked over to have a closer look. There was no roof, but otherwise the building looked like a church. The brickwork rose about eight feet off the ground. There were squares for windows and an entryway leading into a large open area that would one day be the sanctuary, a sanctuary larger than that of the cathedral. Paul pointed to a brick press under a nearby tree. "We have made all these bricks ourselves. The brickwork is done, but we have no money for the roof." While he was at BGC, Paul had tried to raise money for the roof from some of the wealthier members of a Dinka congregation in Juba. He had some success but not enough to finish the work.

Our presence had attracted a growing audience of about a dozen children under the age of ten who had seen a *khawaja* in the area. "Where do these children go to school?" I asked.

Paul shook his head. "There is no school in New Site. Some can go all the way into town, but it is far and that is expensive. Our congregation wants to start a school for this neighborhood but. . . ." He shrugged again. Paul's limited ability in English and my nonexistent Dinka meant that many complex thoughts were going unsaid. But I understood the point he was trying to make. A school was a major undertaking. It was not so much the expense involved—in Abyei, after all, I had seen lessons under a tree—as the talent necessary to teach. Paul had gone to school in refugee camps, which likely made him more educated than many members of his congregation. But he was at BGC most of the year. New Site probably did not have the personnel necessary to teach the children crowding around us.

Paul took me over to a stick hut not far from the lean-to church. It was a square, about eight feet on a side and had a pointy thatch roof. The door was about four feet tall and I bent over to get inside. There was room for two beds. "This is my home," Paul said. He pointed to four of the children gathered around us. "These are my children." We went back outside, and Paul introduced me to his wife, who had been working in a cooking area I had not seen. We sat under a shady tree and ate a meal together. The language barrier meant our conversation was clipped and limited so I had time to reflect on what I was seeing. New Site had almost no social services for its growing population—no school, no clinic, nothing. In other places I had visited, it was the church that stepped in to fill these holes in the social fabric. But Paul's church was almost brand new and the demands on it were intense. It was impressive enough that in a handful of years they had gone from meeting under a tree to a lean-to and now almost to a brick church. But the need was overwhelming and no match for the congregation's limited resources. Everyone in the congregation could come together to make bricks by hand. They were not going to be able to run a clinic that way, however.

I asked Paul about stewardship. The bricks demonstrated the congregation could offer their time and talent. What about their treasure? Paul shook his head. "It is very little," he said. "People do not have a lot to give." This I knew from personal experience. When I preached at the church in Bachure in Yola to a congregation of fourteen, the collection receipts had been about twenty-five dollars. In South Sudan, I would preach at a church where attendance was over nine hundred. The collection receipts were less than one hundred dollars, ten percent of which I had given. During the clergy conference we had just completed in Aweil, Abraham had used a break in my lessons to address the clergy on exactly this question. "I want you to encourage people to give one Sudanese pound"—about thirty cents—"each Sunday," he had told them. "If they can do that and continue to do that, then you will begin to have money to improve your buildings and the diocese will have money to purchase a vehicle so I can visit more of the congregations in this diocese." Abraham had told me about confirmation visits he made to distant villages, where he traveled from place to place, confirming hundreds every day. The church was taking root in a place where a generation ago almost no one had been Christian, but it needed clergy and episcopal support. Abraham's plan was a hopeful one and it might work, but it would still take ages before he had a vehicle that could withstand the punishment of the roads in this part of the country.

Sitting with Paul under the tree, I thought back to Nigeria, where money coursed through congregations. Nigeria was a much richer country, of course, so there was more money to go around. Prosperity gospel theology had created a culture in which Nigerian churchgoers routinely gave more money. Perhaps, I realized with a start, what Aweil needed was a dash—if such a thing was possible—of the prosperity gospel. The thought made me laugh to myself. I bemoaned the prosperity gospel while I was in Nigeria. Now I wanted to import it to Aweil.

The larger question, though, was about the role of the church. The South Sudanese government was overmatched and could not meet the obvious needs of its people. The church could fill some of these gaps—as I had seen it begin to do with agriculture, for instance—but how much was too much? What was the proper role for the church in this context? They were important questions, I knew, and they were only beginning to be asked.

There was one final place I needed to visit before I left Aweil. The children of the school had been a constant presence during the clergy conference, primarily as background noise when they were let out of class. A few brave ones poked their heads through the door of the cathedral to see what the *khawaja* was doing. But it was not until just before I left that I was able to pay a visit of my own. My guide was Angelo, the head teacher. He had been displaced to Khartoum during the war and had lived in the informal settlements that had sprung up to house the southerners who moved north during the war. He had been educated and ordained there and was now one of the senior clergy in the diocese.

Though it was early evening, the school was still in use. The younger students had gone home, but when I crouched over and worked my way through the grass door, I found a class of students, all of whom were in their twenties. Angelo explained that the class was for people who had not been educated during the war. I looked at the students and greeted them. Their faces told of a weariness and exhaustion that went far beyond their years. Some of the men had been soldiers, Angelo told me. The women had a variety of experiences of displacement during the war, but were now back in Aweil trying to make their lives work again. The class was focused on basic skills—reading, writing, and arithmetic—that they had never had an opportunity to learn. In this one central location, the diocese had been able to marshal its collective resources for this ministry. But I wondered how many other people like these students there were who lived in communities where the resources were insufficient for this sort of education.

This was a quick tour and Angelo wanted to let the class get back to work. But before we left, he asked me if I had any words of encouragement for them. I thought again about the teaching on the catholicity of the church I had read while I was at Bishop Gwynne College, that the church is catholic because it teaches everything people need to know. This was the church catholic in front of me, the church being the church. But I could not figure out how to make that into a short message of encouragement that could be easily translated for the students. Instead, I said the most true thing I could think of: "I'm praying for you. I'm going to tell my friends about you, and they'll pray for you as well."

In the face of the challenges the church in a place like Aweil faces, it did not seem like much. But it was, I hoped, a start.

CHAPTER 15

The Countercultural Unity of a Worldwide Communion

Not long after my conversation with the clergy wives at Trinity Theological College in Umuahia, Nigeria, Oliver, my host, took me to visit a rural archdeaconery in the diocese. Our first stop was the area's largest Anglican church, a small cinder-block building in a little town. The priest and a few members of his congregation were there to greet me and ask questions. Conditioned by my experience at Trinity, I was expecting to talk about homosexuality. Instead, the priest's first question caught me off guard. "We hear a lot about globalization," he said. "What effect will it have on the church?"

Struggling for an answer, I turned the question back on him. He was only too eager to answer. "It is making it harder to be together as Anglicans," he said. "We keep hearing about what you Americans are doing—having gay bishops, letting gay marriages happen in your churches." That prompted a question about homosexuality, and the conversation quickly moved to more familiar terrain. But later that day as I reflected on the visit, I thought that the priest was spot on in his diagnosis of the situation the Anglican Communion now faces. We cannot talk about the Anglican Communion in the twenty-first century without also talking about globalization—and in thinking about globalization, we might start finding a way to a future Anglican Communion.

"Globalization" is contested, almost as much as a definition as a process. The Internet, transnational corporations, the World Trade Organization, Islamist terrorism, and outsourcing—to name just a few—are all referred to as aspects of globalization and characteristics of life in our "global village" and "flat" world. The word can be used so frequently and imprecisely that it is hard to determine just what it means. As I understand it, there is a single dynamic at the heart of globalization: the bringing together of a local particularity and a universalizing norm. This interaction is the result of technological advances that have brought people around the world into closer contact with one another. In college I studied the Zapatistas, an indigenous group in Mexico that protested the way a free-trade agreement—a universalizing norm—had the potential to destroy their traditional culture—a local particularity. This local-universal dynamic is characteristic of the Anglican Communion as well. From one perspective, the decision to ordain Gene Robinson as bishop of New Hampshire was a local, contextual response to the needs of a particular church community. From this perspective, the response from leaders in some Anglican provinces is an attempt to impose universal standards for the selection of Anglican bishops. From another perspective, however, these same Anglican leaders are seeking the freedom to pursue ministry in their own context, unencumbered by the burden of the "gay church" label. Whatever the perspective, the dynamic, that of globalization, remains the same.

Although phrases like "global village" might make it seem that globalization promotes mutual understanding among diverse people, in fact the practical effects of globalization are more often fracture, discord, and division. Few people, Anglican or otherwise, seem willing to genuinely engage with someone who is different than them—even though globalization is constantly bringing us into contact with these people. Our default posture to the other is hostility, not relatedness. Examples of true dialogue across intercultural and international lines of difference are rare. On a shelf in Bishop Marcus's office in Yola, I found a book by the late Polish journalist, Ryszard Kapuściński, who wrote that rather than being like a global village, "society on our planet . . . is more like the anonymous crowd at a major airport, a crowd of people rushing along in haste, mutually indifferent and ignorant." If globalization is the hallmark of the twenty-first century, division is its shadow. The priest in the town outside Umuahia was right: globalization makes it hard for Anglicans to be together in the world.

It is not only globalization that has increased fracture and conflict in the world; such division is increasingly the case in other aspects of our life as well. I was in Nigeria at the same time the United States Congress was debating raising the debt ceiling and permitting the American government to borrow more money. When Internet access allowed, I read about that fraught debate. Democrats and Republicans sought to gain the upper hand to advance their particular view of the government. This is not in itself unusual, but the bitterness of the debate and the unwillingness to meaningfully engage with what the other side was thinking were notable. It was as though the two sides were talking past one another, completely oblivious to the fact that the other party even existed.

Then I would turn away from Congress and turn back to the Anglican Communion—and find more or less the same thing. In Internet posts, news articles, and comments on blog items, I found a debased discourse. Each side insisted its version of events was definitive and its beliefs were right. Mutual anathemas abounded. The rhetoric seemed like an imagined and alternate world compared to the hopeful and relationally rich reality I was encountering. The debate was a mirror of the division and discord of the debt ceiling debate and the broken relationships of a globalized world. Something about it felt so deeply, depressingly, distressingly wrong, like somehow the church was missing the point. The church is not supposed to be like the world around it; it is supposed to be different than the world around it.

The biblical witness is clear that God's people are to be out of step with the world around them. As St. Paul instructed Christians in Rome, "Do not be conformed to this world." Only then could they discern "the will of God—what is good and acceptable and perfect" (Romans 12:2). But it is not just a New Testament idea. The Israelites understood the law codes God gave them as a tool that made them distinctive in the world: "You shall be holy to me; for I the LORD am holy, and I have separated you from the other peoples to be mine" (Leviticus 20:26). To be holy is, in some senses, to be different. This countercultural ideal is embodied by Jesus, who challenged many of the social mores of his time and reminded his followers they "do not belong to the world" (John 15:19). The trouble is in determining just what it means to be countercultural, particularly when there are so many different cultures in the world and so many different understandings of what it means to be counter to them. Some people see a growing tolerance of homosexuality in parts of the world and conclude that for the church to be countercultural, it must oppose this trend. Others see continued repression and exclusion of gay people and conclude that if the church is to be countercultural, it must be a welcoming place for all.

The Bible makes clear that the most significant way in which Christians demonstrate their distinctiveness is in the nature of their life together. How the Christian community's members interact with one another, engage in discourse, and welcome others, for instance, are all part of their witness to God. The holiness to which God called Israel was to be found in a law code that focused on care for widows, orphans, and others who were left out in society. It was these relationships that mattered in creating the community's countercultural life. Jesus made a similar point when he told his followers that "by this everyone will know that you are my disciples, if you have love one for another" (John 13:35). The apostolic church was noted for its distinctive relationships. The life of the early Christians—"all who believed were together and had all things in common" (Acts 2:44)— was countercultural in the context of a Roman society stratified by divisions of wealth.

The importance of relationships within the Christian community has its most explicit articulation in the writings of St. Paul. In his first letter to the Corinthians, Paul sees the societal divisions that had crept into the Corinthian church, particularly in the community's commemoration of the Last Supper. He lambasts them for mirroring the fissures of the world: "When you come together as a church, I hear that there are divisions among you. . . . Do you show contempt for the church of God and humiliate those who have nothing?" (11:18, 22). Instead, Paul explains, all Christians actually need one another—no matter how unlikely that may seem—if they want to follow Jesus. This is what it means to be the body of Christ, an idea Paul articulates most fully immediately after chastising them for demeaning their common life. Every member of the Corinthian community actually already is linked by a common baptism—"you *are* the body of Christ" (12:27), Paul writes, not "you *should* be the body of Christ"—and each member has gifts others need to receive if they truly want to follow Jesus. Difference is a blessing to the Christian community, not a curse.

But Paul also understands that the structure of the world makes this mutuality and interdependence a challenge. When he tells the Romans not to be conformed to the world, he also reminds them of the significance of the body of Christ and the diverse gifts each person has. Not being conformed to the world is closely connected to acknowledging our relatedness in the body of Christ. Throughout his writings, Paul pleads with Christians to seek togetherness, to learn from one another, and to determine just what each has to receive from other followers of Jesus. No matter how much we might like to, Paul writes, we cannot say to one another, "I have no need of you" (1 Corinthians 12:21), if we truly want to follow Jesus. Belonging to the church, then, means believing that other people—no matter how different they may seem—have something to offer to us, and us to them. Community is where Christians find truth. This is a deeply countercultural idea.

This biblical teaching explains why it is disastrous for the church to so closely mimic the world around it. There is nothing countercultural about having an internecine debate about sexuality, particularly not one that pits different parts of the world against each other. There is nothing countercultural about ignorance of the other's position. At times in recent years, it has seemed as if some Anglican leaders have come to take pride in asserting, essentially, "I have no need of you." In doing so, the church has become a mirror of the fractured world around us, mimicking its homogeneity, rather than modeling a holy heterogeneity.

With this in mind, the connection Jesus makes between unity among his followers and their witness to the world makes sense. "That they may all be one," he prayed, "so that the world may believe that you have sent me" (John 17:21). Fracture and division were the nature of the times. But if followers of Jesus lived a countercultural lifestyle of unity, they would be testifying to the glory and wonder of God. When Jesus offered that prayer, his followers were confined to a small part of the world. In the early twenty-first century, there are followers of Jesus across the world, living at a time when fracture, division, and discord are heightened and widespread. In this context, unity among Christians could be a powerful countercultural witness, a message to the world that another way exists and that division is not the necessary outcome of our increased interconnectedness. From time to time, it has been said among Anglicans that unity can be found "in mission." In fact, however, unity *is* mission: our unity as Christians is a core part of our witness to the world. Christian unity is good news to a divided world.

But we are failing. Anglicans live a life that is marked more by conformity to this world than nonconformity. And the world is watching. In China, my student group visited a Bible college in the Inner Mongolia Autonomous Region, a sparsely populated, remote, and impoverished part of the country. During a question and answer session, one student asked if any of our group was Anglican. When he found out I was, he asked me, "What is going on in your church with homosexuality? We read about it here, but we just do not understand what is happening." I was stunned. Here, in the proudly nationalist, postdenominational, definitively non-Anglican church, was someone who was paying attention to global Anglicanism. Later, when I spoke with the questioner individually, I learned how closely he and other students used the Internet to follow developments in the Anglican Communion. Anglicans are on a world stage.

By failing to live a countercultural lifestyle of unity, Anglicans are missing a singular opportunity to witness to the truth of the gospel we proclaim. Just imagine if instead of looking at the Anglican Communion and seeing a reflection of its own fracture and division, the world looked at the Anglican Communion and saw a body that was living together in its diversity, not by papering over its differences and divisions but acknowledging them and still together seeking the reconciled life. Just imagine if instead of seeing a group of people that fled from each other's difference, the world saw a group of people who were constantly asking how that difference could enrich their common life. Just imagine if instead of seeing members of a body that tried to outdo one another in shouting, "I have no need of you," the world saw a body that was pointing the way to that glorious future foretold by the author of Revelation who saw "a great multitude that no one could count, from every nation, from all tribes and peoples and languages, standing before the throne and before the Lamb, robed in white, with palm branches in their hands" (7:9). Imagine! Everyone in the church, together, praising God! Imagine what that might mean for the witness of the church to the world.

Such a future seems either impossible or hopelessly naïve. After all, if saying, "Why can't we all just get along?" worked, the world would have solved its problems long ago. Nor do we want unity of only Anglicans. The unity of all the baptized is the goal toward which we are called. But unity has to begin somewhere and Anglicans, perhaps more than any other Christians, are in a position to make this countercultural unity a reality.

⟲∞⟳

Early in Jesus' ministry, the Gospel of John tells us, Jesus left Judea and returned to Galilee. The route took him through Samaria, an unusual place for a Jewish teacher to be, as John reminds his readers: "Jews do not share things in common with Samaritans" (4:9). Jesus rests at a well and begins talking with a woman there. Before long, the conversation has become so significant that the woman runs to find her neighbors and tell them the good things she has heard from this stranger at the well. Her life has been transformed by the experience of meeting Jesus. There are many ways to understand this story and much we can learn from Jesus' interaction with the woman at the well. But when I read the story there is one question that remains with me. What would happen if we did what Jesus did: show up in places where no one expects us to be and start talking with people who seem different than us?

Jesus' meeting with the woman at the well is a microcosm of the act underlying his ministry: Incarnation. The Old Testament tells of a God who loved and cared for God's chosen people and spoke to them through prophets, rulers, and the occasional cataclysmic event, like exile. All was to little avail. God's people continued in their ways. The norms of God's way of life clashed with the particularities of what it meant to be a community in the ancient Near East. The miracle of the Incarnation is that the barrier between human and divine was breached: an omniscient, omnipotent, and almighty God voluntarily took human form in Jesus Christ to love, teach, heal, and save humankind in his ministry, death, and resurrection. Jesus Christ, as fully human and fully divine, represents in his being the reconciliation of the universalizing norms of God's law and the local particularities of each human life. The Incarnation is the divine "showing up" in a new place in a new way among people who were not expecting it.

The Incarnation represents a new use of power or, rather, weakness. The almighty God became human not in a palace or the center of a kingdom but in a manger in a stable in a town in a backwater province of the world's mightiest empire. Christ's life and ministry were marked by a striking degree of vulnerability, uniquely encapsulated in the cross, in which Christ willingly chose a degrading death. It is an idea expressed in the hymn in Philippians: Christ "emptied himself, taking the form of a slave, being born in human likeness . . . he humbled himself and became obedient to the point of death" (2:7–8). In willingly giving up power, God was able to bring about the reconciliation that is at the core of God's purposes for the world.

Our world places little value on vulnerability; strength and dominance are preferred. But that is not an option for Christians. The body of Christ to which we belong is one that was pierced, broken, and weak. Anglicans are called to vulnerability, no matter its nerve-jangling, mind-warping, and uncomfortable implications. This is not the forced vulnerability of the abused spouse or exploited worker but the freely chosen vulnerability of one who trusts in God's purposes and is sure of God's love. As we encounter one another, we seek not the security of inns but the vulnerability of the manger.

The divine "showing up" of the Incarnation also represents a deep commitment to relationship. Rather than withdrawing from God's people in the face of generations of disobedience, God chose to relate to us in a whole new way. By coming among us as one of us, God demonstrates that our relationships matter. But these relationships do not spring up overnight. They are the result of patience and of time. The very fact that it took thirty years between the Incarnation and the beginning of Jesus' ministry should be a reminder to us that God's time is not our time. Rushing headlong toward action and decision, particularly when such a rush comes at the expense of relationship, is not the answer of the Incarnation.

These ideas—Incarnation, vulnerability, and relationship—are hallmarks of Anglican theology. At least since the late nineteenth century, Anglicanism has been known as a religion that stresses the Incarnation. There are many aspects to this belief, not all of them helpful, but Charles Gore, an early twentieth-century English bishop and one of the chief exponents of the theology of the Incarnation, stressed the importance of the "method" of the Incarnation, particularly the way in which it gives one "the power to think one's self into another's thoughts, to look through another's eyes, to feel with another's feeling, to merge one's self in another's interest—this is the higher power, the power of love, and we owe it to the Incarnation." This is precisely what Christians are called to do—to stand in the place of others—and it follows from the model of Christ's self-emptying Incarnation.

The Anglican emphasis on relationship reached its peak in "Mutual Responsibility and Interdependence in the Body of Christ," the document that came out of the 1963 Anglican Congress in Toronto. MRI asserted that the pictures Anglicans had of one another "are utterly obsolete and irrelevant to our actual situation." Instead, Anglicans needed to recommit themselves to seeking communion with others in the worldwide body of Christ. Stephen Bayne, the Anglican executive officer who was closely involved with drafting MRI, said that the way forward for Anglicans was "through the common, shared life of Christians with different experiences and different backgrounds, who pray and work and think together, who do in fact share a common life and, supremely, share a common Sacrament." In other words, relationships matter. We pursue them as Christians because it was God in Christ who first pursued a deep, intimate relationship with us in the Incarnation.

Anglicans have understood these ideas in structuring our common life. The system of autonomous provinces allows each to pursue independence in its own area while still remaining in deep communion with other Anglicans around the world. In the provincial system, Anglicans strike a balance between the strict hierarchy of the Roman Catholics, but also the more dispersed and loosely connected federations that are common in Protestant denominations. The growing number of networks and relationships between dioceses are another way in which these deep relationships are formed. Meetings of Anglican leaders—Lambeth Conferences, Primates Meetings—are designed to allow conversation and relationship-building between participants. They are emphases that serve as reminders that Anglicans are united, but also different.

But Anglicans of all kinds have shifted away from these historic emphases. "Mutual Responsibility and Interdependence" represented a high mark in American commitment to the world church. The half century since has seen not a working out of the principles articulated in MRI but a withdrawal from them. For many reasons, the processes that followed the Toronto Congress emphasized financial aspects of relationships, the least incarnate and committed form of relationship. The mainstream of the American church began increasingly to withdraw from incarnate mission relationships. Domestic needs began to take precedence over global connections. There were sporadic attempts to stir up interest in the world church but such efforts were the exception that proved the rule. By the early 1990s, the church's General Convention seriously considered defunding overseas missionaries altogether. The practical result of this is that when sexuality-related issues came to the fore in the late 1990s, many American church members were largely caught off guard by the discord because they had withdrawn from their sisters and brothers in Christ around the world. Relationships actually matter. But only the people who invest in them will see their benefits.

There are other ways of minimizing relationship as well. In Nigeria, I was briefly introduced to a bishop's wife. When she asked what brought me to her country, I mentioned my interest in unity, which, I said, was a deeply biblical concern. "Unity of *orthodox* Christians," she tartly replied. She is not the only one who uses the word "orthodox"; it is increasingly common in discussions of Anglican futures. Underlying her response was the idea that Christian unity can be found by everyone agreeing to the same set of beliefs. Orthodoxy literally means "right belief." From this perspective, disagreements between faithful Christians about what the Bible says about homosexuality are a death knell for unity.

But as I traveled, I found myself wondering if orthodoxy was truly the right goal. When I talked with people like Paul in Owerri or Bishop Marcus in Yola or the students at Bishop Gwynne College, it was clear that we disagreed about any number of issues. But it was equally clear that we recognized in each other a life that was shaped by the good news of Jesus Christ. This mutual recognition depended on the relationships we had developed, relationships that were the fruit of the time we had spent together. Our relationships were undergirded by an implicit agreement that we would be vulnerable with one another—honest, open, and prepared to listen to the other. Christian unity is not really about what we think. It is about what we feel and perceive. In my travels, I encountered scores of people with whom I disagreed. Yet these disagreements did not impede deep relationships that were marked by the grace of God.

There will never be a day when all Christians will be able to write down what we believe. Attempts to do so in the past have invariably split the church. But we can pray that there will be a day when Christians around the world will recognize in one another the elements of a life shaped by the cross and resurrection of Christ. Instead of concentrating on orthodoxy, we might start pursuing "orthopathos," or "right feeling," and sharing the joy of relationship more broadly. This is not to say that what we think does not matter. But concentrating exclusively on orthodoxy has impoverished our search for unity.

None of this is to say that Anglicans will not continue to disagree with one another. It is just that when we do argue, we might realize that there are higher goods than prevailing in one's position, namely the recognition that our supposed enemy is a fellow member of the same body. Our common baptism actually does make us one body, no matter how often we are told otherwise. Sometimes these fellow members have to be corrected, reproofed, and challenged, but always in a way that is undergirded by the love, mercy, and forgiveness made known to us in Christ and in a spirit that recognizes there is something greater at stake than one's own position. We cannot walk away from those with whom we are joined. Instead, Anglican disagreements can become an opportunity for witness to the world by demonstrating that our life and ministry is rooted in relationships that are different than those that others in the world share.

The institutions of the Anglican Communion—Lambeth Conferences, Primates Meetings, and so forth—will not solve the Communion's problems. Instead, it is networks of mutual, vulnerable, and honest relationships that will begin to move us in directions we can barely imagine. The challenge for Anglicans, then, is the same one St. Paul gave to the Corinthians: "discerning the body" (1 Corinthians 11:29). Are we able to see that our baptism actually already unites us with other people not just in our local congregation, not just in our country, but all over the world? Can those bonds that already exist be used to challenge the fracture and division that characterize our world? Can we turn away from our drive toward independence and like-mindedness and turn again toward our sisters and brothers in Christ? Can we see that unity is not some optional extra we can build in when we feel like it, but something that already exists and which is God's gift for us to reveal? These were the questions Stephen Bayne asked of Anglicans in the early 1960s: "If we cannot discern that body," he said, "then we are only playing at Church."

⟨⟩

One of the most striking contrasts I experienced in my travels around the world church occurred not when I was immersed in a foreign culture, worshipping in a different fashion, singing new hymns, or eating unusual foods. The most striking contrast came when I returned home from a trip abroad. I would come back full of vim and vigor, excited at what I had encountered and wanting to tell others about it: The church around the world is vibrant and alive! I had a conversation about sexuality with people who disagreed with me and it deepened our relationship, not fractured it! There are dioceses and churches that want to be in relationship with us regardless of what other people say! But then I would read up on news of the Communion and realize the same old fights were still happening. My energy left me; I felt like a deflated balloon. Why was this narrative of disunity still strong when it is just so wrong?

There is little joy in the Anglican Communion any more. The lines of conflict are deeply drawn and no one shows any signs of moving. For all the energy and enthusiasm of a service in Nigeria, the largest province of the Communion, one of the overriding emotions in the church is fear of what the future holds. In this, it is not all that different than an American church that is getting ever older and ever smaller. But joy is precisely what I felt when I was standing in a classroom in Juba talking about sexuality. Joy is what I felt when I was hiking up a mountain to visit people in Waciri who did not even know they were Anglican. Joy is what I felt when Maple told me the story of her baptism in Nanjing. It is the joy of coming to know a fellow member of the body of Christ, of being in a holy relationship, of revealing the unity that is God's gift to God's people. Anglicans, I believe, can lead the way to reclaiming this joy. It is part of who we are. Incarnation, relationship, time, vulnerability, mutuality: these are central to what it means to be Anglican.

It is easy for me to write this. I come from a privileged position. I am not seriously threatened by making myself vulnerable. Moreover, nothing I have encountered will lessen the challenge facing Anglicans. The dynamics of globalization will only continue to intensify.

The challenge of holding together a global Communion in the face of differing contexts will not go away. Anglican partisans around the world continue to be exceptionally skillful at exploiting the Internet to deepen divisions and harden positions. The men—and it is, depressingly, almost entirely men—whose voices are heeded in conversations about the Anglican Communion may decide that their highest good lies elsewhere than in membership in a global family of churches.

But as these debates continue, I will continue to think of that rural archdeaconery in Umuahia where the priest asked me about globalization. After our initial meeting in the small church with the priest and a few of his congregants, Oliver took me to some of the parishes in the area. "Parish" is an august word for what I found. The archdeaconery is in an area where Anglicans have historically been weak as a result of agreements in the colonial period that parceled out the region to other denominations. Most of the Anglican churches I saw were small rented rooms overseen by elderly lay leaders who had long since given up any hope of attracting any more than five or ten people on Sunday.

Our final visit was to a small village with a large Methodist church on the main street. A smaller but still substantial Catholic church was nearby. Our destination was a ten-foot-square room with three pews and a small altar. Four elderly parishioners—two-thirds of the Sunday attendance—turned out on this weekday afternoon to meet the American visitor who had come to see their church. We talked a while, sharing stories about our churches and praying together. Before long, Oliver indicated it was time to go. As I thanked them for their hospitality and prepared to leave, one of the old men stood up. He had something to say. "Sometimes, we are ashamed to be Anglicans in this village. Other churches are much bigger and we only have this little room." He paused, leaning on his cane. Cataracts clouded his eyes. "But today you have come here. It is evangelism for you to come here. People in our village will be talking, 'That white man came all the way from America to go to that little Anglican church!' We will be the talk of the town."

I struggled to find an adequate response. All I could think to say was that we were both members of the worldwide body of Christ. In the Anglican Communion, I said, there are millions more like us around the world to whom we are connected. There is nothing to be ashamed of in that.

No matter what bishops decide or what meetings they boycott, no matter what vitriol surges around the Internet, no matter how often Anglicans mouth platitudes about being committed to the Communion and then fail to match their words with deeds, I will continue to believe in the reality of a worldwide Communion because of that man in that village in Nigeria. The bond that he and I share is a bond based not on agreement on contentious issues or a shared cultural background. It is a bond that is rooted in our common baptism and a like commitment to die daily with Christ and be risen to new life in him who is the author of all true and abundant life.

"It is evangelism for you to come here," he told me. Indeed. Our Anglican portion of the worldwide body of Christ has incredible potential to be a witness of unity to a divided and fractured world. When—if—we begin to show up, to see other Christians as people we need to deepen our faith, to see difference not as a barrier but a blessing, then we will begin to live out the reality of Christ's prayer for unity and the world will more fully know the truth of the good news of Jesus Christ.

Author's Note

My deepest and most sincere thanks are due first to the huge number of Anglicans around the world who welcomed me into their homes and lives in the course of these travels. In their hospitality and humor, they have shown me the face of Christ. Time and again, I got in a car, a bus, or a plane, not knowing entirely what would greet me at the other end of the journey, only to be welcomed with open arms by people who knew nothing about me but that I was a Christian and Anglican. The body of Christ truly is the best travel agency one could ever hope for! Some of these sisters and brothers are mentioned in this book, but most are not. To name them all would be impossible, but I give thanks for their witness.

In the course of writing, I have altered some chronological details to maintain narrative flow. In the chapter on Bishop Gwynne College, John is a composite character. To the best of my knowledge, the details I report are accurate as of my visit. Much, of course, may have changed in the interim. When I travel, I routinely post pictures and stories to a blog. While some of that material was incorporated into this book, much was not; all remains online at www.jessezink.com.

I was supported in these travels by a number of people who encouraged me before I left and helped me debrief when I returned home, including Duleep de Chickera, David Copley, Robin Denney, Ian Douglas, Megan Holding, Stephanie Johnson, Matthew Kellen, Matthew Lindeman, Ashley Makar, Jim Munroe, Gordon Scruton, Carolyn Sharp, John Simpson, and Chloë Starr. Rebecca Coleman, Doug and Elaine Culver, Lawrence Duffy, Chris Morck, and Trevor and Tina Stubbs helped orient me to the church abroad. When I lived in Mthatha, Joe and Anna Sawatzky first helped me come to grips with Christianity outside the Euro-Atlantic world. Joseph Britton took me to Canterbury and first made me think of the significance of that pile of rocks on Augustine's grave.

I have been assisted in my travels by a wide variety of individuals and organizations that thought it was a wise idea to fund me—some on multiple occasions—when I said I wanted to meet other Anglicans and "do" nothing with them other than listen and learn. In particular, I am grateful to the Fund for Theological Education, the Evangelical Education Society of The Episcopal Church, the Seminary Consultation on Mission, the Diocese of Western Massachusetts, the Elizabeth Bonham Mission Fund of the Episcopal Church of St. John the Baptist in York, Pennsylvania, as well as the whole host of individuals and congregations that supported me while I lived in Mthatha.

Many people helped me hone my prose and navigate the publishing process, including Andrew Davison, Oliver Igwe, John Peterson, and Lauren Winner. Anthony Poggo read the entire manuscript and offered helpful feedback. The spiritual writing workshop at Yale Divinity School in the spring of 2011 saw an early draft of some chapters. Their comments helped guide the direction of the project in its early stages. Nancy Bryan and the team at Church Publishing helped get the book off my computer screen and into the hands of readers. All mistakes remain my own.

My parents, Tom and Beth, had me baptized at the age of fourteen weeks, likely not knowing that it would set me off on such a journey in the body of Christ. Nonetheless, their support has been as constant as it has been unwavering as I have pursued this vocation.

Debbie entered this journey when it had already begun but has become the best kind of travel partner in life and ministry I could hope for.

To all, my deep thanks.

Notes

I first developed some of the ideas in this book in limited form in other places. I am grateful to the following publications for permission to use selected portions of the following: "Bringing in the Sheaves," *Sojourners* (May 2011); "Changing World, Changing Church: Stephen Bayne and 'Mutual Responsibility and Interdependence'" *Anglican Theological Review* 93, no. 2 (2011): 243–262; "'Anglocostalism' in Nigeria: Neo-Pentecostalism and Obstacles to Anglican Unity" *Journal of Anglican Studies* 10, no. 2 (2012): 231–250; and "Patiently Living with Difference: Rowan Williams' Archiepiscopal Ecclesiology and the Proposed Anglican Covenant," *Ecclesiology* 9, no. 2 (2013): 223–241.

The dialogue in this book is based on my journals and the notes I made while traveling. In many cases, early drafts of these chapters were written shortly after the events took place to ensure my memory was fresh. Listed here are sources for direct quotations from books and other writings.

epigraph "How can we show forth the one body of Christ": Stephen F. Bayne, "Organizing for Action," in *The Church in the 60's*, ed. P.C. Jefferson (Greenwich, CT: Seabury Press, 1962), 115, 116.

p. ix "more mosquito bites than I could count": Howard Johnson, *Global Odyssey: An Episcopalian's Encounter with the Anglican Communion in Eighty Countries* (New York: Harper & Row, 1963), 12.

p. 8 "There are not many bodies in many cities": Stephen Bayne, a sermon preached at the opening service of the General Synod of the Anglican Church of Canada, Kingston, Ontario, August 22, 1962. In Stephen Fielding Bayne, Jr., *An Anglican Turning Point: Documents and Interpretations* (Austin, TX: Church Historical Society, 1964), 270.

p. 76 "teaches universally and without fail all the doctrines": Cyril of Jerusalem, *Catechetical Lectures*, 18.23, quoted in Michael Ramsey, *The Anglican Spirit*, ed. Dale Coleman (London: SPCK, 1991), 126.

p. 112 "The Bible is to be translated, read, preached, taught and obeyed": The Jerusalem Declaration is available in many places and online at http://gafcon.org/news/gafcon_final_statement.

p. 182 "Society on our planet . . . is more like the anonymous crowd": Ryszard Kapuściński, *The Other* (New York: Verso, 2008), 75.

p. 188 "The power to think one's self into another's thoughts": Charles Gore, *The Incarnation of the Son of God: Being the Bampton Lectures for the year 1891* (London: J. Murray, 1912/1891), 160.

p. 189 "utterly obsolete and irrelevant": MRI was published as *Mutual Responsibility and Interdependence in the Body of Christ, with related background documents*, ed. Stephen F. Bayne, Jr. (New York: Seabury Press, 1964).

p. 189 "through the common, shared life of Christians": Stephen F. Bayne, Jr., "The Anglican Communion and the World Mission of the Church," *The Episcopal Overseas Mission Review* 3, no. 3 (1958): 7

p. 192 "if we cannot discern that body": Stephen Bayne, a sermon preached at the opening service of the General Synod of the Anglican Church of Canada, Kingston, Ontario, August 22, 1962. In Bayne, *An Anglican Turning Point*, 270.

Lightning Source UK Ltd.
Milton Keynes UK
UKOW03f0624190114

224797UK00001B/15/P